GW01607233

The History of Rugby League Football

By the same author

The Rugby League Game

The History of

RUGBY LEAGUE FOOTBALL

Keith Macklin

Stanley Paul
London

Stanley Paul & Co Ltd
3 Fitzroy Square, London W1

An Imprint of the Hutchinson Publishing Group

London Melbourne Sydney Auckland
Wellington Johannesburg Cape Town
and agencies throughout the world

First published 1962
Revised edition 1974

Set in Monotype Baskerville

Printed in Great Britain by
R J Acford Ltd, Chichester, Sussex
and bound by Wm Brendon & Sons, Tiptree, Essex

ISBN 0 09 120780 0

Dedicated to

THE PLAYERS, OFFICIALS
SPECTATORS AND PRESSMEN

of a great game

Contents

Notes on Author

KEITH MACKLIN first wrote and compiled *The History of Rugby League Football* in 1962. In this book he brings the story of the game completely up to date to 1974.

All the major events are fully and graphically covered. The famous 'Rorke's Drift' Test of 1914, when 10 Britishers beat 13 Australians. The equally sensational 1958 Brisbane Test, when Great Britain's captain Alan Prescott led his side to victory with a broken arm dangling uselessly at his side.

The waterlogged 1968 Wembley Cup Final, with the dramatic last-minute, unbelievable goalkicking miss that lost the Cup.

These, and many more outstanding moments, woven together in a narrative that traces every important game, law change and vicissitude in Rugby League since the old Northern Union broke away from the Rugby Union in 1895.

For the past five years Keith Macklin has been Soccer and outside broadcasts commentator with Yorkshire Television. He was a member of the ITV commentary team for the 1974 World Cup and was a member of ITV's London-based team for the 1972 Olympics.

Previously he was with the BBC based in Manchester, and while with BBC broadcast commentaries on Rugby League and Rugby Union. He is the only commentator ever to have broadcast networked TV commentaries on both Rugby codes and Soccer.

In addition he has become a familiar television figure with programmes like Yorkshire Television's 'Sunday Quiz' and 'Indoor League' and the BBC 'Songs of Praise' and 'A Spoonful of Sugar'.

Illustrations

The Castleford team hoisting up their coach Derek Turner after their Challenge Cup win at Wembley in 1968.

Warren Ayres, Wigan half-back, romps round for a try near the posts.

Between pages 136 and 137

Alan Smith, Leeds and Great Britain winger, on his way to the posts for a try.

Terry Clawson, the man whose kicking helped Leeds to a great Championship Final win in 1973.

At the bottom of the pile, but triumphant, John Bevan gets his first try.

Superb action picture of John Bevan, Warrington's signing for Welsh Rugby Union. Bevan, a British Lion, soon settled down in Rugby League.

Controversial but brilliant leader of St Helens, Leigh and Warrington, Alex Murphy boots the ball into touch.

Oh, my aching head! Murphy and Stephens (St Helens) hold their heads after colliding with Gregory of Warrington.

Between pages 184 and 185

Bobby Fulton, outstanding Australian player in the triumphant 1973 tour of Britain.

Cliff Watson, St Helens and Great Britain forward, charges into a ruck of Aussie defenders in a Test match at Headingly.

Hull Kingston Rovers star half-back Roger Millward gets Great Britain's sole try in the Third Test of the 1973 tour.

Australian centre Starling crashes through a tackle by Hynes (Leeds) for one of Australia's five tries in the deciding Third Test of 1973.

The Australian hooker helps himself to one of a nap hand of tries in the 1973 Third Test win.

New Zealand players perform their war dance before a Test match at Swinton in the last World Cup series.

1

Birth and Breakaway

Two world wars, the development of competitive spectator sports and now the emergence of the armchair sportsman and the counter-attractions of the affluent society—all these things have threatened the stability and popularity of the game of Rugby League. Yet the game survives and holds its popularity in Britain, France, Australia and New Zealand.

The great games still command the crowds: 95 000 at Wembley, 70 000 at Sydney. These are not figures that indicate a wilting game: they show the strength and appeal of an individual handling game that had its first stirrings nearly 70 years ago.

The English Rugby Union was formed in 1871, nearly 40 years after William Webb Ellis, a scholar of Rugby School, first picked up a football and ran with it instead of kicking. The handling game rapidly caught on, and by the closing years of last century there were more than 400 clubs in Rugby Union membership.

In 1893, however, storm-clouds began to gather in the North. In the industrial towns of Northern England time off from work to play rugby often meant loss of hard-earned pay, and many clubs were faced with demands from workmen players for 'expenses' to cover loss of work. Northern clubs began to agitate for 'broken-time' payments for the miners, the mill-workers and the glass-blowers whose sport was tough on the already moderate pay-packet.

To the officials of the Rugby Union the issue was plain. The Northern clubs were trying to open the door to a form of professionalism, and the very thought was anathema to the officials of the Rugby Union.

A clash could not be avoided, and at the annual general meeting of the Rugby Football Union in London on 20 September 1893, two Yorkshire representatives, Messrs J. A. Millar and M.

Newsome, proposed that 'players are to be allowed compensation for bona-fide loss of time'. This proposal, put in the form of an amendment, was defeated, but 136 people voted for it out of a total of 418 representatives.

The division rapidly widened. Northern club officials, encouraged by the 136 votes at the annual meeting, decided to meet informally at frequent intervals, and eventually a special meeting of interested clubs was called at the George Hotel, Huddersfield, on 29 August 1895.

Representatives of 21 clubs attended that first historic meeting. It was presided over by Mr H. H. Waller, of Brighouse, and clubs represented were Oldham, Halifax, Leeds, Bradford, Hull, Huddersfield, Hunslet, Wakefield, Widnes, Broughton Rangers, Batley, St Helens, Leigh, Warrington, Tyldesley, Wigan, Manningham, Rochdale Hornets, Liversedge and Dewsbury. At the end of the meeting all these clubs, with the exception of Dewsbury, decided on the tremendous step of resigning from the Rugby Union to form a Northern Rugby Union in which legitimate broken-time expenses would be paid.

The breach was made, never to be sealed, and when Stockport and Runcorn joined the other dissentients, Dewsbury having decided against it, 22 clubs formed the Northern Union. They lost no time in getting cracking, playing the first matches on Saturday, 7 September 1895, the Saturday before the official opening of Rugby Union fixtures.

Rules and regulations were evolved by a quickly formed committee. Two senior competitions were formed, one in Lancashire, one in Yorkshire, with provision for 'second' competitions. A sub-committee to consider rules and bye-laws was to meet alternately at Huddersfield and Manchester.

It is interesting to record the first-ever Northern Union fixtures on 7 September 1895. They were Bradford *v.* Wakefield Trinity, Leigh *v.* Leeds, Tyldesley *v.* Manningham, Batley *v.* Hull, Stockport *v.* Brighouse, Warrington *v.* Hunslet, Liversedge *v.* Halifax, Runcorn *v.* Widnes, St Helens *v.* Rochdale, Broughton Rangers *v.* Wigan.

The reaction of the English Rugby Union was to forbid clubs in membership from playing matches with Northern Union clubs, and to evolve even stricter rules against monetary payments to players.

The issue on which the breach had formed was broken-time payment for loss of employment, and this was fixed at the rate of 6*s.* a day, hardly a generous sum, but worth a great deal in terms of wages standards in 1895. It was not long before wealthier and more successful clubs began to pay a little more than 6*s.* a day, but this was the originally stipulated figure at the birth of Northern Union.

At the end of the first season of Northern Union rugby football, which still retained the playing rules of the parent Rugby Union, gates had been good and competition keen. Runcorn became the first winners of the Lancashire Senior Competition, and Manningham, the Bradford club, first winners of the Yorkshire Senior Competition.

After winning the matches which decided the championship both clubs returned to their home towns amid scenes of wild rejoicing. Crowds lined the streets of Bradford to cheer Manningham home in horse-drawn vehicles, while in Runcorn a torchlight procession met the team at the railway station and led a triumphal tour by horse-coach and four-in-hand throughout the town.

The Union had fired the enthusiasm of Northern rugby towns, and many more rushed to join the original 22 pioneers. At the first annual general meeting at the George Hotel, Huddersfield, on 27 August 1896, Mr H. H. Waller announced that 59 teams were in membership, and applications were continuing to pour in.

In the 1896–7 season Swinton, Salford and Morecambe joined the Lancashire Senior Competition, while Bramley, Castleford, Leeds Parish Church, Holbeck and Heckmondwike were admitted to the Yorkshire competition. Other clubs on the fringe of the senior competitions were later formed into 'second' competitions in both Lancashire and Yorkshire.

The 1896–7 season brought a major development in Northern Union football with the launching of the Northern Union Challenge Cup for all member clubs. This competition aroused terrific interest, and the first final was scheduled for 1 May 1897, at the handsome Headingley enclosure at Leeds, one of the finest grounds in the country. The honour of taking part in the first-ever cup final fell to Batley, nicknamed the 'Gallant Youths', and St Helens.

A crowd of between 13 000 and 14 000 paid £620 to see the match, an excellent attendance for those times, and they saw Batley beat St Helens by 10 points to 3, two tries and a dropped goal to a try.

Lancashire Senior Competition champions in the second season of Northern Union were Broughton Rangers, while Brighouse Rangers won the Yorkshire section.

The second annual meeting was held in 1897, with Mr Waller again presiding, and at this meeting the Northern Union widened further the gap between the Rugby Union and the Northern clubs by adopting sweeping changes in the rules of the game. Under the new rules every goal, however kicked, would count only two points. This ended the Rugby Union anomaly of four points for a drop goal, three for a penalty and two for a conversion.

The line-out was abolished to make way for a kick-in, or 'punt-out', from touch, and scrum-halves were ordered to retire behind the scrimmage or risk a penalty. Discipline was tightened by the insistence that matches should start on time, with fines for late starts. The Northern Union was making no bones about the fact that spectators were of primary importance.

The annual report, presented by the secretary, Mr J. Platt, was again optimistic. Enthusiasm for Northern Union continued to grow, and the number of clubs in membership had increased to 80. The credit balance of the Union stood at the tidy figure of £420.

The third season began in September, 1897, under the new rules system and the chairmanship of Mr J. E. Warren, of Warrington. Among the new clubs playing in the Lancashire Senior Competition were Lancaster, Millom, Crompton, Birkenhead Wanderers, Radcliffe, Barton, Walkden, Barrow, Ulverston, St Helens Recreation, Altrincham and Fleetwood.

The early part of the season was given interest by county matches, arranged from the birth of the Northern Union in 1895. Large crowds attended matches between Lancashire, Yorkshire and Cheshire. Lancashire won the title in 1895–6 and 1896–7, and there was great delight in the county of the broad acres when Yorkshire won the tourney in 1897–8.

Oldham won the Lancashire competition in 1897–8, Hunslet taking the Yorkshire title in a play-off with Bradford. Once again, however, it was the newly instituted Challenge Cup competition which provided the excitement for the ever-increasing army of spectators.

The mighty Batley 15, the redoubtable 'Gallant Youths', again reached the final and played at Headingley on Saturday, 23 April 1898. Their opponents were Bradford, and before a crowd of 27 941, paying £1506, they retained their hold on the Challenge Cup by a score of 7 points to 0, a try and two drop goals providing the points. J. B. Goodall scored a try and dropped goal, Davies adding another dropped goal.

The teams were:

Batley: Garner; Davies, Fitzgerald, J. B. Goodall, Fozzard; Oakland, H. Goodall; Shackleton, Gath, Maine, Spurr, Fisher, Stubley, Munns, Rodgers.

Bradford: Patrick; Cooper, W. Murgatroyd, F. Murgatroyd, Dobson; Wood, Prole; Broadley, McLoughlin, Toothill, Fearnley, Holt, Holden, Robertson, Kelsey.

Referee: J. H. Smith (Widnes).

The size of the crowd and the gate receipts indicated the remarkable growth of the game as a spectator sport, and this factor was inevitably leading towards the establishment of another major cleavage between Northern Union and Rugby Union. Professionalism was irrevocably becoming part of the game.

By 1897–8 many talented players, realizing their worth as crowd-pullers, were asking for more than mere expenses. This trend was opposed by many officials on the grounds that professionalism would drive smaller clubs out of existence.

It was little use swimming against the tide. Many of the wealthier clubs were paying over and above agreed 'expenses' to their star players, and the forecasts of the Rugby Union pundits were coming true.

Recognizing the position, the Northern Union established a sub-committee to look into the facts, and the result at the annual meeting of the Union in 1898 was the adoption of a policy which made professionalism a fundamental part of the Northern Union code.

The meeting was held in July at the George Hotel, Huddersfield, and a four-point charter was thrashed out and approved. This decreed that professionalism would be adopted, that players should be properly registered, that players must have legitimate employment in a full-time job other than football and that severe penalties would be imposed for offences against the above conditions.

The rule concerning 'legitimate employment' showed the determination of the Union to make professionalism respectable. No player was to be allowed to make a living purely and simply out of rugby football.

The 1898 annual meeting reported further expansion. Cumberland clubs like Whitehaven, Maryport, Wath Brow and Seaton were entering the ranks, and Cumberland were admitted to county championship fixtures. Membership of the Union stood at 98 clubs, and the season had ended with a credit balance of £1525.

Season 1898–9 was the first season of full professionalism. Players were registered on forms to be sent to the Union secretary, Mr J. Platt, and players could be transferred from club to club only if proper terms were agreed and drawn up and no illegal approach was made. All agreements were in writing, and no player received close-season payment.

The rule regarding legitimate employment caused many headaches. It was not completely clear in its definition of such employment, although 'shady' jobs like bookies' runner, billiard-marker or public-house waiter were definitely taboo!

This rule, known as the 'working clause', was applied with great severity. Booth, of Radcliffe, had his registration suspended when he was found to be a public-house waiter. A Swinton player who visited a sick relative, absenting himself from work, was barred from playing on Saturday, and Fitzgerald, the Batley centre was suspended for nearly two seasons for failing to find full-time employment.

Throughout the 1898–9 season the Union continued to grow. The Lancashire second competition was split up into North Lancashire and Cumberland and South Lancashire sections, allowing new clubs to be admitted in both areas. In Yorkshire,

York, Normanton, Rothwell and Featherstone were admitted to the Union.

Attendances increased, and as more money poured into club coffers, successful clubs began to pay bonuses for victory. The *Athletic News* reported that some Northern Union players were better paid than soccer professionals, with wages varying between 30*s*. and £4.

Club officials began to turn their eyes to the fruitful fields of talent in Rugby Union strongholds. Amateur players, in their turn, weighed up their chances of making money from their sport. As a result, Northern Union club representatives began to make signings in South Wales, the West Country and the North-East, aggravating the already strained relationship between the Rugby Union and the Northern Union.

Opposition to professionalism was particularly bitter in Wales, where the targets were often players of international standard. Two early signings were the brilliant half-back brothers James, of Swansea, who joined Broughton Rangers. Others followed. Anger seethed, and when a Wigan scout was recognized in Penarth he was ducked in the sea and rolled in the sand. But he got his man, Smith, the Penarth winger! Woodhead, of Elland, and Harry, of Torquay Athletic, were suspended by the Rugby Union for accepting Northern Union terms.

Despite the constant friction between the codes, little could be done to prevent the flow of recruits from Rugby Union. Then, as now, players recognized the prospect of rewards in Northern Union, and Rugby Union was often merely a stepping-stone to the professional ranks.

The clamour for admission to the Union continued. Newly admitted clubs in 1899 included Melbourne, Fairburn, Ossett, Alverthorpe, Doncaster Town, Whitehaven Town, Whitehaven Recreation, Hebden Bridge, Kirkstall St Stephen's and Windhill. Junior and amateur organizations sprouted like mushrooms throughout the Northern counties.

In the 1898–9 tournaments Broughton Rangers won the Lancashire championship, and Batley the Yorkshire championship, while Oldham and Hunslet fought out the final of the

Challenge Cup at Fallowfield, Manchester, before a crowd of 15 763, paying £1065.

The teams were:

Oldham: Thomas; Davies, T. Fletcher, S. Lees, Williams; A. Lees, Lawton; Moffatt, Frater, Telfor, Bonser, Broome, Ellis, J. Lees, Barnes.

Hunslet: Mitchell; A. Goldthorpe, W. Goldthorpe, Hannagh, Wright; Robinson, E. Fletcher; O. Walsh, Leach, Harrison, Young, Rubrey, T. Walsh, Ramage, Wilson.

Referee: T. H. Marshall (Bradford).

Oldham gave a brilliant display of running, handling and kicking to win the game by 10 points to 9, scoring five tries to one by Hunslet. The Yorkshire side, playing what the critics dubbed a 'kick-and-rush' game, led 9–5 at the interval, but in the second half the brilliant Oldham combination led to four fine tries.

The 1899 annual meeting, held in Manchester in July, brought the familiar reports of prosperity and development, with the credit balance of the Union now standing at £2033. For the first time the Union turned down applications for membership, as it was felt that the existing leagues were big enough.

One or two rule changes were made at the meeting. Previously, the kick-off after a try had been from the defending club's 25. Under the new ruling it was to be taken more fairly, from half-way.

The Rugby Union play-the-ball rule, which stated that when a man was tackled he had to put the ball down in front of him and play it, had caused a lot of trouble and scrappy play, and the new rule stated that 'if a man and ball be fairly held the referee awards a scrum. If the ball is not held the tackled man can pass or drop it at his feet, provided the ball is not dropped in a forward direction.' This rule proved as unsatisfactory as the previous one, and down the years the play-the-ball rule has been a consistent problem to the rule-makers.

2

The First Northern League

THE Union's healthy finances led to one or two monetary gestures in 1900. The Challenge Cup finalists for the previous two seasons were voted £50 each for their achievement, which went down well with the clubs, with the exception of Batley, who felt that the payment could have included the 1897 final. A similar sum was voted for each of the county unions, with Cheshire and Cumberland, the poorer counties, receiving the same as their wealthier brethren in Lancashire and Yorkshire. The sum of £100 was shared between various junior clubs struggling for existence, and philanthropic donations were made to Boer War charities.

The 1900 annual meeting had its usual optimistic start, with a credit balance of £1544, despite the various donations. Then came a barrage of proposals and amendments to rule, each of them requiring a three-fourths majority.

Certain changes were approved. In the case of a deliberate obstruction the free kick was to be awarded at the place where the ball dropped instead of at the place where the offence was committed, thus increasing the penalty. Goalkickers benefited from the next rule change, for defending sides were no longer to be allowed to charge. They had to stand on the mark until the kick was taken. Not unexpectedly, this change of rule led to an increasing number of successful kicks at goal and the emergence of the 'star' goal-kickers.

Runcorn won the Lancashire Senior Competition in 1899–1900, and Bradford the Yorkshire tournament. It was a good season for Lancashire, for the Red Rose county won the county championship, and local rivals Swinton and Salford fought out the Challenge Cup final at Fallowfield, Manchester, on 29 April. The attendance for this parochial type of final was 17 564, paying £1106.

The teams were:

Salford: D. Smith; Pearson, T. Williams, Harter, Hadwen; Grey, Griffiths; Rhapps, J. Williams, Gledhill, Tunney, Shaw, Shore, Fisher, Brown.

Swinton: Chorley; Lewis, Messer, R. Valentine, Hampson; D. Davies, Morgan; J. Valentine, C. Pollitt, Vigors, J. Evans, Preston, Harris, Murphy, G. R. Jones.

Referee: Mr F. Renton (Hunslet).

Swinton won the trophy by beating their local rivals by 16 points to 8 after a Tom Williams try and Griffiths goal had given Salford the lead. A dummy and try by Messer, converted by Jim Valentine, equalized the scores, but an unconverted try by Pearson regained Salford's lead. A try by Lewis made it 8—8 at the interval and after Brown, the Salford forward, had been sent off the field, Swinton took control in the second half, and tries by R. Valentine and Davies, and a goal from J. Valentine, gave them victory.

In the later stages of the 1900–1 season occurred two developments of immense significance in shaping the course of Rugby League. The first agitation among the clubs was for a reduction in the number of players on the field. The second was for the fusing of the Lancashire and Yorkshire Senior Competitions into one major league with attractive inter-county fixtures.

In January, 1901, a meeting of the professional sub-committee of the Union met at Manchester under the chairmanship of Mr H. Hutchinson to consider suggestions from several clubs that the number of players in a team should be reduced from 15 to 12. The idea of the clubs was to make the game faster and more open, and the professional sub-committee passed the buck to the county unions for 'observations'.

Several clubs played friendly matches in 12-a-side football, among them Oldham, Halifax, Broughton Rangers and Widnes in Lancashire, and Dewsbury and Heckmondwike in Yorkshire. In May, 1901, two sides styling themselves England and Wales played a 12-a-side benefit match for a player stricken with consumption.

The campaign for a 'super' league quickly gathered momentum in 1901. Tired of parochial county competitions, and remembering that the inter-county club games in the Challenge Cup whipped up terrific enthusiasm, clubs campaigned for a combined Northern

League to contain the cream of the top clubs in the senior competitions.

Opposition to this campaign came from those clubs who felt that they would be unable to find a place in such a league for top-class clubs. Their argument was that a 'super' league would skim the cream from the senior competitions and kill the smaller and less glamorous clubs. The powerful voices of the Northern Union's top clubs were insistent, however, and in May, 1901, the first Northern Rugby League was born.

The speed with which it was launched staggered opponents of the scheme. Hardly had the 1900–1 season ended than 12 club representatives met at Huddersfield to discuss the proposed formation of a Northern League. At the close of the meeting they drew up a resolution that a Northern League be formed consisting of the 12 clubs represented at the meeting, with power to add to their number. The 12 clubs were Bradford, Batley, Broughton Rangers, Halifax, Huddersfield, Hull, Hunslet, Oldham, Runcorn, Salford, Swinton and Warrington.

Naturally there were howls of protest from those clubs left out of the new league, and accusations of treachery and perfidy were levelled at the 12 clubs. They were accused of attempting to sabotage the senior competitions, of wanting to kill off smaller clubs to achieve their own selfish ends. Smaller clubs, it was pleaded, would lose their star fixtures against top clubs and would soon go out of existence.

A head-on clash came at a full meeting of the management committee on 4 June 1901. When the matter was put to the vote the 12 clubs threw their combined weight into the issue, and the Northern League squeezed through by the narrowest possible margin of 12 votes to 11.

While the Northern League was smouldering into life, the Northern Union trophies of 1900–1 ran their course. Oldham won the Lancashire Senior Competition in its last year of major importance, and Bradford again won the Yorkshire championship. In the Challenge Cup the Gallant Youths from Batley entered their third final in four seasons, and won once again by beating Warrington.

The final was played at Headingley, Leeds, on Saturday, 27

April 1901, despite comments from Lancashire that the venue favoured nearby Batley. The choice was justified in terms of crowd and gate receipts, for a 30 000 crowd paid £1650. The teams were:

Batley: Garner: Davies, Fitzgerald, Goodall, Auty; Oakland, Midgley; Fisher, Judge, Rodgers, Stubley, Spurr, Maine, Fozzard, Hollingworth.

Warrington: Hallam; Fish, Isherwood, Dickenson, Harris; Bate, Duckworth; Boardman, Fell, Edmondson, Scholtze, Eden, Cunningham, Morrison, Swift.

Referee: Mr J. Kidd (Millom).

The Batley side again showed their power and consistency, and not even the speedy and redoubtable Warrington winger, Jack Fish, could pierce the dour defence of the Yorkshiremen. Davies and Auty scored well-worked tries for Batley, who won by 6 points to 0.

The close season of 1901 was a hectic one. Fifteen clubs were now in membership of the new Northern League—Hull, Hunslet, Huddersfield, Halifax, Batley, Bradford, Brighouse Rangers, Oldham, Swinton, Salford, Broughton Rangers, Warrington, Leigh and Runcorn—and they set to work to evolve rules for the new competition. It was agreed that in order to avoid accusations of 'closed shop' the bottom club in the Northern League each season would drop out to make way for the winner of a play-off between the top teams in the Lancashire and Yorkshire Senior Competitions. This crumb of consolation to the sides left out of the new league did not appease clubs in Yorkshire, and those clubs left in the Yorkshire Senior Competition decided on a boycott of fixtures with the 'new leaguers'. Lancashire clubs were more sensible. Realizing that the Northern League was inevitable, they bravely reconstructed the Lancashire Senior Competition by inviting Lancashire Second Competition clubs to join their number. An unexpected and brave addition to the ranks came from Hull Kingston Rovers, who tired of the Yorkshire clubs' attitude to the élite in the new league and joined the Lancashire Senior Competition.

The Yorkshire Senior Competition invited Yorkshire Second Competition members to help make up a league, and the 14 sides who competed in 1901–2 were Bramley, Keighley, Manningham, Heckmondwike, Leeds, Wakefield Trinity, Castleford, Liversedge, York, Goole, Dewsbury, Sowerby Bridge, Holbeck and Normanton.

Amid the birth-pangs of the first Northern League, the Northern Union annual meeting at Huddersfield on 19 July 1901, reported a balance of £2334. The noxious punt-out was amended as a compromise. When the ball was carried into touch a scrummage was ordered. When it was kicked into touch a punt into play would still be taken. The knock-on rule was also changed, and those who asked that a player be allowed to make two attempts or more at a clean catch won their way. In addition, there was to be no knock-on if a member of the opposing side caught the ball before it touched the ground.

The close season saw the death of two more clubs, and the admission of a new one. South Shields, a County Durham outpost, were admitted, but founder members Tyldesley withdrew for lack of a ground, and Leeds Parish Church were also forced out when they failed to renew the lease of their ground at Crown Point.

As had been hoped, the inter-county fixtures in the Northern League pulled in the gates in all towns, except those where the home club failed to find form. In the senior competitions the anticipated effect was soon apparent, for the loss of star fixtures hit the gates of all clubs.

The unhappy state of affairs in the senior competitions resulted in the end of the boycott practised by the Yorkshire Senior Competition clubs, who soon realized that they were hurting themselves more than the Northern League.

First champions of the Northern League were Broughton Rangers, who displayed such consistent form that they were declared champions as early as February. Cheshire, with only a handful of teams to pick from, won the county championship for the first time. Wigan were champions of the Lancashire Senior Competition and Leeds of the Yorkshire competition.

It was a great season for Broughton Rangers, who followed up their championship victory with success in the 1902 Challenge Cup. In each case Salford, champion runners-up, had to take second place. The cup final between neighbours was played at

Rochdale on Saturday, 26 April 1902, before a moderate crowd of 15 000, with Mr W. Robinson (Manningham) as referee.

Teams were:

Broughton Rangers: Fielding; Hogg, Harry, Wilson, Widdeson; S. James, W. James; Woodhead, Garretty, Stead, Oram, Trotter, Whitehead, Winskill, Thompson.

Salford: D. Smith; Bone, T. Williams, Davies, Price; Lomas, Griffiths; Heath, Rhapps, Shaw, Brown, J. Williams, Buckler, Gledhill, Tunney.

Rangers played brilliant football, and overplayed their neighbours to the tune of 25 points to 0. Wilson had a brilliant match at centre, scoring a hat-trick of tries, and making another for Hogg after an interception. Widdeson got the fifth try and W. James (4) and Oram landed goals. Amid scenes of Rangers' rejoicing and Salford gloom, the curtain rang down on the Northern League's first season.

3

The Two-divisions Scheme

THE success of the Northern League killed for ever any hope of a return to the parochial county competitions. Consequently, in the close season of 1902, senior competition club officials and those of the Northern League met together to discuss the formation of a second division of the Northern League.

A joint meeting of the Northern League and the senior competitions at Huddersfield resulted in the proposal that the first division should consist of 18 clubs, with 12 in the second. Twenty-three clubs applied for 12 places, and it was obvious that some would have to go to the wall.

The second division was given formal approval at the Northern Union annual meeting at Huddersfield. There was one major rule change: the punt-out was abolished, and in its place was substituted a 10-yard scrimmage.

The Northern League two-divisions scheme was launched in September 1902, under the presidency of Mr J. Clifford, of Huddersfield. The second division had been increased in its suggested size, and there were 18 teams in each division. In the first division bottom club Brighouse Rangers were re-elected, and Wigan, Widnes, St Helens and Hull K.R. were admitted. Leeds were shocked at their failure to gain admission. Despite their runaway Yorkshire Senior Competition championship, the voting clubs did not see them as serious challengers!

The second division contained the following teams: Birkenhead Wanderers, Millom, South Shields, Stockport, Dewsbury, York, Keighley, Barrow, Castleford, Manningham, Bramley, Normanton, Rochdale, Holbeck, Wakefield, Lancaster, Leeds and Morecambe. The early games in the second division became of vital importance, and before long the tendency most feared had become apparent. The successful clubs in the second division pulled in the gates. The unsuccessful ones were soon in the red.

The 1902–3 championship was a thrilling affair, with the lead constantly changing between Runcorn, Salford, Broughton Rangers, Halifax and Swinton. Halifax eventually took the title to Yorkshire in a great finish. At the bottom end of the table the four newly admitted clubs, Wigan, Widnes, Hull K.R. and St Helens, found the going tough and finished in the bottom six, with Brighouse again at the bottom. Winners of the second division were Keighley, with Leeds runners-up.

League form was confirmed in the Challenge Cup when Halifax and Salford, the two top teams, fought out the Challenge Cup final. The match aroused terrific interest, for Halifax fans sought a 'double', while Salford supporters hoped to see an end to Salford's run as the league's perennial runners-up. The match was played at Headingley on Saturday, 25 April 1903, and a record crowd of 32 507 paid receipts of £1820.

Alas, the match did not live up to its billing. It was a scrambling, kick-and-rush affair, with little handling or open football.

The teams were:

Halifax: Little; Wedgwood, Williams, Rigg, Hadwen; Morley, J. Riley; Jack Riley, Bartle, Mallinson, Swinbank, Morton, Hammond, Bulmer, Winskill.

Salford: Smith; Norris, Messer, Lomas, Bell; Harter, Griffiths; J. Williams, Rhapps, Tunney, Heath, Brown, Buckler, Shaw, Shore.

Referee: Mr H. Bruckshaw (Stockport).

The record crowd had to wait until the second half for the first points in a tedious game. Jack Riley forced his way over for a Halifax try, converted by Hadwen, and later Hadwen kicked a penalty goal. Poor Salford tried hard to score, but powerful Halifax tackling kept them out, and the Reds finished as runners-up for the third time in four seasons.

The 1902–3 season brought several problems for the Union's officials. They had the problem of the parlous state of many second division clubs. Professional players were asking for higher wages from successful clubs, and threatening not to play if their demands were not met. The 'working clause', which insisted on players having a bona-fide job outside football, was causing registration headaches week after week.

The end of season had brought a quota of bankrupt clubs leaving the Union. Manningham, first champions of the Yorkshire Senior Competition, and Stockport went out of existence. The loss of these clubs indicated that the golden days of progress were virtually over, and retrenchment, rather than expansion, was now the necessity.

For season 1903–4 St Helens and Brighouse were relegated, and Leeds and Keighley were promoted. There were 17 clubs in the second division, Manningham and Stockport having dropped out, with Pontefract coming in. Mr J. Platt remained as secretary of the Union, with Mr J. H. Houghton as Northern League secretary. President of the Union was Mr R. Collinge, of Rochdale.

The county matches of 1903–4 put 12-a-side on trial. Five counties were now playing in the championship with the admission of Durham and Northumberland, and there were plenty of matches to give the experiment a thorough airing.

The 1904 annual meeting brought interesting rule changes. Clubs were forbidden to pack down with more than three men in the front row of the scrum, a move to stop 'wheeling' and barging. The knock-on rule was further amended, allowing opposing sides to gain possession even if the ball had touched the ground.

The three-fourths majority rule and the 'working clause' were attacked as usual, and success came at last for those who thought a three-fourths majority to be too excessive a demand. A vote was taken, and the new ruling reduced the necessary majority to two-thirds. The attack on the 'working clause' was less successful, and the iniquitous clause, with its constant headaches for secretaries responsible for their players' bona-fide jobs, was retained.

South Shields, the North-Eastern outpost side, left the League after a short and unsuccessful stay.

League champions in 1903–4 were Bradford, with Salford in the customary position of runners-up. At the other end of the table Huddersfield and Keighley were relegated, the latter after only one season in higher company. Wakefield Trinity topped the second division, and St Helens and Holbeck, who tied for second place, had to play-off for the right to accompany them into the first division. St Helens won, a result whose sequel had remarkable repercussions. Holbeck, who had been toying for some time with the idea of changing from Northern Union to soccer, decided the time was ripe for the change, and Holbeck Northern Union side went out of existence to be replaced by Leeds City soccer club. It was a big blow for the Northern Union.

The 1904 Challenge Cup final was a dual between Halifax and Warrington at Salford on Saturday, 30 April, before a crowd of 17 041 paying £936. This was a considerable drop on the previous year's attendance and takings. The powerful Halifax side took the trophy home for the second successive year by a score of 8 points to 3.

The teams were:

Halifax: Little; Hadwen, Joe Riley, W. Williams, Hartley; Morley, Nettleton; Bartle, Bulmer, Langhorn, Mallinson, Morton, Jack Riley, Swinbank, Winskill.

Warrington: Hallam; Fish, Harris, Isherwood, Dickenson; D. Davies, Hockenhall; G. Thomas, Boardman, Morrison, Naylor, Cook, Jolley, Lunt, Edmondson.

Referee: Mr J. H. Smith (Widnes).

Halifax scored the only points of the first half when Joe Riley went under the posts after passing between half-backs Morley and Nettleton. Hadwen converted. In the second half Warrington made a great effort, and a terrific burst by Fish made a try for Davies. Harris, the Warrington centre, stumbled and fell with the line at his mercy, and Halifax came back to secure the game with a try by Morley.

Second division club Dewsbury went through a remarkable sequence of events in 1904–5. There was a smallpox scare in the town early in the season, and other clubs refused to play at Dewsbury. Eventually, after a huge backlog of fixtures had been built up, the scare subsided, and Dewsbury set to their task of clearing their fixture list. They did so with such success that they won the second division championship!

The first division championship was won by Oldham, with St Helens and Runcorn at the foot of the table. In division two Barrow were runners-up to Dewsbury. The Challenge Cup brought consolation to Warrington, beaten the previous year, when they beat Hull Kingston Rovers 6—0 at Headingley on Saturday, 29 April 1905. In squally weather, 19 439 paid £1261 to see the match.

Teams were:

Hull K.R.: Sinclair; West, Phipps, Robinson, Madley; Barry, Gordon; Starks, Kemp, Windle, Osborne, Spackman, Ellis Gorman, Read.

Warrington: Hallam; Fish, Isherwood, Dickenson, Kenyon; Brooks, Davies; Thomas, Boardman, Naylor, Jolley, Shugars, Swift, Belton, Harmer.

Referee: Mr H. Bruckshaw (Stockport).

The game was not a particularly exciting one, due to rain and a strong wind, and Warrington were content to prevent Hull K.R. from scoring during a first half in which they faced the elements. In the second half, with wind and rain behind them, Warrington piled on the pressure and Fish went over at the corner after a fine threequarter movement. Then the Warrington scrum-half Brooks broke through the middle with Fish in support, and sent the winger clean away for his second try.

The annual meeting of 1905, held in July, brought an end to the ill-fated and short-lived two-divisions scheme. It was obvious that to continue the second division would 'kill off' more struggling clubs, and the clubs at the annual meeting decided that the two divisions should be combined to form one big division in 1905–6.

The close season of 1905 also brought an end to the 'working clause', which was at last ruled out by the management committee. No longer need a player prove that he had worked at a bona-fide job during the week before he could play on Saturday.

Season 1905–6, under Mr J. H. Smith's presidency, saw further shrinkage of the Northern Union. Northumberland and Durham and Cheshire, weakened by withdrawals from the Union, quit county championship fixtures, leaving Lancashire, Yorkshire and Cumberland to fight it out. However, in an attempt to create further interest, Lancashire and Yorkshire county challenge cup competitions were introduced, and good crowds saw Wigan beat Leigh at Broughton to win the Lancashire trophy for the first year of competition, while Hunslet beat Halifax at Bradford.

The fusing of the two divisions into one did not prove a success in 1905–6. Former second division clubs fared no better in the new league than they had done in division two, and gates did not increase.

The fixture mix-up also caused many a tangle. Some clubs had fixed up fewer fixtures than others, with the result that the championship had to be decided on a percentage basis. Leigh were awarded the championship on this percentage basis after a comparatively easy season in which they made few visits to Yorkshire to face tough Yorkshire sides. Hunslet, runners-up, were among those clubs who complained that Leigh's 'easy' fixture list had made them a present of the title. These complaints led to a meeting of clubs in April, 1906, which thrashed out an acceptable fixture formula for 1906–7. This made provision for a top-four play-off, in which the top four clubs would pair off in semi-finals, with the winners meeting for the championship on a neutral ground.

If Leigh's championship win was greeted with surly grunts everywhere except in Leigh, the Challenge Cup tournament held its interest and excitement. Fine crowds saw the ties, and Salford aroused great interest when they once again reached the final. The big question was: Can the 'champion runners-up' do it this time?

The match was played at Headingley on Saturday, 28 April 1906, a moderate attendance of 16 000 paying £920. The referee was Mr W. McCutcheon and teams were:

Bradford: Gunn: Dechan, Heseltine, Sinton, Connell; Marsden, Brear; Laidlaw, Feather, Greenwood, Turner, Grayson, Smales, Sharratt, Francis.

Salford: Cochrane; Hampson, Lomas, Thomas, McWhirter; Preston, John; Rhapps, E. J. Thomas, Spencer, Lewis, Warwick, Brown, Foster.

The match was a big disappointment, scrum following scrum with monotonous regularity in a dull game. The first half brought no score, and when the second half was equally scrappy, with defences on top, the crowd began to get impatient. Then, with 15 minutes left, poor Salford were shattered when the Bradford half-back, Brear, dodged over the Salford line. As Salford fans disconsolately trudged from the ground, Laidlaw kicked a penalty goal for Bradford to make the final score 5—0. The Salford hoodoo still persisted.

In the 1906 close there was a buzz of excitement throughout the League when it became known that a large number of clubs would be pressing for a reduction in the size of teams at the annual meeting. St Helens proposed the dropping of one player, Whitehaven Recreation proposed reduction from 15 to 12. Warrington, backed by Leigh, suggested teams of 13-a-side as the best compromise, and it was this proposal which won the day at the annual meeting at Huddersfield in June. In the interests of open football it was decided that the two men would disappear from the 'spoilers', the forwards, in 1906–7.

The annual meeting gave formal approval to the 'top-four' championship plan, creating a semi-final and final play-off for the title at the end of each season. These moves, it was hoped, would make Northern Union more attractive as a game, and help the code hit back at the increasing popularity of soccer. They came, however, too late to save two more clubs from extinction, for Brighouse Rangers and Morecambe gave up the increasingly hard struggle against apathy and lack of success. Against these losses a new club, Liverpool City, were admitted, with disastrous results for the new hopefuls.

The 1906–7 season, under the presidency of Mr J. B. Cooke (Wakefield), began well enough for the 13-a-side game, the novelty of the move being sufficient to bring in the crowds in the early stages. Liverpool City's progress was less happy, for the new club conceded more than 100 points in their first three games, and were soon in the unwanted role of chopping-block for the rest.

Most people agreed that 13-a-side was faster and more open, but it was still success that counted, and the continuing financial plight of the less successful clubs caused many furrowed brows at Union headquarters.

The flagging spirits of Northern Union officials were revived by the first season of championship play-offs. The semi-finals and finals between them attracted a total of £1319 in gate receipts, while the Challenge Cup drew an attendance of 18 500 in bad weather. In the championship semi-finals Halifax, the top club, beat fourth club Keighley, and Oldham, runners-up, beat the third club, Runcorn.

The final between Halifax and Oldham took place at Huddersfield, and Halifax confirmed league form by beating Oldham 18—3 before a 16 000 crowd. Bartle, Bulmer, Morley and Riley scored tries for Halifax, Little kicking three goals, while Ferguson got a try for Oldham.

Oldham reached the Challenge Cup final by beating Salford in the semi-finals, while Warrington hammered Swinton 21—0 to earn the right to meet them. The weather was unkind to the final, played at Broughton on Saturday, 13 April, before 18 500 people. The teams were:

Oldham: Thomas; Tyson, Dixon, Irvin, White; Lees, A. Yewlett; Avery, Ferguson, Smith, Vowles, Topham, Wilkinson.

Warrington: Tilley; Fish, Isherwood, Taylor, Brooks; Lees, S. Hockenhall; Thomas, Shugars, Bolton, Boardman, Heath, Naylor.

Referee: Mr F. Renton (Hunslet).

The heavy rain and slushy conditions spoiled the game, and one newspaper described it as being 'all pack, possession and kick'. Oldham scored first near the end of a scrappy first half when Arthur Lees sent Avery over, and just before half-time Fish kicked a goal for Warrington. In the second half play improved slightly, and Warrington scored a fine try through S. Lees after Isherwood and Fish had broken through. The brilliant Fish kicked the goal, and then scored a superb try from inside his own half, converting his own great effort. Hockenhall scored another Warrington try, converted by Fish to give Warrington the cup by 17 points to 3.

The season was rounded off with some immense news from New Zealand. A syndicate of sportsmen, impressed with Northern Union play and organization during a New Zealand Rugby Union 'All Blacks' tour, were planning to sponsor a team to visit the Northern Union in 1907–8. An historic development was just about to take place.

4

New Zealand, Australia – and Wales

LIVERPOOL City quit the League after a disastrous only season, but Bradford, after a shaky season, re-formed on a new ground and with a new name, Bradford Northern.

The parochial problems of the Northern Union and League were, however, pushed into the background by immense news from elsewhere. In Wales, hotbed of the handling code, several clubs were anxious to change over to Northern Union, and Ebbw Vale and Merthyr Tydfil were admitted in 1907–8. But the really exciting news was from New Zealand, where leaders of the Rugby Union game were corresponding with Mr J. Platt, secretary of the Northern Union, regarding the development of the 13-a-side code 'Down Under'.

The interest stemmed from the last All Blacks tour of Britain. The All Blacks had made many friends among Northern Unionists, and their fast, open style of play had endeared them to the players and spectators of the professional game. Among the New Zealand pioneers were A. H. Baskerville, of Wellington, and George Smith, an All Blacks winger, who were the prime movers in the plan to bring a touring team to Britain to play Northern Union. These two rapidly gathered round themselves a core of enthusiasts, including many All Blacks players, and in June 1907, the Northern Union announced that arrangements had been made for a New Zealand tour of Britain. It was agreed that the tourists would receive 70 per cent of gate receipts and would receive guarantees of £50 for a mid-week game and £100 for a Saturday game. A 'guarantee fund' would be opened to insure the tour against loss.

In New Zealand there was controversy and consternation at the news. The All Blacks were stated to have signed assurances that they would do nothing contrary to the laws and spirit of Rugby Union, and grave doubts were cast on the likelihood of international Rugby Union players risking their status and reputations on a Northern Union tour.

However, a party of players set off by sea in midsummer, among them four All Blacks—George Smith, D. McGregory, W. Johnston and W. H. Mackrell. Also in the party were two young players destined to become all-time greats: H. H. Messenger, an Australian 'guest' from Sydney, and Lance B. Todd, a 22-year-old half-back. This first touring party from Australasia, 'Baskerville's team' arrived in Britain in October 1907.

Meanwhile, great developments were taking place in Australia. A similar situation to that which led to the Northern Union breakaway had blown up in Australia, with clubs in New South Wales at odds with their officials over 'broken time' and other payments. This rumble of revolt was fanned into a flame when the New Zealand pioneers returned in 1908.

The arrival of Baskerville's team, under the captaincy of H. R. Wright, of Wellington, aroused terrific interest throughout the Union. They played their first 13-a-side game at Bramley in midweek, and despite the unfamiliarity of the surroundings and rules, won handsomely. They followed this up by beating Huddersfield by 19 points to 8, although six-a-side scrummaging obviously troubled them.

A crowd of 24 000 saw the New Zealand party beat Broughton Rangers 24—14, followed by a draw at Wakefield and an 8—2 victory against Leeds. After this the Northern Union clubs began to get the measure of the tourists, and Wigan beat them 12—8, with the tourists once again showing their inability to cope with Northern Union scrummaging techniques. By now the English weather was at its rainy, snowy, slushy worst, and defeats at Barrow, Leigh and Oldham were sustained in dreary conditions. Runcorn, Bradford and Halifax took their turn in beating the tourists, and the shine of the tour had pretty well been knocked off. From New Zealand came the news that all members of the touring party had been suspended *sine die* by the New Zealand Rugby Union, but this came as no surprise to the players, who had realized they were burning their boats.

Three representative matches were played against the New Zealanders, styled 'Test' matches after cricket. With pioneering zeal, the Northern Union played two of them for the South of England as propaganda matches, and these were played at Cheltenham and Stamford Bridge, Chelsea. The first Test in Northern Union history was at Headingley on 25 January 1908, but the gate of 8000 proved a great disappointment.

The tourists' loss of form after a bright start was almost certainly the cause, and the result of the first Test confirmed current form, the Northern Union winning by 14 points to 6. Robinson (Halifax) scored two tries, and Leytham (Wigan) and Llewellyn (Oldham) one each for Britain, Jolley (Runcorn) kicking a goal. Turtill and Wynyard scored tries for the New Zealanders. Teams for this first Test match were:

Northern Union: Taylor (Hull); Hogg (Broughton Rangers), Llewellyn (Oldham), Jenkins, Leytham (Wigan); Jolley (Runcorn), Thomas (Wigan); Ruddick (Broughton R.), D. Jones (Merthyr), A. Smith (Oldham), A. Robinson (Halifax), Wilson (Hunslet), Warwick (Salford).

New Zealand: Turtill; G. W. Smith, Rowe, Lingley, Todd; Wynyard, Kelly; Wright, Cross, Pearce, Johnston, Gilchrist Trevarthen.

The second Test was at Stamford Bridge, Chelsea, on Saturday, 8 February 1908, and a crowd of 15 000 turned up at the soccer stronghold. In the home side Eccles (Halifax), Baxter (Rochdale) and Thomas (Warrington) came in for Hogg, Thomas and Robinson. New Zealand had Messenger, Tyler and Dunning for Rowe, Kelly and Wright.

Against all expectations the New Zealanders turned on a great display to win by 18 points to 6, G. Smith, Todd, Johnston and Wynyard scoring tries and Messenger three goals, against tries by Leytham and Eccles.

Todd's try was a memorable one. After Smith had run strongly just over the half-way line Todd came up on the inside, and the half-back ran like the wind for the posts with the defence trailing in the rear. The 15 000 crowd applauded enthusiastically as Toddy, known as a 'five-eighth' because of the odd position he took up as link between the threequarters and halves, walked back to the centre line.

The surprise New Zealand victory shook the Northern Union, who took the third Test at Cheltenham on 15 February very seriously indeed. Eccles, Llewellyn, Leytham, Baxter and four forwards, Ruddick, Jones, Thomas, and Warwick, were replaced by Batten (Hunslet), P. Thomas (Leeds), Tyson (Oldham), P. White (Oldham), Clampitt (Broughton R.), Birch (Leeds), Spencer (Salford) and Holder (Hull). The New Zealanders happily made no changes.

Conditions were poor, and only 5000 saw New Zealand complete the shaking-up of Northern Union complacency by winning the Ashes at the first attempt, 8 points to 5. A try by Jolley and goal by White gave Britain an interval lead, but the tourists slammed away in the second half, and after a Messenger try, converted by Wrigley, Johnston heaved himself over the home line for the winning try. It was a remarkable and unexpected climax to the tour, in which the tourists had played 35 games, winning 19, including two out of three Tests. Financially, they had broken even, and the party returned to New Zealand dedicated to the development of the Northern Union game in their own continent.

At the end of the third Test it was revealed that Oldham had signed winger-cum-centre George Smith, still a great player at the age of 35, while Wigan had scooped their rivals by signing half-back or five-eighth Lance B. Todd, beginning Northern Unions career that was to make him the most famous player, administrator and commentator of his era.

In 1908 came the Australian breakaway from Rugby Union. The New South Wales Rugby Union, dissatisfied with rulings on broken time and compensation payments, decided to set up their own set of rules, and, more significantly, to send a team to Britain in 1908–9. Proceeds of this tour would be used to set up a New South Wales Rugby League.

Mr J. J. Giltinan, secretary of New South Wales Rugby Union, kept in constant contact by mail with the Northern Union secretary, Mr J. Platt. After the New Zealand tourists had played three successful games in Australia under Northern Union rules, a

Batley, first winners of the Rugby League Cup

The 1908 Australian touring team

1908 New Zealand touring team, the 'Pioneers'

Rorke's Drift 1914 N.U. touring team to Australia

The team believed by many to have been the greatest club side ever. The great 1914–15 Huddersfield 'Team of all the Talents'. The legendary Harold Wagstaff is in the centre of the picture behind Rosenfeld (with ball)

Brian Bevan, Warrington's magician on the wing

Jim Sullivan, Wigan's legendary full-back

momentous meeting took place at Sydney at which the New South Wales president, Mr Harry Hoyle, gave his casting vote for the adoption of Northern Union rules. The first clubs came from the Sydney area, but interest soon spread to other areas, notably Newcastle, and eventually interest was whipped up in Queensland.

In midsummer, 1908, 12 months after the departure of the New Zealand pioneers, the first Australian tourists to play Northern Union set sail for Britain. With them was H. H. 'Dally' Messenger, one of the great successes of the New Zealand tour.

The excitements of the New Zealand tour and the great news from Australia did not entirely cloud over the Union's major trophies. The Northern Union Challenge Cup final between Hull and Hunslet was played at Huddersfield on Saturday, 25 April, and despite a continuous storm of snow and sleet, 18 500 spectators paid £903 to see the match. The teams were:

Hull: Taylor; Parry, Cottrell, Cook, Rogers; Wallace, Anderson; Herridge, Owen, Carroll, Kilburn, Fulton, Holder.

Hunslet: Place; Farrar, Eagers, W. Goldthorpe, Batten; A. Goldthorpe, H. Smith; Wilson, Brooks, Jukes, Randall, Higson, Walsh.

Referee: Mr J. H. Smith (Widnes).

The constant blizzard spoiled the game, but Hunslet came nearest to overcoming the awful conditions with some brave, lively handling moves. After Eagers had dropped a goal, Smith scored a try converted by Albert Goldthorpe, and at half-time Hunslet led 7—0. In the second half Hull made a fitful rally, but then Albert Goldthorpe kicked another goal, and finally Farrar scored a try improved by Goldthorpe to give Hunslet a 14—0 victory and the cup.

Hunslet also reached the championship final, and they and Oldham had to meet twice before the trophy was won.

The teams drew 7—7 at Weaste, Salford, on 2 May, and the replay was at Wakefield the following Saturday, giving the Northern Union its longest-ever season. Hunslet won by 12 points to 2, and in doing so achieved the magnificent feat of winning four major trophies in a season, adding the championship to the Yorkshire League, the Yorkshire Cup and the Challenge Cup. Walter Goldthorpe scored two tries, Albert Goldthorpe two goals and Place a dropped goal for Hunslet, while White landed a goal for Oldham.

The 1908 annual meeting was a cheerful one, and the news from Australia and New Zealand had undoubtedly given the game a shot in the arm. More good news came from Wales, for although Ebbw Vale and Merthyr Tydfil had only moderate records in 1907–8, new clubs in Barry, Aberdare, Mid-Rhondda and Treherbert were admitted for 1908–9.

The Australians, with J. J. Giltinan as secretary-manager, and Dennis Lutge as captain, arrived at Tilbury on Sunday, 27 September 1908, and began their tour against the new Welsh club, Mid-Rhondda.

Three Tests had been arranged, with 'propaganda' venues, and the first was at Park Royal, London, on 12 December 1908. As propaganda the match was a flop, only 2200 turning up to see it, but the game provided a brilliant spectacle, the final score of 22 points each reflecting a superbly fought and exciting struggle. The teams for the first Britain *v.* Australia Test were:

Northern Union: Gifford (Barrow); Batten (Hunslet), Jenkins (Wigan), Dickenson (Warrington), Tyson (Oldham); Thomas (Wigan), Brooks (Warrington); A. Smith (Oldham), Longworth (Oldham), Jukes (Hunslet), Robinson (Halifax), Mann (Bradford), Higson (Bradford).

Australia: M. Bolewski; W. Heidke, J. Devereux, S. Deane, H. H. Messenger; A. Butler, A. Holloway; J. Abercrombie, L. O'Malley, A. Burdon, S. Walsh, A. Pearce, J. Courtney. Lutge, who had not been in good form, was replaced as captain by Messenger for the Test.

The match provided end-to-end excitement throughout. After a Messenger goal for Australia, tries by Thomas and Batten gave Britain a 6—2 lead. This was cut down by a try by Devereux, but suddenly the Northern Union got on top, and after a fine try by Brooks, converted by himself, beautiful combination between the backs saw Batten squeeze in at the corner for his second try to make it 14—5 at the interval.

Tyson made it 17—5 with another try, but then the Australians made a wonderful rally. Devereux got his second try, and forward O'Malley dribbled through for another, Messenger converting both to make the score 17—15. A passing movement from inside the home half ended with a Robinson try, but Messenger intercepted and made a try for Devereux, his hat-trick. Messenger converting to equalize the scores 20—20. Another Messenger goal gave Australia the lead, but in the last minute a penalty to Northern Union saw Brook land the goal.

The second Test match was played at another soccer stronghold, St James Park, Newcastle, on Saturday, 23 January 1909. This time the match was a much greater propaganda success, for 22 000 paid £568 to see the game. The match, however, never reached the heights of the first Test, and the Northern Union won 15—5 in comparative comfort.

In the Northern Union side Lomas (Salford) and Silcock (Wigan) came in for Dickenson and Jukes. Australia brought in A. Rosenfeld, F. Frawley, J. Morton, A. Conlon and T. McCabe. The home side, having had nearly all the play, led 8—0 at the interval, with tries from Thomas and Lomas and a goal from Lomas. In the second half Messenger scored one of his 'specials', a superlative effort in which he caught a high kick and swerved throughout the whole of the home defence to put the ball down under the posts and convert. He got a terrific ovation from the crowd.

Messenger's great effort was not enough to turn the tide, for Tyson scored another home try and Lomas kicked two more goals.

The third Test was an anticlimax. It was played for the third time on a soccer ground, Villa Park, Birmingham, on Monday, 15 February 1909. The Northern Union won 6—5 before a crowd of only a few thousand, and the game itself produced little excitement and interest.

At the end of their first tour the Australians had played 46 games, winning 22 and drawing six. Financially the tour had been a failure, but the Northern Union had underwritten the tour's losses, and there was no lack of spirit in the Australian camp as they set off for home in March 1909.

Inevitably, English clubs went for the Australian players as signings. Deane and Anlezark went to Oldham, Devereux and Morton joined Hull, and Albert Rosenfeld, a winger with a great future, joined Huddersfield.

The Australians proved their optimism following this 1908–9 tour by inviting the Northern Union to send a touring team to

Australia. The invitation was accepted, with 1910 scheduled as the year for the first-ever overseas tour by the Northern Union. In the meantime the Australian and New Zealand leagues set about consolidating their position. A New Zealand representative side visited Australia in 1909, and the first two games brought total gate receipts of over £2000.

In the Northern Union's domestic sphere Hull again reached the final of the Challenge Cup, with fellow-Yorkshire side Wakefield Trinity as their opponents. The match took place at Headingley on Saturday, 24 April, and the Northern League's biggest-ever crowd of well over 30,000 attended, producing receipts of £1,489 15*s*. 3*d*. There were astounding scenes before the kick-off, for large numbers of spectators queueing outside became impatient, and several thousand rushed the gates and broke in. The match was a triumph for the Wakefield Trinity lads, a team of local products, many of whom worked six successive night shifts before the final. 'If we want them fit we send them to work,' a Wakefield official commented.

The teams were:

Hull: Taylor; Rogers, Connell, Cottrell, Dechan; Anderson, Wallace; Herridge, Holder, Boylen, Havelock, Britton, Carroll.

Wakefield Trinity: Metcalfe; Bennett, Lynch, Sidwell, Simpson; Slater, Newbould; G. Taylor, Auton, Crosland, Kershaw, Walton, Beaumont.

Referee: Mr J. F. Smirke (Wigan).

Hull, despite their pull in greater experience, were soundly thrashed, 17 points to 0, by the young and enthusiastic Trinity side. Newbould had a great game for Trinity at half-back, scoring the first try and starting a four-man passing movement which gave Bennett the second. In the second half Newbould and Slater worked a move for Crosland to score, Metcalfe goaling, and Newbould and Slater made Bennett's second try. Newbould crowned a great performance with a cross-kick for Simpson to score the fifth and final try.

After the great crowd at Headingley the championship final at Salford the following Saturday attracted only 12 000. Wigan, who had scored more than 700 points during the season, beat Oldham 7—3 in a game which never reached great heights.

5

Australian Tours; Vintage Huddersfield

THE annual meetings of the Northern Union and of the Northern League brought a slight check on this new wave of optimism, for the news from Wales was not as bright as had been hoped. Barry, Mid-Rhondda and Aberdare left the League after moderate seasons, reducing Welsh membership to the trio of Merthyr Tydfil, Ebbw Vale and Treherbert.

Throughout the close season clubs continued to import players from 'Down Under'. H. S. Turtill, New Zealand full-back, joined St Helens; Frawley, O'Malley and Stuntz, Australians, joined Warrington; H. Rowe, an All Blacks winger, signed for Leeds and New Zealand forward Trevarthen joined Huddersfield. This spate of Colonial signings caused indignation in Australia and New Zealand, where League officials saw their strength being drained, and after negotiations between the Northern Union and the two Australasian leagues certain laws were adopted. Transfers could not be effected without the approval of the home club, or without two years' residence in Britain.

Arrangements for the 1901 tour of Australia were announced at the start of the 1909–10 season. The British team were to receive a guaranteed figure to cover expenses, plus a percentage of gate receipts. The managers for the tour were chosen on 22 February 1910, and the first pair of touring managers in Northern Union history were nominated. They were Messrs. J. H. Houghton (St Helens), president of the Union, and J. Clifford (Huddersfield), a former president.

Excitement grew among players as the summer of 1910 approached. The thrill of an overseas tour was dangled in front of players like a carrot before a donkey, and clubs were asked to nominate players who would 'be a credit to the Union both on and off the field'. Within a few weeks 150 players had been nominated. Two trial matches were played at Headingley and Wigan and the following players were finally chosen for this first great Australasian tour: Ruddick (Broughton Rangers), Shugars (Warrington), Farrar, Smith, Jukes and Batten (Hunslet), Winstanley (Leigh), Davies and Bartholomew (Huddersfield), Riley (Halifax), Jenkins (Ebbw Vale), Lomas and Curzon (Salford), Newbould and Kershaw (Wakefield Trinity), Young, Webster and Ward (Leeds), Boylen (Hull), Helm and Avery (Oldham), and Ramsdale, Sharrock, Leytham, Jenkins and Thomas (Wigan). Two sailings were arranged, the first for the bulk of the party, the second for players whose clubs were concerned in cup and championship matches.

In order to clear the decks for the tour, the Union brought forward the Challenge Cup final to Saturday, 16 April, the same day as the championship semi-finals. The cup final at Fartown, Huddersfield, produced the oddity of a very late start, for both Hull and Leeds, the finalists, were delayed by faulty train services between Leeds and Huddersfield. The teams took the field at 4.20 p.m., 50 minutes after the scheduled starting time.

The teams were:

Hull: Taylor; Cottrell, Devereux, Morton, Rogers; Wallace, Anderson; Herridge, Osborne, R. Taylor, Connell, Holder, Walton.

Leeds: Young; Fawcett, Goldthorpe, Gillie, Baron; Ware, Sanders; Biggs, Jarman, Harrison, Topham, Webster, Ward.

Referee: Mr H. J. Priestley (Salford).

For Hull, their third successive Challenge Cup appearance simply had to be a winning one to satisfy their long-suffering supporters. Leeds were seeking victory at their first attempt. Hull played great football in the early stages, and after a drop goal by Wallace, Cottrell scored a try and Rogers a goal. However, a goal by Young and a second-half try by Walter Goldthorpe made it 7—5 and another Young penalty equalized the scores. Hull had missed their chance, for Leeds played most of the game without their injured half-back Sanders.

The crowd at this game was 17 000, and when the replay took

place on the following Monday 11 600 attended, a good mid-week crowd. Both teams had injury changes, Taylor and Anderson dropping out of the Hull side and Rowe replacing Sanders in the Leeds line-up.

It was the Hull side which was hardest hit, and Leeds piled on the agony of Hull's third successive Challenge Cup defeat with a record 26—12 victory. At one stage Leeds led 26—0, and only a late burst by Hull when Leeds relaxed made the score look reasonably respectable. Webster, Topham, Goldthorpe and Rowe scored tries for Leeds, and Young seven goals. Hull's consolation points came from tries by Walton and Connell, Rogers landing three goals.

After three years of disappointment Oldham won the championship by beating Wigan 13—7 at Broughton. Dixon, McCabe and George Smith got the Oldham tries, and White two goals, while a Todd try and goals from Leytham and Ferguson completed Wigan's total.

With the end of the Northern Union home season, thoughts turned towards the momentous pioneer tour of Australia. The first party of tourists arrived at Sydney at the end of May, 1910, and the remaining members landed on 2 June. After their enthusiastic welcome by the New South Wales League the tourists played their first game at Sydney against New South Wales on Saturday, 4 June.

Not surprisingly, the tourists lost 28—15, but the gate of £1300 cheered them up. Two days later New South Wales won again, 27–20, and again the gate was good. The third game was also against New South Wales the following Saturday, and this time the tourists recorded their first success with the score 23—10. Total gate receipts for the first three games were £3600.

The eagerly awaited first Test on Australian soil was at Sydney on 18 June 1910. An immense crowd of nearly 50 000 saw the match in which the sides were captained by James Lomas and Dally Messenger. Lomas and Messenger preceded the game with a private goal-kicking competition. Lomas won this, and the Northern Union side followed this up with a great 27—20 win in the Test. Hickey (try) and Messenger (goal) put Australia ahead, but Leytham touched down after a dribble and Lomas converted.

A fine Messenger try, and two goals by the Australian star, put Australia 12—5 ahead, but Thomas nipped over for a try to Britain, and another try from Leytham made it 12—11 at the interval. There was no holding the brilliant tourists in the second half, and Jukes, a mighty Hunslet forward, scored a hat-trick of tries, Batten getting Britain's seventh try. Lomas completed three goals for Britain. The match had been well won when two late tries and a goal to Australia made it 27—20 at the finish.

Following the first Test win, the tourists beat Newcastle and Queensland, and the total gate money in the kitty reached £6000. The finances of the tour were safe.

This good news was before the representatives of the Union clubs when they met for the annual meeting at Huddersfield on 29 June 1910. The balance sheet reported sound finances, and the only unhappy note again came from Wales, where Treherbert decided to call it a day. To balance this, Coventry entered a team for 1910–11, thus opening up the Midlands for the first time.

The second Australian Test took place at Brisbane on Saturday, 2 July, and the tourists scored another brilliant victory after trailing 11—0 at one stage. The Northern Union revival against this deficit began when Leytham scored a fine try, converted by Lomas and then Leytham's Wigan team-mate Thomas also scored, Lomas again adding the goal. In the second half Britain played brilliantly and Kershaw and Leytham (3) scored further tries in a final score of 22—17.

As the Northern Union tourists had won the Test series, it was decided that the third Test should be played against a combined Australia–New Zealand side. This match was played at Sydney on Saturday, 9 July, before yet another crowd of 50 000, gate receipts totalling £1850.

Australasia scored first with a try by V. Farnsworth, Lomas replying with a penalty goal. A goal from Messenger and a nicely worked try for Courtney put Australasia further ahead, but a Leytham try made it 8—5 at the interval. McKivatt scored a try and Messenger a goal to make it 13—5, and things looked black for Britain when Batten was carried off injured. But the Northern Union players pulled off a grandstand finish, and tries by Avery and Winstanley and a goal from Thomas equalized the scores.

An extra match against Australasia was arranged for Wednesday, 13 July, and the home side achieved revenge for Test beating with a victory of 32 points to 15. From Australia the tourists went on to New Zealand, where they played several games, running up big scores against the Maoris, Auckland, Rotorua and New Zealand, the latter match being won by 52 points to 20. The gate for this Test match at Wellington was £520, bringing total tour receipts to over £11 000, of which the Northern Union received £6500, a bumper return.

After a final match with New South Wales on Saturday, 6 August, the tourists set sail from Melbourne in the S.S. *Otranto.* They won this last game 50—12 and set the seal on a magnificent and memorable first-ever tour of Australasia.

Hardly had the tourists returned than a cablegram from Australia requested an invitation to tour Britain in 1911–12. The invitation was soon forthcoming from the Northern Union.

On the home front the Union suffered another Welsh setback when Merthyr Tydfil gave up the fight against lack of success and apathy in January 1911. In the Midlands Coventry were not faring too happily, but with one or two scalps under their belt were making a better show than Liverpool City had done.

The Challenge Cup final of 1911 brought together two Lancashire teams, making a change from the all-Yorkshire finals of 1908. 1909 and 1910. It also brought about a game which proved almost a complete flop, for Wigan and Broughton Rangers met at Salford on Saturday, 29 April, on a day on which torrential rain had fallen since early morning. The pitch was like a swamp, and Wigan lodged a protest, calling for a postponement. However, the Union committee decreed that the match should go on, and 8000 hardy souls saw a travesty of a game in a continuous downpour on a pitch ankle-deep in mud and water. Wigan, normally a fast, attractive side, were literally all at sea in these conditions, and Rangers sloshed home by dubious virtue of two first-half penalty goals by Harris. The teams for this ill-fated match were:

Broughton Rangers: Davidson; Bouch, Wild, Harris, Scott; Barlow, E. Jones; J. Clampitt, B. Clampitt, Ruddick, Gorry, Hirst, Winskill.

Wigan: Sharrock; Leytham, Jenkins, Todd, Miller; Thomas, Gleave; Seeling, Williams, Cheetham, Ramsdale, Whittaker, Silcock.

Referee: Mr J. F. May (St Helens).

Wigan's hopes of consolation in the championship final a week later were dashed once again by their rivals from Oldham. The venue was Broughton, the weather much kindlier and a crowd of 20 000 saw Oldham play consistently against an erratic and disappointing Wigan to win 20—7. Oldham's star was Test captain Jim Lomas, transferred from Salford, who scored two tries, kicked four goals and made tries for White.

At the 1911 annual meeting Mr G. Taylor (Wigan) took over from Mr J. Wood (Leeds) as chairman of the Northern Union under the presidency of the Earl of Derby. The most interesting news of the close season was the announcement of the names of the Australian tourists, who included several New Zealanders in their ranks. The name of the great Dally Messenger was missing, due to business reasons, a big disappointment for British fans. The players left for England on 5 August and were welcomed at Tilbury on 16 September 1911.

Managed by Messrs. C. H. Ford and J. Quinlan, the tourists numbered 24 Aussies and four New Zealanders: F. Woodward, A. H. Francis, C. Savoury and G. Gillett. Captain was C. McKivatt, and the remainder of the party were C. McMurtrie, P. McCue, W. Noble, A. Broomham, J. Murray, V. Farnsworth, W. Farnsworth, R. Stuart, D. Frawley, C. Russell, H. Gilbert, R. Craig, E. Courtney, R. Williams, C. Sullivan, W. Cann, P. Burge, A. Holloway, T. Berecry, S. Darmody, C. Fraser, W. Neil, H. Hallett.

The tourists started well, beating Midlands and South at Coventry, Broughton Rangers, Wales at Ebbw Vale and England at Fulham soccer ground. They then beat the Northern League at Goodison Park soccer ground, and continued to have the best of matters against club sides. Their first defeat was at the hands of Wigan before a 25 000 crowd, but their form was still good enough to arouse great interest for the first Test match. Oddly, the Union still persisted in making these great games serve the ends of propaganda rather than keeping them within the Union, and the match was played at St James Park, Newcastle, on Wednesday, 8 November 1911, before a gate of 6000.

Teams were:

Northern Union: Sharrock (Wigan); W. Davies (Halifax), Wagstaff (Huddersfield), Jenkins, Miller (Wigan); Thomas (Wigan), Smith (Hunslet); Harrison (Leeds), Burgham (Halifax), J. Clampitt (Broughton R.), Gronow (Huddersfield), Winstanley (Wigan), Avery (Oldham).

Australasia: Fraser; Broomham, Gilbert, Hallett, Russell; V. Farnsworth, McKivatt; Francis, McCue, Cann, Courtney, Williams, Craig.

Davies beat Fraser to put Britain ahead, but Farnsworth gathered a cross-kick from Russell to score. Thomas, who had converted Davies's try, added a penalty, then suddenly Australia took charge. Brilliant passing movements along the backs dazzled and bewildered the home defence, and Francis, Farnsworth, Hallett and Cann ran in superb tries, Francis converting two. It was 19—7 at half-time, and the only score of the second half was an unconverted try by Davies for Britain. The tourists' win was quite a blow to home complacency.

The second Test was played at Edinburgh on Saturday, 18 December, 1911, before a poor crowd of only 8000. The Australians were out for an Ashes-winning victory, and the Northern Union were lucky to escape with an 11—11 draw in a match which the tourists claimed to have won with a disallowed penalty goal.

Britain had several changes, Wood (Oldham), Jenkinson (Hunslet), Lomas (Oldham), Batten (Hunslet), Davies (Huddersfield), Clark (Huddersfield), Ramsdale (Wigan) and Woods (Rochdale Hornets) replacing Sharrock, W. Davies, Jenkins, Miller, Thomas, Burgham, Clampitt and Avery.

The Northern Union side had the better of things in the first half and good tries by Wagstaff (2) and Lomas, plus a goal from Wood, gave them an 11—3 half-time lead, Frawley touching down for an Australasian try. In the second half the visitors tied at 11—11, with tries by McKivatt and Russell, Francis landing one goal.

Then came the controversial decision that robbed Australasia of victory. Francis took a shot at goal, and one touch-judge, an Australian, put up his flag. The other touch-judge, appointed by the Northern Union, disallowed the shot, and the referee ruled 'no goal'. The Australasians claimed unavailingly that the shot had gone between the posts.

This draw made the third Test vital, and it took place at Villa Park, Birmingham, on New Year's Day, 1912. The Union brought in Jenkins (Wigan) for Wagstaff and Australasia played tall winger T. Berecry for Russell. This third match resulted in a complete and crushing victory for the tourists, who won in masterly fashion. At one stage the home side led 8—0, but then Ramsdale hurt his ankle and left the field. Australasia took complete charge, and in the end the Northern Union were licked 33—8, V. Farnsworth, McKivatt (2), McCue (2), Berecry (2) and Frawley (2) scored tries, Gilbert and Frawley (2) kicking goals. This victory gave Australasia the series, and made up for the 'robbery' of two points which cost them the second Test.

It was an Australian who hit the headlines in the Union's domestic season—Huddersfield's flying winger Albert Rosenfeld notched 80 tries in 1911–12, a superlative record which still stands. Huddersfield also set up a team record by scoring 1183 points, and reached the championship final in cavalier style.

Headingley was the venue for the 1912 cup final, played on Saturday, 27 April 1912, between Dewsbury and Oldham. The attendance of 15 721 (£853) was a big disappointment, but the game brought joy to Dewsbury, who won their first trophy since joining the Northern Union. Teams were:

Dewsbury: Jackett; Rhodes, Ware, Ward, Sharples; Neary, Milner; Richardson, Garnett, O'Neill, Hammill, Abbishaw, Evans.

Oldham: Wood; Cook, Dean, Davies, Williams; Lomas, Anlezark; Ferguson, Smith, Avery, White, Wise, Wiltshire.

Referee: Mr B. Ennion (Wigan).

At half-time, in a dour and unspectacular game, a try by Cook and a goal by Ferguson, against a goal by Neary, had given Oldham a 5—2 lead. The second half was rugged and grim, and there were only 10 minutes to go when Avery, the Oldham forward, was sent off, and Dewsbury snatched a try by Rhodes. With two minutes left, Dewsbury won a scrum on the Oldham line and Rhodes squeezed over to give Dewsbury an 8—5 victory.

On Saturday, 4 May, two great footballing sides, Huddersfield and Wigan, met at Halifax for the championship. A crowd of 15 000 saw the expected fast, exciting game, won by the Huddersfield 'team of all the talents' by 13—5. Rosenfeld, Clark and Davies got the tries, and Longstaffe and Grey the goals. Holland scored Wigan's try, Thomas converting.

Colonial signings stole the thunder at the start of the new season. By financial agreement with Australasian clubs several fine players came to England, among them H. Gilbert and S. Darmody to Hull, W. Farnsworth to Oldham and A. H. Francis to Wigan. These signings reopened hostilities between the Union and Australia, and the Union ruled that no player could sign for an English club without a two-year residence qualification.

Huddersfield's wonderful teamwork was again the talk of the Union in 1912–13. With no tour of Australia scheduled until 1914, the Union's competitions came into their own again, and Huddersfield underscored their glorious attacking football by reaching the final of both Challenge Cup and championship.

The cup final took place at Headingley on Saturday, 26 April before a crowd of 22 754 (£1446).

Teams were:

Huddersfield: Holland; Rosenfeld, Gleeson, Wagstaff, Moorhouse; Grey, Davies; Higson, Lee, Clark, Gronow, Longstaffe, Chilcott.

Warrington: Jolley; Brooks, Tranter, Renwick, Bradshaw; Dainteth, Nicholas; G. Thomas, Chesters, Skelhorne, Fearnley, R. Thomas, Cox.

Referee: Mr J. F. May (St Helens).

Everyone expected brilliant Huddersfield to spreadeagle the Warrington defence, but Warrington soon showed otherwise. At half-time their fierce-tackling, determined defenders had kept the Fartowners out, and a Bradshaw try and Jolley touchline goal had given Warrington a 5—0 lead. In the second half Huddersfield threw everything into the attack and Moorhouse snatched two tries after all-out attacks. Gallant Warrington had shot their bolt, and Wagstaff and Moorhouse did a magnificent interpassing act for Moorhouse to get his hat-trick.

On the following Saturday the 'team of all the talents' ended a great season by once again beating Wigan in the championship final at Wakefield. Before a 16 000 crowd, Huddersfield laid on a display of sparkling football, and although Wigan kept the score to 3—2 at half-time, they were afterwards overwhelmed. A Clark try against a Thomas goal provided the first-half scoring, but after the interval the Fartowners turned on their full flow of sweeping movements. Davies sold a dummy and romped over, Holland converting, and two minutes later 'Waggy' kicked ahead, followed up and sent Clark over again, Holland once more converting.

The romp went on, and Wagstaff made a try for Moorhouse. Then, in quick succession, Clark and Rosenfeld (2) rubbed it in with more tries, Holland landing another goal in a 27—2 victory. It had been another fine year for this vintage Huddersfield outfit, established by now as a team of all-time greats.

The early stages of the 1913–14 season, which was to end with the second tour of Australia, brought the dawn of the big transfer fee in Northern Union, and overseas players set the standard.

Wrigley was transferred from Huddersfield to Hunslet for £500, and Lance Todd went from Wigan to Dewsbury for £400.

Huddersfield continued to break records in 1913–14. They hit up the highest individual score when they pulverized a junior club, Swinton Park Rangers, 119—2 in a Challenge Cup game. Just when they seemed likely to sweep all before them again, Hull surprisingly beat them 11—3 in the Challenge Cup semi-final at Headingley, and Hull went on to meet Wakefield Trinity, their conquerors in 1909. With players scheduled to leave on the Australasia tour, the Challenge Cup was brought forward to Saturday, 18 April 1914, and again the championship semi-finals were held the same day.

The Challenge Cup final was played at Halifax before a crowd of 19 000 (£1035), and with the following teams:

Hull: Rogers; Harrison, Batten, Gilbert, Francis; Devereux, Anderson; Herridge, Holder, Taylor, Hammill, Grice, Darmody.

Wakefield Trinity: Land; Johnson, Lynch, Ponyton, Howarth; J. Parkin, Millican; Dixon, Crosland, Beattie, Kershaw, E. Parkin, A. Burton.

Referee: Mr J. F. May (St Helens).

Hull at last gained the Challenge Cup victory that had eluded them so many times, and in doing so won revenge for 1909. The game was keenly fought, but never reached any great heights of brilliance, and at half-time there was no score. The second half followed a similar pattern until Kershaw, the Wakefield captain, was sent off the field. Hull got the upper hand and after 72 minutes Devereux, Gilbert and Batten handled to put Harrison over. Two minutes from the end Devereux and Gilbert went through again and Francis made the match safe.

The championship final the following week brought to an exciting finale the Cinderella-like story of a club's struggle against adversity. Salford, the club once dubbed 'champion runners-up' had been on the verge of bankruptcy and dissolution. Their directors had struggled on, a team had been brought together which suddenly blossomed into a rugged power and the reward was the 1913–14 championship. To add to the thrilling nature of this triumph, their opponents at Headingley were the mighty Huddersfield.

Only a moderate crowd turned up for what was expected to be a formal victory for Huddersfield. Victory for the favourites seemed confirmed when Wagstaff, Rogers, Gleeson and Wagstaff again paved the way for a Gleeson try, but Salford fought tigerishly and Rees forced his way over the Huddersfield line for Mesley to convert. In the second half the courageous Salford defenders fought a glorious backs-to-the-wall action against non-stop Huddersfield attacks.

Time and time again Huddersfield seemed certain to score, but always a last-ditch tackle saved the day, and when the final whistle blew the bruised, battered but triumphant Salford side, winners by 5—3, were chaired off the field by their enthusiastic supporters—victors at last!

With the championship final over, the second party of tourists went off to join their colleagues, who had sailed before the Challenge Cup final. Managers for the tour were again Messrs. J. H. Houghton and J. Clifford, with Wagstaff as captain, and the full party was: H. Wagstaff, J. H. Rogers, S. Moorhouse, F. Longstaff, D. Clark and J. Chilcott (Huddersfield), W. Hall, A. E. Wood and D. Holland (Oldham), G. Thomas, B. Jenkins, A. P. Coldrick and R. Ramsdale (Wigan), F. Smith, J. W. Guerin and J. Smales (Hunslet), W. A. Davies and W. Jarman (Leeds). F. Williams, S. Prosser (Halifax), J. E. Robinson, W. Roman (Rochdale Hornets), A. J. Francis (Hull), J. O'Garra, A. Johnson (Widnes) and J. L. Clampitt (Broughton Rangers).

6

'Rorke's Drift'; First World War

THE 'Rorke's Drift' tour began on Saturday, 6 June 1914, with a 26—10 beating by Metropolis at Sydney. Then came defeat against New South Wales, but the tourists soon found their land legs and beat Queensland, Ipswich and Northern Districts. This put the tourists in a cheerful frame of mind for the first Test that set in train eight days of remarkable incident. In this eight-day period three Test matches and a minor game were played by the tourists, a terrific row blew up which almost wrecked the tour and the Northern Union side won one of the most fantastic and courageous victories ever to be won in any sport.

Before the first Test Britain lost with injuries both full-backs, Wood and Gwyn Thomas, and Leeds forward Bill Jarman was pressed into service. Despite this handicap, the tourists played superb football before a 40 000 crowd at Moore Agricultural Ground, Sydney, and won by 23 points to 5. The Northern Union scored five tries through Moorhouse (2), Clark, Robinson and Hall, while Longstaff and Robinson scored two goals each.

The second Test match had been rather unwisely arranged by the Australians for the King's Birthday, two days later. This meant that the tourists were further weakened by injuries to Jarman, Moorhouse, Longstaff and Bert Jenkins, sustained in the first Test.

In a reshuffled side Hall played in the threequarters and Rogers played out-half. Even with these enforced changes Britain fought hard and were level 7—7 at the interval. However, Robinson was injured shortly afterwards, and Australia took command to score a second-half try and goal to clinch victory at 12—7. The Test series was even.

It was after this second Test at Sydney that the Australian League threw the whole series into chaos. The third Test was scheduled for later in the tour, but the New South Wales League suddenly decided that the time was ripe to rearrange it for the following Saturday in place of a New South Wales *v.* tourists game. This would mean that the Northern Union team, badly hit by injuries and with a mid-week fixture to be played, would be in a desperate state. The Australian officials offered as explanation for their remarkable about-face the claim that interest was at fever pitch and that a huge gate would be recorded on 4 July.

Mr Clifford refused to accept the New South Wales decision. The Australians promptly cabled the Northern Union in Britain. The result was a hastily convened management committee meeting which, in stiff upper-lip fashion, ordered the tourists to play on Saturday as requested.

The message added: 'England expects that every man will do his duty.' The Nelson touch won the day, and the team agreed to take the field, handicapped as they were.

Before the match Mr Clifford addressed the players in the dressing-room. It was a stirring call to action, and Harold Wagstaff later wrote that every player's eyes filled with tears as Mr Clifford spoke. They then went out to make history. Typical of their spirit was the action of full-back Alf Wood, who played with a patched-up broken nose.

The teams for this stirring contest were:

Australia: Hallett; Frawley, Deane, Tidyman, W. Messenger; Fraser, Holloway; Cann, Courtney, Craig, Sullivan, Burge, Pearce.

Northern Union: Wood; Williams, Hall, Wagstaff, Davies; Smith, Prosser; Holland, Coldrick, Ramsdale, Johnson, Clark, Chilcott.

A crowd topping 40 000 saw this memorable game, given the title 'Rorke's Drift' after a British rearguard action which, in its courage against overwhelming odds, recalled a battle of the Zulu War in which two officers and 80 men repulsed 4000 Zulu warriors at Rorke's Drift, Zululand, in January 1879. In the first two minutes of the game the tourists' plight worsened when winger Frank Williams twisted his leg, but despite this the visitors played attractive football and led 9—3 at half-time, Percy Coldrick scoring a try and Wood three goals.

Early in the second half Clark, the Huddersfield forward, fell and broke his collar-bone. He tried to resume, but the pain was too great, and he left the field with tears in his eyes. Then Frank Williams's leg gave out, and he too had to leave the field. Then Hall, of Oldham, received concussion going down for a loose ball, and the Northern Union had 10 men against 13. It was a hopeless position.

There were 30 minutes to go, and for 10 men to hold out against 13 seemed beyond the bounds of reason. Yet the miracle happened. Time and time again the Aussies attacked, only to be pulled down and thrown back by men who tackled with superhuman strength. The four-man pack of the British heeled the ball from the scrum in fantastic fashion, and in the makeshift back division forwards Johnson and Coldrick ran themselves into the ground, covering and tackling.

With 20 minutes left, Wagstaff found a gap in the stranglehold and broke through. He gave the ball to Johnson, forward-turned-winger, who put the ball to his toe, dribbled half the length of the field defying pursuit and touched down for a try which brought the house down. Wood kicked the goal, a dazed and dizzy Hall came back to give the tourists 11 men and although Deane got a late try to make the score 14—6, the glorious fight against crippling odds won the day and the series, and the Sydney crowd applauded Wagstaff's men off the field.

With the praises of all Australia and England ringing in their ears, the tourists left for New Zealand, where they beat Hawkes Bay, Wellington, Taranaki, Auckland Province, Wanganui, Auckland and the New Zealand Test team 16—13 at Auckland. After playing a match at Melbourne against New South Wales the tourists set off for home after playing before a total number of spectators exceeding the 1910 tour and with gate receipts £2000 up on the previous tour.

Everything was set to give the returning tourists the heroes' welcome they deserved when almost without warning an event took place which pushed all thought of sporting success into the background. After a series of international squabbles Britain entered the war against Germany in August 1914, and even as the tourists were sailing home their country was pitched into the most devastating war the world had known in its history.

The outbreak of war caused consternation everywhere, and the Northern Union management committee had to decide whether the season would begin as scheduled for 1914–15. Many clubs were denuded of players by the rush to join the forces, and Mr J. Platt, the Union secretary, made it clear in a statement that 'serving King and country is more important than winning medals on the football field'.

Amid the disorder, the Union decided to open the season as usual, to allow recruiting on grounds, and to regard the game as a form of wartime entertainment for the forces and for munitions workers at home.

The best-known players in the game continued to join the forces, among them Gwyn Thomas and Bert Jenkins (Wigan) Chick Johnson (Widnes) and G. Ruddick (Broughton). The news was often unhappy for early casualties included Midgley (Bramley), Twigg (Rochdale Hornets) and Tom Williams (Salford). Many more fine players fell in action during the 1914–18 war. One town. St Helens was stated to have provided no fewer than 13 000 volunteers for various forms of war service.

Despite dwindling crowds and interest the 1914–15 season finished with the Challenge Cup and championship finals. The great Huddersfield side did the double again beating St Helens in the Cup and Leeds in the championship as the swan-song in a great era of open football.

The championship final was played first at Wakefield before a 16 000 crowd. Huddersfield were at their superlative best and Leeds were beaten 35 points to 2. On Saturday 1 May Huddersfield met St Helens at Oldham seeking the four-cup feat having already won the Yorkshire League and Cup and the League championship.

Only 8000 people saw the Challenge Cup final which was almost called off before it started. The St Helens players dissatisfied with their terms refused to play, and were persuaded to do so only by their wing threequarter and captain, Tom Barton, a gallant sportsman. Perhaps the disgruntled St Helens players were in the wrong mood for a cup final, for Huddersfield romped home 37—3, scoring 9 tries and 5 goals. The goals for Huddersfield were kicked by forward Ben Gronow, who thus beat the League record of 138 previously set by A. Carmichael (Hull K.R.).

Teams for this last Challenge Cup final before the resumption of peacetime football were:

Huddersfield: Holland; Rosenfeld, Gleeson, Wagstaff, Moorhouse; Rogers, Ganley; Longstaff, Clark, Gronow, Banks, Lee, Higson.

St Helens: Roberts; Barton, Flanagan, White, Greenall; Trenwith, Creevey; Daniels, Durkin, Farrimond, Myers, Jackson, Shallcross.

Referee: Mr R. Robinson (Bradford).

Huddersfield's four-cups season was the last full season of the war. Warrington announced in May 1915, that they would close down for the duration of the war, and their decision anticipated the annual meeting of the Union in June 1915. At this meeting the Union decided that there would be no more professional football in wartime, and that competitive tournaments would be suspended. Matches could be played on a friendly basis by arrangement between clubs.

With 1500 players serving in the forces, and attendances down to rock bottom, this was the only possible decision. The Yorkshire clubs were first to try to make the best of a bad job. They held an informal meeting, and decided to create inter-club 'friendlies', with players receiving 2*s*. 6*d*. 'tea money' as expenses. Lancashire clubs quickly followed suit with the plan for friendly matches, and these began in September 1916, with scratch sides and before small crowds. The Northern Union had been reduced to an emaciated amateur tournament, but at least the game was being kept alive.

Although there were no big tournaments in 1916–17, several representative matches were played for war charities. Yorkshire met Lancashire, and a Yorkshire *v.* New Zealand XV played under Rugby Union rules.

Sad news continued to arrive from the front of great players killed in action. They included Bill Jarman (Leeds), Fred Longstaffe (Huddersfield), Walter Roman (Rochdale), George Thom

(Salford), J. Harrison (Hull), J. H. Turtill (St Helens) and George Thomas (Warrington).

At the end of the emergency 1917–18 season the Northern Union seemed on its last legs. Clubs were so hard-up that Oldham, Broughton Rangers and Wigan had to sell their grandstands to raise funds. Other clubs dubbed them 'the timber merchants'. Although the end of the war with Germany was not far away, prospects of its end were not bright in June 1918, and Mr J. H. Smith, presiding at the annual meeting, needed all his powers of eloquence to convince clubs that there was any purpose in carrying on. Some clubs started in September, some in October, and few of them really believed they could survive another season of friendly matches and poor crowds. Mercifully, the end of the First World War was in sight.

7

Post-war Revival

THE war with Germany ended officially on 11 November 1918. At a Northern Union meeting of representatives on 5 December the question of a revival of full-scale tournaments was raised and, wisely, it was agreed that there could be no full resumption until 1919–20, when the country had had time to get back to normal and players had returned from overseas service. It was decided that during the final makeshift season of 1918–19 the Lancashire and Yorkshire League and cups would be played, but that there should be no Challenge Cup or championship. Players would be paid their 2*s*. 6*d*. tea money, plus up to 10*s*. for broken time.

With the promised resumption of full-time activities in 1919–20, clubs which had closed down for the war began to come back into the game, although there was one unhappy casualty. Founder members Runcorn, first winners of the Lancashire Senior Competition, did not resume, and Cheshire's last team disappeared.

The transfer market buzzed in December and January, and registrations of new players poured into the office of the Union secretary, Mr J. Platt. The Lancashire League and Yorkshire League programmes opened on Saturday, 8 January 1919, and the size of the attendances surprised and delighted officials. Northern Union had not lost its support from the terraces.

Teams playing in the revived competitions at this time were Barrow, Wigan, Widnes, St Helens Recreation, Leigh, Oldham, Rochdale, Salford, Swinton, St Helens, Broughton Rangers, Warrington, Hull, Halifax, Bramley, Batley, Leeds, Hull K.R., Dewsbury, Hunslet, Wakefield Trinity, Bradford and York—a bumper return to peacetime football.

Australia and New Zealand shared in the quick post-war revival, and the Australian authorities lost no time in asking Britain for a touring team. The Northern Union Council, equally anxious to set the ball rolling again agreed to send a team at the end of the 1919–20 season.

Rochdale Hornets won the first post-war trophy when they beat Oldham 22—0 in the final of the Lancashire Cup before a £1700 gate at Salford, while in Yorkshire the famous Huddersfield side carried on where they had left off by beating Dewsbury 14—8 at Headingley before a splendid 21 500 crowd. The league championships were won by Rochdale, who secured the double, and Hull.

The brief but successful 1918–19 season, with its surprisingly big crowds and smooth return to competitive football, closed on a happy note with the report to the 1919 annual meeting that the majority of clubs were free from debt and rarin' to go in 1919–20.

The great post-war boom reached new heights, with huge crowds in 1919–20. In several centres, including Hull, Rochdale, Widnes, Halifax, Swinton and Warrington, new ground records were set up. A crowd of 26 000 saw Huddersfield beat Leeds 24—5 in the Yorkshire Cup final at Halifax, and 19 000 saw Oldham avenge their previous year's cup defeat by beating Lancashire rivals Rochdale 7—0.

The coming of the first post-war tour was approached with great enthusiasm and confidence, and names of the tourists were announced in March 1920. Managers were Mr John Wilson (Hull K.R.), Northern League secretary, and Mr Sidney Foster (Halifax). The 26 players were: *Backs:* G. Thomas, H. Wagstaff, J. Rogers (Huddersfield), A. E. Wood, E. Davies (Oldham), E. W. Jones (Rochdale Hornets), D. Hurcombe (Wigan), W. J. Stone (Hull), J. Doyle (Barrow), C. Stacey, E. Lloyd (Halifax), S. Stockwell, J. A. Bacon (Leeds), J. Parkin (Wakefield T.); *Forwards:* A. Milnes (Halifax), J. Cartwright (Leigh), J. Bowers (Rochdale Hornets), W. Cunliffe, J. Skelhorne (Warrington), S. Rees (Leeds), A. Johnson, W. Reid (Widnes), B. Gronow, D. Clark (Huddersfield), H. Hilton (Oldham), F. Gallagher (Dewsbury). Of this party, Wood, Wagstaff, Rogers, Johnson and Clark were 1914 tourists. As always, the tourists sailed in two parties, Huddersfield and Wigan players leaving after the Challenge Cup final.

There was still no holding Huddersfield on the Union's home

front. They reached the Challenge Cup final again, and met Wigan at Headingley on Saturday, 10 April 1920, in the first cup final since 1915. The attendance was disappointing 14 000 paying £1935. Teams were:

Huddersfield: Holland; Pogson, Wagstaff, Gleeson, Todd; Rogers, Habron; Swindon, Naylor, Fenwick, Sherwood, Gronow, Clark.

Wigan: Jolley; Smith, Hurcombe, F. Prescott, Hall; Hesketh, Jerram; Seeling, Coldrick, Ramsdale, Shaw, T. Prescott, Lowe.

Referee: Mr F. Mills (Oldham).

The game did not live up to expectations, and the first try was a scrappy affair, Hall being awarded an obstruction try for Wigan after a kick ahead. This roused Huddersfield, and Rogers and Pogson made a try for Wagstaff. Then Pogson got a try, Gronow kicked a goal for Huddersfield, and Jolley one for Wigan to make the interval score 8—5. Wigan restored their lead with a Jerram try and Jolley goal, then suddenly Huddersfield had an unbroken spell of fine football. The Wigan defence was cut to pieces by swift, scientific moves and Habron, Todd and Pogson went over for tries, Gronow landing two goals. Huddersfield had done it again 21—10.

The championship play-offs had an air of anticlimax about them. They were played after the tourists had left for Australia, and Huddersfield and Hull were without their tourists for the final at Headingley on 24 April. Huddersfield were worst hit by tour calls, and before a crowd of 12 513 they were beaten 3—2 in an unexciting game, Batten scoring a try against a Holland goal.

The 1920 close season brought to an end a wonderful record of service with the Northern Union when Mr J. Platt, tireless and zealous secretary for 25 years, and founder-secretary of the Northern Union, announced his retirement.

At the 1920 annual meeting the story of the great post-war boom continued. The balance sheet showed a surplus of £4641, and Mr W. Fillan (Huddersfield), the new chairman, said there was no sign of the boom receding. Mr Platt's great service was praised, and Mr John Wilson, of Hull Kingston Rovers, was named as his successor. Mr Wilson was not present to witness his election—he was on the Australian tour as co-manager of the British side!

This 1920 tour was designed to put the game back squarely on its feet in the international sphere. In this it succeeded magnificently, for no fewer than 65 000 people, a world-record attendance, saw Sydney meet the tourists at the Cricket Ground in the first match. Receipts of £5500 were also a record.

After a successful series of club and state games, with only one lost, against New South Wales, the tourists met Australia at Brisbane in the first Test on 26 June 1920. Australia were handicapped by injuries, but the Northern Union team were unable to take advantage of this and played well below form. Two goals from Gronow set up a 4—0 lead, but Australia were always more dangerous in attack, and Fraser, the home marksman, got a try. In the second half Australia piled on the pressure, and it was just reward when their brilliant winger, Harold Horder, cross-kicked and forward Frank Burge dashed up and touched down for Fraser to goal. Australia had won the first Test 8—4, and were one up.

The second Test was played at Sydney a week later, and the evidence of the first Test was confirmed when Australia won a fine victory by 21 points to 8 and regained the Ashes. The tourists' pack was hammered into the ground by the home six, and the Australian backs displayed some beautiful moves, spearheaded by half-back Duncan Thompson. For Australia, Potter, V. Farnsworth, Vest, Horder and Gilbert scored tries and Burge three goals, against tries by Johnson and Gallagher and a Gronow goal.

The tourists salvaged a little prestige from the Tests by winning the third Test, at Sydney on 10 July, by 23 points to 13. Australia were able to rest on their laurels in this game, and the Northern Union side came into their own in an entertaining and open game. Hilton (2), Stone (2) and Bacon scored tourists' tries, and Rogers (3) and Stockwell goals. Gray, Thompson and Burge replied with tries and Burge also kicked two goals.

One aspect of the Test series delighted the tourists. Attendances were large at all three Tests, and a thumping profit was assured. From Australia the party went to New Zealand, where all three Tests were won: 31—7 at Auckland, 19—3 at Christchurch and 11—10 at Wellington.

When the tourists set sail for Britain, with an arrival date of 17 October, they sailed with the knowledge that, financially at least, the tour had been a triumph. Takings amounted to more than £28 000, ensuring a handsome profit and bonus for the players. On the playing side 21 matches had been won and four lost, two in Tests, and 763 points had been scored against 339. Top scorer was Ben Gronow, 65 goals and two tries, while in the try-scoring lists Stone had 24, Bacon 23 and Parkin 19.

Season 1920–1 saw the post-war boom in full spate, with a record aggregate total of 181 070 spectators at 11 matches during the second-round Challenge Cup ties in March. The Challenge Cup final was an inter-county battle between Leigh, making their first appearance, and Halifax, and 25 000 saw the game at Broughton Rangers' ground. Teams were:

Halifax: Garforth; Turnbull, Ackroyd, Stacey, Todd; Lloyd, S. Prosser; Gibson, Milnes, Broadbent, Whiteley, Beames, Schofield.

Leigh: Clarkson; Hurst, Heaton, Thomas, Braund; Mooney, Parkinson; Cartwright, Winstanley, Darwell, J. T. Prosser, Boardman, Coffey.

Referee: Mr F. Renton (Hunslet).

Unfancied Leigh, who had had a poor League season, soon knocked Halifax out of their complacency. They hustled and bustled Halifax out of the picture, and the Yorkshiremen never settled down. Mooney broke from a scrum to give Ackroyd a try, and then the Leigh half-back repeated the move for Parkinson to score, Clarkson goaling. Halifax tried desperately to open out play, but Leigh tackled like tigers, and just before half-time a fumble by Stacey gave Thomas a gift try.

Halifax stormed the Leigh line in the second half, but the Leigh defence refused to give an inch, and a Clarkson goal was the only score, giving Leigh a well-deserved, if surprise, victory, by 13 points to 0.

The championship final, played at Headingley on 7 May, was a 'derby' match, a repeat of the Yorkshire Cup final between Hull and Hull K.R. The Rovers had won the county trophy, and Hull were all out for revenge against their neighbours. Only 10 000 saw them achieve their aim by 16 points to 14 in a great fight, the parochial nature of the game reducing its interest for all except Hull supporters. It was a splendid game, in which Rovers fought back after being 14—4 down to 16—11. Then Cook scored a try to make it 16—14, and, with everyone holding their breath, Gibson missed the conversion which would have tied the scores.

In Britain a new side entered the senior ranks, wartime members Featherstone Rovers taking their place in the Northern League.

Season 1921–2 had been fixed for the first post-war Australian tour of the Northern League, and so great was Australian interest that in July 1921, Sir James Joynton Smith, president of the New South Wales Rugby League, visited Britain to make arrangements. July was also busy in the transfer and signings market, and Wigan made a capture destined to become world-famous when they signed a young Welsh full-back, James Sullivan, from Cardiff. This 17-year-old lad was destined to become one of the greatest full-backs and goal-kickers the game had known.

The 28 Australian tourists arrived in Britain on 5 September 1921, with their managers, Messrs S. G. Ball and W. A. Cann, a former player. Captain was Les Cubitt, and the party consisted of *Backs:* C. Fraser, L. C. Cubitt, G. Carstairs, T. Norman, N. Broadfoot, H. Horder, R. Vest, J. H. Craig, E. S. Brown, C. Blinkhorn, H. Peters, C. Caples, A. Laing, D. F. Thompson, A. Johnston; and *Forwards:* J. Watkins, T. Pearce, B. Gray, F. Burge, R. Townsend, N. Potter, F. Ryan, W. Schultz, B. Latta, E. McGrath, J. C. Ives, C. W. Prentice, W. Richards.

The Aussies set off magnificently, sweeping all before them against Salford, Keighley and Hull K.R. In these three matches alone the tourists rattled up a total aggregate of more than 100 points, and the Northern Union selectors were worried men as they chose the team to tilt for the Ashes in the first Test at Headingley on Saturday, 1 October 1921.

The match aroused great interest, and a crowd of 32 000 paid receipts of £3884.

The teams were:

Northern Union: G. Thomas (Huddersfield); W. J. Stone (Hull), H. Wagstaff (Huddersfield), J. A. Bacon, S. Stockwell (Leeds); J. Rogers (Huddersfield), J. Parkin (Wakefield Trinity); W. Cunliffe (Warrington), J. Cartwright (Leigh), J. Skelhorne

(Warrington), E. Morgan (Hull), J. Baemes (Halifax), J. Price (Broughton R.).

Australia: C. Fraser; H. Horder, R. Vest, J. Craig, C. Blinkhorn; D. Thompson, A. Johnston; C. Prentice, F. Ryan, T. Pearce, F. Burge, B. Gray, J. Watkins.

Within 10 minutes Britain were in the lead, Stone making a great interception to break away and score. Australia struck back when Vest served Blinkhorn and the winger outpaced the home defence to score. Craig converting. At half-time Australia led 5—3, and looked good for victory, but the Northern Union side controlled the scrums in the second half and battered the tourists' line. However, the Australians defended magnificently, and despite the roar of the home crowd, the British team could not break through.

Then, with three minutes to go, Wagstaff made a typical burst. When he was tackled, Rogers, Parkin, and Bacon got the ball out to winger Stockwell. The winger had Horder between him and the line, but he ducked under his opponent's arm and dived over to give Britain a dramatic last-gasp win.

The second Test was played at Hull on Saturday, 5 November, and by this time the tourists' reputation had been dented by several club defeats. The crowd was once again a good one, 28 000 paying £3007 in the hope of seeing Britain regain the Ashes. The Australians brought in Carstairs, Caples, Schultz and Latta for Craig, Johnson, Ryan and Gray, and Britain had Batten back for the injured Wagstaff.

The home side suffered a blow in the first minute when Stockwell injured his hand, and Australia took the initiative right away. Goals from Thompson for Australia and Rogers for Britain were the only scores of a first half largely fought out between the Northern Union defence and the tourists' attack. Seven minutes after half-time Vest intercepted between Bacon and Stockwell to score, and then Horder, the great Australian winger, sidestepped and weaved his way through for a brilliant try. Blinkhorn scored two more tries as Australia rammed home their advantage, and one more Thompson goal gave Australia a 16—2 victory to tie the series.

Shaken by this defeat, Britain made six changes for the third

Test at Salford on 14 January 1922. Wagstaff, J. Owen (St Helens Recreation), D. Hurcombe (Wigan), H. Hilton (Oldham), R. Taylor (Hull) and F. Gallagher (Dewsbury) replacing Batten, Stone, Stockwell, Morgan, Beames and Price.

This match, played before 20 000 spectators, should have been an exciting and vital struggle, but Australia suffered a crippling blow minutes after the start. Full-back and captain 'Chook' Fraser broke his leg and was taken off the field, and though the tourists fought with great courage, Great Britain took command of the Ashes decider. Forwards Cunliffe, Hilton and Taylor combined for Hilton to score the first try, and only courageous defence saved further tries. The second half followed a similar pattern, with Australia defending desperately, and only one more try was scored by Britain, Gallagher tackling Thompson so hard that the half back lost the ball and Gallagher touched down. It was rough luck on the Aussies, but Britain could point to the injury which robbed them of a fit Stockwell in the second Test.

Although the tourists had lost the Test series, they had won 27 of their 36 matches, scoring 763 points against 253, and Horder, Blinkhorn and Burge had each scored more than 30 tries. The tour had not made any fabulous profit, but it had paid its way.

The 1921–2 Challenge Cup final was played at Headingley on Saturday, 29 April, with Rochdale Hornets and reigning champions Hull as contestants. This match, with its inter-county appeal, attracted a record attendance in Britain of 35 500, with receipts of £2964. The gates were closed with thousands clamouring outside, and officials finally ordered the gates to be reopened. Thousands then encroached on the pitch and had to be pushed back by mounted police to allow the game to start. Here was conclusive evidence of the pulling power of the Union's showpiece game. Teams for the day were:

Hull: Holdsworth; Wynne, Kennedy, Batten, Stone; Caswell, Charles; Beasty, Oliver, Morgan, Wyburn, Taylor, Garratt.

Rochdale Hornets: Prescott; J. Corsi, McLaughlin, Wild, Fitton; Kynan, Heaton; Woods, Bennett, Harris, Edwards, Paddon, H. L. Corsi.

Referee: Mr R. Jones (Widnes).

Hull were first to score when Kennedy charged down a Heaton

kick and touched down. Rochdale piled on the pressure, however, and after two Paddon goals had given them the lead, Fitton bored over for a try. Just before half-time Batten scored a typical try for Hull. He raced away brilliantly, and when Prescott went to tackle him he made a spectacular leap over the full-back's head to touch down. At half-time Hornets led 7—6, and play went from end to end in an exciting second half. Heaton and Wild gave Fitton a second try for Rochdale. Then Taylor broke through superbly and crashed over for a try. As Stone took the kick, the crowd breathed in. The international winger was wide, and Rochdale had won the cup 10—9.

The championship final was held at Broughton the following week, 26 000 paying £1825 to see Wigan beat Oldham 13—2 in a moderate final. The Wigan score was made up of goals from Sullivan (4) and Howley and a try from Shea, Farrar kicking a goal for Oldham.

8

Goodbye to the Northern Union

THE 1922 annual meeting brought two important decisions. The outdated and parochial title of 'Northern Union' was changed to 'Rugby League' with little opposition, and the goal-kick from a mark, which had provided many a too-easy goal, was abolished.

The financial report to the annual meeting showed a still-handsome surplus of £15 164, but there were signs that the post-war boom was beginning to subside in the gate returns from clubs. Top clubs were still reaping big dividends in crowds, but at the bottom of the table the crowds were becoming choosy of their fare. Still, with such a balance in hand, the finances of the Rugby League were gilt-edged.

First chairman of the Rugby League under its new name was Mr John W. Counsell, and one of his first functions was the summer conference of the Rugby League Council at Keswick in July 1922.

When the 1922–3 season opened it was expected that the abolition of the mark would handicap goal-kickers, but one young kicker soon disproved this theory with a superb display of place kicking.

Jim Sullivan, Wigan's young Welsh full-back, while still under 20, landed 172 goals, beating Ben Gronow's previous seasonal record of 147 goals set up in 1919–20. It was a great achievement for the young Welshman, who also scored 10 tries, and was particularly notable in view of the fact that he had not had the assistance of shots from the now-defunct mark.

The Rugby League Challenge Cup final, the first under the new name, was held at Wakefield on Saturday, 28 April 1923, before a crowd of 29 350 (£2390). Hull were in the final for the seventh time, with only one victory to their credit, and their opponents were Leeds. Mr F. Mills (Oldham) was referee and the teams were:

Hull: Samuel; Stone, Kennedy, Whitty, Holdsworth; Caswell, Gwynne; Oliver, Bowman, Beasty, Morgan, Taylor, Garratt.

Leeds: Walmsley; Buck, Bowen, Bacon, Lyons; Binks, Brittain; Trusler, Jackson, Dixon, Davis, Thompson, Ashton.

The match was a triumph for the famous 'Busy B's' of Leeds' back division. Binks at half-back prompted move after move, and Buck and Bowen scored first-half tries converted by Thompson. In the second half Hull faded out of the picture and Davis, Brittain and Ashton scored tries, Thompson landing two more goals. After a brief Hull flash in which Kennedy got a try, Walmsley scored Leeds' sixth try after interpassing with Buck from his own half, and Thompson kicked the goal for a 28—3 Leeds win.

Hull K.R. went one better than their neighbours in the championship final at Headingley on 5 May. They beat Huddersfield, no longer the 'greats' of a few years before, by 15 points to 5 before a crowd of 15 000. The game never reached great heights, with too much kicking spoiling open play. The only score of the first half was a dropped goal by Osborne for Rovers, but in the second half feeble Huddersfield tackling let in Rees for a try goaled by Osborne. Williams touched down for Huddersfield and Gronow converted, but another defensive weakness let Rovers in again. Gwyn Thomas, the Huddersfield full-back, misfielded the ball, and Cook touched down. Then Hoult scored a try after a kick ahead, and Osborne goaled.

Season 1923–4, under the chairmanship of Mr H. Dannatt (Hull), got under way with a new club in commission. Wigan Highfield joined the League, determined to prove that there was room for two sides in rugby-minded Wigan, and their ground was established at Pemberton.

Managers for the 1924 tour were Messrs Dannatt and E. Osborne (Warrington), and after two trial matches the party was selected. It included the young Welsh wonder, Jim Sullivan, at full-back. The other *Backs:* J. Ring, T. Howley, D. Hurcombe (Wigan), E. Knapman, S. Rix (Oldham), W. Bentham (Broughton R.), J. Bacon (Leeds), C. Carr (Barrow), C. Pollard, J. Parkin

(Wakefield Trinity), F. Evans (Swinton), S. Whitty (Hull) and W. Mooney (Leigh); and *Forwards:* W. Burgess (Barrow), W. Cunliffe (Warrington), H. Bowman (Hull), J. F. Thompson (Leeds), J. Bennett (Rochdale H.), B. Gronow (Huddersfield), A. Brough, R. Sloman (Oldham), J. Darwell (Leigh), F. Gallagher (Batley), J. Price (Wigan), D. Rees (Halifax). Parkin was skipper, and he, Hurcombe, Gronow, Cunliffe and Gallagher had made the trip in 1920.

The Rugby League Challenge Cup final brought together two Lancashire clubs for the first time since 1911. The old rivals Oldham and Wigan qualified, and the crowd scenes at Rochdale broke all records for numbers and drama. Half an hour before the kick-off the crowd invaded the pitch, and it took mounted policemen and officials all their time and effort to get them behind the touchlines. The official attendance was a record 40 786, and several times during the game the touchlines had to be cleared.

The Rev. Frank Chambers of Huddersfield, a famous disciplinarian referee, was in charge, and the teams were:

Oldham: Knapman; Rix, Hall, Woodward, J. Corsi; Hesketh, Bates; Collins, Tomkins, Baker, Sloman, Brough, Hilton.

Wigan: Sullivan; Ring, Howley, Park, Van Heerden; Jerram, Hurcombe; Webster, Banks, Brown, Van Rooyen, Roffey, Price.

In the Wigan team were two great South Africans, former Springbok international Van Heerden and Van Rooyen, who came to Britain in return for substantial fees. Before moving to Wigan Van Rooyen was with Hull Kingston Rovers. Oldham opened the scoring with a Knapman goal, but Webster, Roffey, Brown and Price swept play to the Oldham line and Roffey scored. Then Van Heerden showed his class with as brilliant a try as could be wished. He kicked ahead from his own half, gathered the ball, handed off several defenders and finally ran round a mounted policeman to touch down behind the posts for Sullivan to goal. In the second half Wigan really went to town, and fine precision handling brought tries to Parker, Ring and Price, Sullivan kicking two more goals. Oldham's reply consisted of two goals, one from Knapman, one from Brough.

Wigan were also in the championship final at Broughton on 3 May, but on this occasion the loss of five tourists proved too much, and Batley beat Wigan 13—7. Murray, Leeming and Murray again scored tries, and Rees kicked two goals for Batley, while Armstrong (try) and Oakley (two goals) replied for Wigan.

The British tourists arrived in Melbourne on 20 May 1924, and four days later beat Victoria 45—3. Victories followed against Cootamunda, Newcastle, Tamworth and then New South Wales before a 50 000 Sydney crowd. Then the tourists were pulled up with three successive defeats against New South Wales, Queensland and Toowoomba. Ninety points were conceded in these three games, a poor reflection on the tourists' defences.

A win against New South Wales restored morale in time for the first Test at Sydney on Monday, 23 June 1924. The match was played before a 60 000 crowd at the famous Cricket Ground, and significant of the growth of the game in Queensland was the fact that the Australian side included a good proportion of Queensland players. Sullivan gave Britain the lead with a penalty, and when Australia attacked the tourists' forwards tackled mercilessly. Sullivan kicked a second goal, but a try by Aynsley made the score 4—3 at half-time.

Five minutes after the restart the Aussies suffered a crippling blow when Potter, the Queensland forward, was ordered off the field. Immediately Britain pounced and took charge of the game, with Parkin a brilliant captain and schemer. Price, Parkin (2) and Rix ran in tries, and Sullivan landed five goals in a 22—3 win for Britain.

The second Test gave little breathing space to the teams. It took place at Sydney five days later, Saturday, 28 June. In the Australian side Thompson, Hunt and Armbruster replaced Blair, Blinkhorn and Oxford as the Kangaroos sought a team to retrieve the Ashes and repeat the 1920 Australian success. Heavy rain made the pitch muddy and slippery, but despite the conditions there was a crowd of nearly 50 000.

The game provided a tough struggle, mainly fought out between the mud-covered packs, and the only score of a tenaciously fought first half was a try for Australia by Aynsley. Under the conditions, with mud bogging down both sides, this could have proved a winning lead, and Australia fought to hold it in the second half. Britain attacked desperately and muddily, but Australia held out until 10 minutes from the end with the crowd on tenterhooks. It was Parkin who did the trick, spotting the slight hole in the Australian defence through which he nipped to touch down. The sure boot of Jim Sullivan did the rest, and Britain had retained the Ashes with a narow 5—3 victory.

As so often happens, the third Test brought victory to the side beaten in the series. Played at Brisbane, with Paten (Queensland) replacing the great Horder on the Australian wing, it attracted a 40 000 crowd. Britain led 5—4 at half-time through a Frank Evans try and Sullivan goal against two goals from Aynsley. In the second half the Australians hammered the tourists' line, and the British defence finally caved in.

Paten, Armbruster and Oxford scored tries, forward Oxford running clean through from inside his own half, and Thompson (2) Aynsley and Oxford landed goals. In a late burst from Britain, Parkin and Evans scored tries for Britain in a 21—11 victory for Australia.

The Ashes had been retained, and the receipts were higher than on the 1920 tour. The tourists went off to New Zealand in high spirits—to face a series of shocks and reverses that shattered their complacency. After the usual comfortable victories against club and provincial sides, the tourists played the first Test at Auckland on 2 August. Britain had to reshuffle the side through injuries, with Gallagher at stand-off and Rix in the centre, but, even so, victory was anticipated. The result was a salutary and chastening defeat by 16 points to 8, and to make matters worse W. Cunliffe, the Warrington forward, was sent off the field.

The tourists were just a little less confident for the second Test, at Wellington, on 9 August. Reports of improvement in New Zealand Rugby League were once again proved true, for the Kiwis fought back brilliantly after being 11—0 down to pull back to 11—10. Then, in the last few minutes, New Zealand scored the winning try to win the series against Britain for the first time. The third Test at Dunedin on 16 August saw the tourists win 31—18, but the cock-a-hoop Kiwis had made their mark.

Leading scorer for the tourists was full-back Jim Sullivan, whose 84 goals beat the 65 kicked on the 1920 tour. His Wigan clubmate, Johnny Ring, scored 23 tries. Receipts for the tour amounted to more than £30 000, the Rugby League share was £16 000 and the players' bonus was just less than £100.

Season 1924–5 contained no tour, giving a welcome respite, but there was an international development when an Other Nationalities side met England and included men like Van Rooyen and Van Heerden, of South Africa, and J. Beattie, the Scottish forward from Halifax. This fixture provided a home break from the traditional England *v.* Wales fixture and paved the way for a home triangular tournament.

Early 1925 brought a problem for the Rugby League. Both Australia and New Zealand asked for invitations to visit England in 1926. The Australians thought such an invitation would be the usual formality.

They were in for a shock, for the Rugby League, remembering that New Zealand had won two out of three Tests against the 1924 tourists, decided to invite the Kiwis to prove themselves in Britain. In vain the Australian Board of Control protested. The Rugby League replied that the New Zealanders had done what Australia could not do in 1924—they had won a Test series. So 1926 was scheduled as the date for the first full New Zealand Rugby League tour of Britain, for the first, in 1907–8, had included Australian 'Dally' Messenger.

The star team of 1924–5 were Hull K.R., who reached both Challenge Cup and championship finals, but the biggest feat of the season was recorded by Wigan, who set up a club scoring record by butchering the luckless Cumberland junior team, Flimby and Fothergill, 116—0 in the Challenge Cup. This was only three short of Huddersfield's record 119 against Swinton Park. Here was another brutal illustration of the wide gulf between senior and junior Rugby League football.

The first of Hull Kingston Rovers' two finals was played at Headingley on Saturday, 25 April 1925, with Rovers seeking to record their first-ever Challenge Cup win against Oldham, beaten finalists the previous year. The crowd was 28 200 with receipts of £2878. The teams were:

Hull Kingston Rovers: Osborne, Harris, Cook, Hoult, Austin; McIntyre, Raynor; J. Wilkinson, Boagey, J. R. Wilkinson, Westerdale, Bielby, Carmichael.

Oldham: Knapman; J. Corsi, Rix, Davies, Farrar; Hesketh, Beynon; Collins, Tomkins, Marlor, Sloman, Brough, Hilton.

Referee: Mr R. Jones (Widnes).

The first half was disappointing, with Oldham a little more assertive than a seemingly overawed Rovers side. Oldham scored when smooth passing put Farrar over, and the winger converted to give Oldham a 5—0 interval lead. In the second half poor Rovers continued to fumble and falter, while Oldham swept into full stride. Corsi slipped a pass inside for Brough to score, and Hesketh sent Corsi over from a scrum, Farrar goaling from touch. Davies got a fourth try, and a crumb of consolation for Rovers was provided by an unconverted try from J. H. Wilkinson.

After their bitter Challenge Cup disappointment Rovers sought consolation in the championship final against Swinton at Rochdale the following week. A crowd of 22 000 saw Rovers in a much more determined mood, and though they conceded a 5—0 interval lead once again, they fought back to win.

A goal from Brockbank and a try from Bryn Evans provided Swinton's lead, but in the second half it was Rovers all the way. Rhodes scored a try and Osborne three goals to edge them into the lead, and only bad luck and great Swinton defence prevented further Rovers scores.

The annual meeting of 1925 was a pleasant affair, with the profit on the season reported as £3918 and the credit balance £13 985.

New clubs stole much of the limelight in 1926. In February, months in advance of the annual meeting, Castleford were admitted following several applications, the Yorkshire club reporting the purchase of a ground at the headquarters of Castleford Town soccer club. The admission was to be confirmed for the following season.

Another new club, Wigan Highfield, stole the Challenge Cup thunder. The Highfield club, composed largely of colliers from the Wigan area, had struggled without much success in the League, but in the cup they beat Wakefield, Huddersfield and Leeds, three powerful Yorkshire sides, in the first three rounds. All three matches were played at Pemberton, and Highfield on their own 'midden' proved more than a match for their glamorous visitors.

All good things come to an end, however, and in the semi-final hopes of another sensation were dashed. Highfield left their own Tunstall Lane enclosure to meet Oldham at Salford, and were beaten after a tenacious fight by 15 points to 6.

Swinton beat Hull in the other semi-final and the two Lancashire clubs met in the final at Rochdale on Saturday, 1 May 1926. Heavy rain fell throughout the day, but the crowd still reached 27 000, with receipts of £2551. Oldham were making their third successive appearance, while Swinton had reached the final for the first time since 1900. Teams were:

Oldham: Knapman; Corsi, Higgs, Rix, Brough; Jones, Hesketh; Lister, Marlor, Read, Sloman, Carter, Baker.

Swinton: Pearson; F. Evans, Sulway, J. Evans, Brockbank; W. Rees, B. Evans; Strong, Blewer, Morris, Halliwell, Entwistle, Beswick.

Referee: Mr A. Brown (Wakefield).

Swinton had a strong wind behind them in the first half, and this wind made kicking difficult for both sides. Morris landed a goal for Swinton after the wind had blown shots by himself and Knapman wide of the target, and then Swinton scored a good try. Rees hit the crossbar with an attempted drop goal, and when the ball bounced into play Blewer seized his chance and dived over. Morris goaled to make it 7—0 and then added a penalty goal.

Oldham had the wind at their backs in the second half, but the Swinton defence held firm, and Oldham's only reward was a try by Corsi following a kick through.

In another all-Lancashire final, Wigan easily disposed of Warrington in the championship match at Knowsley Road, St Helens. Ring (3), Van Heerden (2) and Howley scored tries, and Sullivan two goals, in a 22—10 victory.

9

The Way to Wembley

THE years between 1926 and 1929 brought yet another failure in Wales, an ill-fated New Zealand tour and the climax to a search for the perfect Challenge Cup final venue.

At the 1926 annual meeting at Leeds the League decided to try another Welsh experiment, and Pontypridd were admitted. The Welsh club had a good ground, and support at England *v.* Wales League internationals had indicated good potential crowds. With fingers crossed, the League took another plunge in Wales.

The New Zealand tourists arrived at Southampton on 2 September 1926, with Messrs E. H. Mair and C. H. Ponder as managers. Captain of the team was H. Avery, and the vice-captain N. Mouat. The tourists made their H.Q. at Harrogate, and Harold Wagstaff, famous Huddersfield and England captain, was assigned by the Rugby League as their 'adviser'. In order to make the tour a financial success for the Kiwis, they had been allocated 75 per cent of gates, and a £950 gate at Dewsbury on 11 September augured well. The New Zealanders beat Dewsbury and Leigh, but then fell at Halifax, and this was the prelude to 11 defeats at the hands of club teams.

The first Test was played at Wigan on 2 October, and gate receipts were good at £1650. The Rugby League, remembering the surprise 1924 defeats, chose a strong side, and the teams were:

Great Britain: J. Sullivan (Wigan); J. Ring (Wigan), J. Evans (Swinton), C. Carr (Barrow), S. Rix (Oldham); J. Parkin (Wakefield T.), W. Rees (Swinton); W. Burgess (Barrow), J. Bennett (Wigan), W. Cunliffe (Warrington), R. Taylor (Hull), D. Rees (Halifax), F. Gallagher (Batley).

New Zealand: E. Gregory; L. Brown, B. Davidson, H. Brisbane, F. Delgrosso; A. W. Hall, W. Desmond; F. Henry, E. Herring, W. Carroll, L. Mason, H. Avery, N. Mouat.

Great Britain played in the first half like a team determined to wipe out the painful 1924 memories in one big scoring rush. They carved great holes in the Kiwis' defences, and tries by Carr, Rix, Taylor and Gallagher, with four goals from Sullivan, gave them a 20—5 lead at half-time. The tourists' captain, Avery, scored a try in a breakaway, and Mouat converted.

In the second half Great Britain relaxed, and the tourists rallied manfully, Brisbane scoring for Mouat to convert. Britain were roused again, and Taylor and Car ran in two more tries,Sullivan converting one. Finally Mason and Davidson scored tries for New Zealand, and Mouat's conversion made the final score 28—20 to Britain.

The second Test at Hull on 13 November 1926,. was greeted with pessimism and the gate was a trifling £592. Both sides had changes. Britain brought in Wallace (Barrow) on the wing, Fairclough (St Helens) at half-back and Smith (Bradford), Thomas (Leeds) and Fildes (St Helens Recs.) in the forwards. New Zealand brought in H. Cole, J. Kirwin and C. Dufty in the backs, and W. Devine, E. Peterson and W. Singe in the forwards.

The match followed a similar pattern to the first Test, Britain totting up tries through Wallace, Fildes and Thomas, with two goals from Sullivan against a try from Peterson. At 13—3 Britain were coasting home, but quick tries by Avery and Brown and a goal by Gregory rocked them back on their heels. Britain once again pulled out their reserve power, and Thomas and Fairclough ran in tries, another Sullivan goal making the final score 21—11.

Britain had won the series without much difficulty, and the Kiwis' woes continued to multiply.

After the second Test it was revealed that the players and Mr Mair, team manager, had been in dispute. The touring team's finances were running at a loss, interest in the tour had waned, and the playing record showed that the tourists had won 16 and lost 11 of their club programme, an undistinguished record.

The third Test at Headingley on 15 January completed the disillusionment of the New Zealanders. Great Britain did as they liked, running through the faulty and disheartened visitors' defence for eight tries. Britain won 32—17, the tourists' points again coming when the home side relaxed. During this game Jim

Sullivan, who kicked four goals, landed his 100th goal of the season.

The tourists, whose first party had left for home just before the third Test, set off back home with their tails very much between their legs. The tour had been a flop in every sense, and in Australia the opinion was expressed that the Rugby League had been too hasty in granting full status to the Kiwis.

The tour fiasco over, the League turned to the Challenge Cup and championship. The championship was played first at Warrington on Saturday, 30 April 1927, before a 24 432 crowd. St Helens Recreation, top of the table, met Swinton, runners-up, in a match that was, for once, a fair reflection of the season's form. Recs. led 5—2 at half-time, Bowen getting a try and Dingsdale a goal for Recs. against a Morris goal. In the second half Swinton took command, and Bryn Evans, with a brilliant, mazy, jinking run, ran through for a try. When Dingsdale lost possession on his own line Beswick touched down, and then Bryn Evans ran through for another fine try, Morris goaling. Innes got a late try for Recs., but once again the top club had failed at the last hurdle, and Swinton were 1927 champions by 13 points to 8.

This win gave Swinton the chance of the 'double', for they met Oldham in the Challenge Cup final at Wigan on 7 May before a splendid crowd of 35 000 (£3170). Oldham were playing in their fourth successive final. Swinton in their third and the match was a repeat of the 1926 final won by Swinton. Small wonder the interest in the game was terrific.

Teams were:

Oldham: Comm; Johnson, Rix, Higgs, Holliday; Hesketh, Jones; Read, Scaife, Marlor, Sloman, Ashworth, Brough.

Swinton: Leigh; F. Evans, Halsall, J. Evans, Brockbank; B. Evans, Rees; Strong, Blewer, Cracknell, Morris, Halliwell, Beswick.

Referee: Mr R. Robinson (Bradford).

Swinton started off with great confidence, and a swift passing movement put Brockbank over. This, however, was Swinton's first and last try-scoring move. Oldham pulled themselves together, and after a Johnson goal Holliday scored a try converted by Johnson. A Morris penalty made it 7—5 at the interval.

Swinton resumed without centre and captain Hector Halsall, and Oldham went further ahead when Rix swerved through for a great try, Brough goaling. Five minutes later Brough went through at his leisure, and Sloman and Holliday (2) completed the rout. Morris got one more goal for Swinton, who were crushed 26—7.

When the annual meeting of the League was held in June the expected loss on the season was reported. It amounted to £1235, including £890 in underwriting the New Zealand tour flop. This seasonal loss had been anticipated—a decision of the annual meeting on Colonial importations came as a surprise.

Wigan proposed the ending of the two-year residence qualification for Colonial players, pleading that Colonial stars were needed to give renewed punch and life to the game. The annual meeting voted in favour, and immediately the news reached Australia Mr H. R. Miller, secretary of the New South Wales League, urged reconsideration. 'Your gain will be at our expense', said the Australian message, a charge that was certainly justified.

The Australian protests fell on deaf ears, and soon the Colonial stars were flooding in. Wigan bought L. Brown, B. Davidson and L. Mason, of the 1926 New Zealand tourists. Leeds secured Australians A. F. O'Rourke, a centre, and J. Moores, half-back. Huddersfield signed Aussies A. Carr and S. Harris, and Hull brought New Zealand half-back Wilson Hall to Britain.

In August 1927, the League's rulers made another change in the play-the-ball rule in an effort to tidy it up. To stop barging and interference as the ball was played, it was ordered that one player from each side was to act at the play-the-ball, with one player from each side standing immediately behind. All other players must be within a five-yard radius and behind them. Even this rule change did not stop the untidy scrambles at the play-the-ball, a feature of the game which caused as much controversy as the scrimmage.

The 1927–8 season brought to an end the Pontypridd experiment and chalked up another Welsh failure. However, Wales was not entirely abandoned, for a team from Glamorgan and Monmouthshire entered the county championship, players being drawn from Welshmen with English clubs.

After three trial matches the 1928 touring side was announced

Managers were Messrs. E. Osborne (Warrington) and G. F. Hutchins (Oldham), and Wakefield Trinity half-back Jonty Parkin was chosen captain, setting up a record by making his third Australian trip. Sullivan, Sloman, Burgess and Bowman made their second trip, but Gallagher, who would have equalled Parkin's record, had to withdraw at the last minute. The party included the Evans brothers, Jack and Bryn, from Swinton, and the full list was *Backs:* J. Sullivan (Wigan), W. Gowers (Rochdale H.), J. Brough, M. Rosser (Leeds), J. Oliver (Batley), A. Ellaby, A. Frodsham, L. Fairclough (St Helens), J. and B. Evans, W. Rees (Swinton), T. Askin (Featherstone R.), T. E. Gwynne (Hull), J. Parkin (Wakefield T.); *Forwards:* W. Bentham (Wigan Highfield), O. Dolan, B. Halfpenny (St Helens), W. A. Williams (Salford), F. Bowen, A. Fildes (St Helens Recs.), W. Burgess (Barrow), H. Bowman (Hull), W. Horton (Wakefield T.), R. Slowman (Oldham), H. Young (Bradford N.) and J. F. Thompson (Leeds).

The honours for the Swinton players stimulated interest in the achievements of this fine side in 1927–8. They reached the final of the Challenge Cup and championship, and had already won the Lancashire League and Cup. Their ambition was a four-cup season to emulate Hunslet and Huddersfield, and the first match was the Challenge Cup final at Wigan, brought forward to Saturday, 14 April, because of the Australian tour departures.

Swinton's opponents were Warrington, and the teams were:

Swinton: Young; F. Evans, Halsall, J. Evans, Brockbank; Atkinson, Rees; Strong, Blewer, Morris, Hodgson, Cracknell, Beswick.

Warrington: Frowen; Rhodes, Meredith, Perkins, Davies; Flynn, Kirk; Cunliffe, Peacock, Miller, Williams, Tranter, Seeling.

Referee: Mr H. Horsfall (Batley).

Unfortunately for the game as a spectacle, a strong wind blew throughout, making handling mistakes frequent, and the only scoring of a windswept and dourly fought first half was a Brockbank try for Swinton. The second half was even more scrappy, and although Warrington struggled to break through the tough Swinton defence, they were held until a surprising slip in defence let Seeling through for the equalizing try. Weak tackling in an unguarded moment let in Seeling, but Swinton immediately got to grips again and after an assault on the Warrington line Atkinson gave the ball to Jack Evans, who took deliberate aim and dropped the winning goal.

Swinton now needed the championship title to make it a four-cup season, and 16 000 people saw them pull it off against Featherstone Rovers at Oldham on 5 May 1928. Rovers were held in a ruthless grip by the Swinton forwards, while Halsall, Frank Evans and Cracknell (tries) and Young (goal) scored Swinton's 11 points.

The British touring party arrived in Australia at the end of May, 1928, and before long the tour had been established as a financial success. Australian matches had become a byword for large gates and bumper gate receipts, and even though the form of the 1928 tourists was poor at the start, the Aussie crowds rolled up as usual. In three matches against New South Wales, one won and two lost, Great Britain attracted gates totalling more than £9350.

However, there was still the playing form of the tour to straighten, and after moderate showings in state and club matches Great Britain were not too confident of success when the first Test was played at Brisbane on Saturday, 23 June. The crowd was 36 000, receipts £4000. Britain were up against it, for their captain, Parkin, was unfit, as were Bryn and Jack Evans. Brough and Oliver were at centre, and Rees worked the scrums with Fairclough at stand-off. Although second favourites, Britain shook the Kangaroos by running up a 10—2 lead through tries by Fairclough and Horton and two goals from Sullivan against a penalty goal by Craig. When Australia swept back, a lovely passing movement gave Armbruster a try, but equally brilliant football between Fairclough and Brough sent Ellaby over.

In the second half Australia piled on terrific pressure, and pulled back to 13—12 with a try and two goals from Aynsley. It was a tremendous struggle, with the crowd roaring Australia home, but Britain held out and a late penalty goal from Sullivan gave them an unexpected 15—12 win.

After their poor form in minor matches the tourists had pulled off the first Test. They went on to pulverize several 'up-country' sides in Queensland, and the tourists were in much more confident mood for the second Test at Sydney on 14 July. Conditions were not very pleasant, but despite the rain there was a crowd of 45 000 to see Australia fight to save the British-held Ashes. The Aussies wore a new strip for the first time in this game. They turned out in green and gold, colours now famous wherever Rugby League is played.

In the wretched conditions, on a muddy, rain-lashed ground, open football was out of the question, and the game became a tough, no-quarter slog. The only first-half scores were a Parkin opportunist try and a Sullivan goal. In the second half the Aussies fought hard to save the day, but from the only real passing movement of the game the British backs got the ball out to winger Ellaby, who streaked over in the corner. Britain won 8—0, and the Ashes had been retained.

The big interest now lay in Britain's hopes of winning all three Tests for the first time. The third Test was played at Sydney a week after the second, on 21 July, Gwynne and Fairclough coming into the British team for Rosser and the unfit Parkin. The gate was 35 000, and receipts sent the tour proceeds to over £31 000.

Britain were not destined to get the hat-trick. The Kangaroos came with a late burst after Horton, the tourists' forward, had been sent off the field, and Australia won 21—14, after leading 9—7 at half-time. Wearing (2) and Pearce scored tries, and Wearing (3) and Craig (3) scored goals for Australia, while Fairclough got two tries and Sullivan four goals for Britain.

The tourists set off for New Zealand determined to wipe out the memory of 1924. The first Test was at Auckland, and New Zealand included only two men, Delgrosso and Dufty, of the ill-fated 1926 tourists. Once again Britain received a rude shock, for after leading 9—3 at half-time the Kiwis resisted a late rally by Britain to win 17—13. Scott (2) and List scored tries, and Delgrosso (3) and Dufty goals. Britain scored tries through Ellaby (2) and Fairclough, and two goals from Sullivan.

The second Test, at Dunedin, was vital for Britain if they wished to avoid more loss of prestige. Perhaps both sides were too keenly conscious of the nature of the game, for 'needle' crept in, and tough play scarred the game's progress.

After one big bust-up Burgess, the tourists' forward, was sent off the field. Then the balance was restored when Delgrosso was carried off injured. The game swayed from end to end with torrid exchanges, and Britain held on to a 7—5 lead at the interval, thanks to a try by Rees and two goals by Sullivan against a Scott try and Delgrosso goal. In the second half the tourists really got on top for the first time, and Ellaby touched down after a fine passing move. Sullivan made a try for Bowen, and Britain had squared the series at 13—5.

Crowds of 35 000 and 10 000 had seen the first two Tests, and there was another good crowd topping 20 000 for the third Test at Christchurch on 20 August. This game was again a rough, tough battle, gripping to the last, and Britain won by the skin of their teeth, 6 points against 5. At half-time it was 3—2, a Fairclough try against a Dufty goal. Then Askin scored to make it 6—2. Late in the game a forward rush brought New Zealand's O'Brien a try, but Dufty was short with the kick at goal.

The tourists had won both rubbers, total receipts for the tour topped a record £40 000 and the Rugby League's profit was £10 670. After a bad start the tour had proved an outstanding success. A feature of it had been the presentation by the City Tattersalls Club of Sydney of an 'Ashes Cup' to be competed for annually, a happy gesture by these Sydney sportsmen.

The tour's leading scorer had again been Jim Sullivan, with 150 points, while Ellaby ran in more than 30 tries. At the end of the tour Britain invited Australia to tour in 1929–30, and there was a quick acceptance of the invitation.

Late in 1929 a movement began in Rugby League that was destined to have important and far-reaching consequences. Several Council members began an agitation aimed at finding a permanent and worthy home for the Challenge Cup final, the season's showpiece, which was attracting big attendances every year. Existing grounds were proving inadequate to cope with crowds approaching and topping 40 000, and Council members, looking ahead, urged the construction or finding of a ground capable of holding 50 000. The crowd record of over 40 000 had proved too tight a squeeze at Rochdale, and Headingley, stylish and comfortable as it was, was just not big enough.

The Wembley authorities, anxious to use the fine Empire Stadium to full capacity, were only too ready to confer with the Rugby League. Meetings took place, and after weighing up the pros and cons the Rugby League Council took the plunge and announced that the 1929 cup final would take place at Wembley Stadium.

The clubs fought for the right to be the first to play at Wembley, and the 1929 final became a Lancashire *v.* Yorkshire duel when Wigan and Dewsbury beat St Helens and Castleford in the semi-finals. Immediately there was a rush of bookings in and around these two towns, and Council members breathed more easily.

At last the great day arrived, and for the first time the trains and coaches poured into London for a Rugby League cup final. It was not the show of strength seen today, but it was an impressive demonstration of support for the Council's bold decision. Wembley's lush turf and impressive stands and terraces gave the perfect atmosphere to the game, and although Wembley was far from full, the attendance of 41 500 and receipts of £5600 were enough to make the experiment worth while.

In the dressing-rooms there was greater tension than ever before. Mr F. Kennedy, the League chairman, urged both teams to be 'clean and sportsmanlike', for Rugby League was on trial as a national spectacle.

Mr R. Robinson was referee, and teams were:

Dewsbury: Davies; Coates, Hirst, Smith, Bailey; Woolmore, Rudd; P. Brown, Rhodes, Robson, Bland, Malkin, Lyman.

Wigan: Sullivan; Ring, Parker, Kinnear, L. Brown; Abram, Binks; Hodder, Bennett, Beetham, Stephens, Mason, Sherrington.

As might have been expected, the occasion proved just a little too much for the players. The final was hard and clean, but not brilliant. In one of the few natural, flowing moves, Mason, Ring and Abram combined for Abram to score Wembley's first try. A Sullivan goal against a Davies dropped goal made it 5—2 at half-time. In the second half Kinnear sent Brown over, and Binks gave Kinnear a third Wigan try. Sullivan's goal completed the scoring, and Wigan became the first team to win the Challenge Cup at Wembley.

At the after-match festivities Mr Kennedy answered the

An incident in the Third 'Test' at Sydney on 18th July 1936. Wally Prigg, Australia's loose forward, breaks away with Hodgson (England) ready for business. Other Australian players seen are Mick Madsen, Vic Hey, Alan Ridley and Dave Brown (behind Prigg). England won 12–7

The waterlogged Wembley, 1968

The Castleford team hoisting up their coach Derek Turner after their Challenge Cup win at Wembley in 1968

Warren Ayres, Wigan half-back, romps round for a try near the posts

question everyone was asking. He said: 'The Council has been satisfied with the experiment, which will almost certainly be repeated.' The Way to Wembley was signposted.

The championship final between Huddersfield and Leeds attracted 25 604 to Halifax. In a dull game dominated by defences, a goal by Brook for Huddersfield was enough to win the title. It was a tame end to an exciting season.

10

Australia Complains of 'Poaching'

A GREAT Northern Union name returned to the headlines in 1928–9. At the end of the season, in which the Rugby League's surplus soared to £28 000, Salford reported a good financial year after years of struggling. The man behind the revival was none other than Lancelot B. Todd, former New Zealand pioneer half-back, who had returned to Britain to manage the 'Reds'.

The Rugby League Council meeting of 1929 turned its eyes to two important issues. First, it was agreed that the 1930 Challenge Cup final would again be played at Wembley. Secondly, arrangements were made for the 1929–30 visit of the Australian touring team. The Kangaroos, who arrived at Southampton on the *Aquitania* on 28 August, were managed by Mr Harry Sunderland and Mr J. Lorne Dargan.

The tourists, captained by Tom Gorman, a renowned centre, were to receive £4 10*s*. allowance per week, a sum well above the standard of previous touring sides from Australia. The party comprised *Backs:* F. McMillan, J. Upton, T. Gorman, A. Ridley, W. Spencer, W. Shankland, P. Maher, C. Fifield, F. Laws, H. Finch, A. G. Edwards, J. Holmes, E. Weissell, J. Busch, H. J. Kadwell; *Forwards:* G. Treweeke, M. Madsen, A. E. Root, A. J. Justice, G. Bishop, A. H. Henderson, L. V. Armbruster, D. V. O'Dempsey, L. A. Sellers, H. Steinohrt, J. Kingston, W. Brogan, W. Prigg.

The Aussies came with a reputation as a fast, strong, all-round side, and the tourists confirmed this with a series of good wins in their early club matches, the only reverse being a 14—3 beating at Wakefield, who were led by old foe Jonty Parkin. The first Test was played at Craven Park, Hull, on 5 October, and Britain had to turn out without Parkin, Ellaby and Brough. Teams were:

Great Britain: T. E. Rees (Oldham); A. Frodsham (St Helens), R. Kinnear (Wigan), W. Dingsdale (Warrington), E. Gwynne (Hull); L. Fairclough (St Helens), W. Rees (Swinton); H. Bowman (Hull), H. Bentham (Halifax), J. Thompson (Leeds), W. Horton (Wakefield T.), A. G. Middleton (Salford), J. Feetham (Hull K.R.).

Australia: F. McMillan; W. Spencer, T. Gorman, C. Fifield, W. Shankland; E. Weissell, J. Busch; W. Brogan, G. Bishop, M. Madsen, G. Treweeke, L. V. Armbruster, W. Prigg.

Britain opened brightly, and Gwynne was pulled down only a yard short. But then the Australians took charge, and Britain were cut to pieces by brilliant attacking football. Sweeping movements put Treweeke over for Weissell to goal, then Shankland, then a Busch burst put Prigg over and again Weissell converted. Immediately a scintillating piece of inter-passing magic between Gorman, Bishop and Weissell gave Bishop a try and Weissell the goal. Thompson's penalty goal was all Britain could muster, and it was 18—2 at half-time.

In the second half the rout continued. The 25 000 crowd saw Middleton get a try for Britain, but it was brief respite. Shankland beat four men to score, and again Weissell goaled. Spencer and Weissell added further second half tries and although Feetham got a late try for Britain, the Australians won 31—8. It was a shattering blow to British morale, and many changes were made for the second Test at Leeds on 9 November. Only Rees, Dingsdale and hooker Bentham kept their places, and strapping young Castleford centre Atkinson was brought in for the sole purpose of marking Gorman, the Australian centre and captain. Also drafted in were Sullivan, Ellaby, S. Smith (Wakefield T.), Parkin, Burgess, D. Jenkins (Hunslet), A. Fildes (St Helens Recs.) and the Swinton 'back two' of M. Hodgson and F. Butters. The Aussies brought in Steinohrt and O'Dempsey for Brogan and Armbruster.

The crowd of 32 000 witnessed a gruelling struggle quite different in character from the first Test. The British team, having tasted the power of the Australian attack, used stopping and marking tactics to strangle Aussie attacks at birth, and these 'spotting' tactics eclipsed the brilliant moves seen at Hull.

Only once was the Australian attack allowed to get clear, and Shankland got in at the corner to give Australia a 3—2 lead. Thereafter fierce spotting and marking closed up the game, and the rest of the scoring came from Britain. Sullivan landed three goals, and Parkin and Rees sent Atkinson over for a try.

Britain had won a grim battle 9—3, and the series was squared. The vital third Test was played at Swinton on 4 January, and this game became one of the exclusive number of Tests which have carved an individual niche in the game's history. It contained one of the most controversial incidents of all time, and paved the way for a unique decision. Both sides made changes, Halsall (Swinton), Oster (Oldham) and Thomas (Leeds) playing for Britain, and Justice, Brogan, Armbruster and Kingston joining the Australian pack. A crowd of 33 809 came to see the decider, and they saw a fierce, bitter and unrelenting trial of strength of an intensity even greater than at Leeds.

With 15 minutes left there was no score, and in that last quarter of an hour Australia hurled themselves into the assault to try to clinch the Ashes. Twice they were baulked by brilliant last-ditch tackles from loose forward Butters. Then came the incident that has been a controversial issue for more than 30 years. With the game in its closing seconds, Chimpy Busch, the Aussie half-back, made a glorious effort. From the last scrum he jinked past two despairing tackles, saw a narrow route to the right-hand corner flag and went for it. Busch raced with the speed of desperation. Equally desperate in his chase was loose forward Fred Butters. As Busch hurled himself over the line, Butters dived and took his legs from under him, forcing him into touch in goal. As the linesman's flag went up, referee R. Robinson (Bradford) ruled 'no try' and despite excited and strenuous protests that Busch had touched down before being carried into touch, the great effort failed.

It seemed that the Test series had ended in stalemate, one win each, but the touring team's managers had other ideas. The ebullient Mr Harry Sunderland requested permission to approach the Rugby League Council to suggest a fourth Test match, and his persuasive powers, backed by a Press demand for a 'decider', won a fourth Test by a narrow 13—11 vote.

This first-ever fourth Test had to be hastily arranged, and was fixed for mid-week, Wednesday, 15 January 1930, at Rochdale. In the British team T. Blinkhorn (Warrington), S. Brogden (Huddersfield) and B. Evans (Swinton) played in the backs, while W. A. Williams (Salford), A. Crowther (Hunslet) and H. Young (Huddersfield) came into the pack. Once again the match, before a crowd of 16 743, was a terrific struggle, with defences taking a grilling but coming out on top, and it seemed that the result would be another stalemate. Bad luck again struck the Aussies, however. In the second half their centre Fifield broke his ankle, and this unhappy mishap almost certainly cost them the game and the series, for minutes from the end Brogden sent Smith over for the winning try. It was the decisive score in one of the most tenaciously fought Test series ever.

The tourists left for home on 18 January, and immediately interest switched to the prospects for the second Wembley cup final.

When the semi-final rounds had been completed St Helens and Widnes had reached the final—a local 'derby' at Wembley! The local nature of the game caused grave doubts of a bumper Wembley, especially as star-studded St Helens, bristling with internationals and Colonials, were expected to trounce home-grown Widnes with their one solitary Colonial, South African Van Rooyen. The match was played on Saturday, 3 May, and although St Helens and Widnes fans poured into Wembley, the crowd was smaller than the 41 000 of the previous year. The teams were:

St Helens: Crooks; Ellaby, Mercer, Lewis, Hardgrave; Fairclough, Groves; Hutt, Clarey, Houghton, Hall, Halfpenny, Harrison.

Widnes: Fraser; Owen, Topping, Ratcliffe, Dennett; Laughton, Douglas; Silcock, Stevens, Kelsall, Van Rooyen, Hoey, Millington.

Referee: Mr F. Peel (Bradford).

Before the match the St Helens team had been involved in a programme of eight matches in 15 days. This may partly explain their colourless performance, but the major credit must go to the Widnes 'underdogs', who harried and worried the big guns of St

Helens into decisive defeat. St Helens scored first when Houghton touched down an Ellaby kick, but afterwards the Widnes terriers took a grip on the game which never relaxed.

Ratcliffe, the Widnes centre, was badly obstructed as he chased a loose ball over the St Helens line, and was awarded a try which Hoey converted. More shocks were on the way for St Helens, for after 34 minutes Dennett got a good try, and on the interval Ratcliffe kicked a penalty goal to give Widnes a 10—3 lead. In the second half the Widnes defence performed heroically as St Helens fought to save the game, and at the final whistle the score was 10—3 and Widnes had pulled off the victory no one thought possible.

The championship final at Wakefield on 10 May was an all-Yorkshire affair between Huddersfield and Leeds. A crowd of 32 095 saw a dour 2—2 draw, and two days later Huddersfield won the title by beating Leeds 10—0 at Thrum Hall, Halifax.

The 1930 annual meeting at Leeds on 11 June brought one or two important rule changes. The loose forward no longer had the option of packing down at the side of the scrum, and in a further attempt to cut down scrum offences it was ruled that the defending half-back would in future feed the scrum. This would cut down the temptation to offend, particularly near the goal posts.

In the 1930 close season the row over Australasian signings flared up again. Handsome fees were paid for a series of star signings, among them Eric Harris, Queensland winger, to Leeds; Australian Test centre Cecil Aynsley to Rochdale; Bill Shankland, Test winger, and Nelson Hardy, a Sydney centre, to Warrington. Leeds then made another big overseas signing by securing Chimpy Busch, the Australian half-back of the famous Swinton Test-match incident. These signings followed the lifting of the ban on signings overseas, and soon indignation against alleged British poaching flared up in Australia.

The Australian problem was to keep the brightest stars at home. The British problem in 1931 was to whip up enthusiasm for the third Wembley cup final following the small attendance in 1930.

Two Yorkshire clubs, York and Halifax, reached the final, and the attendance on Saturday, 2 May 1931, was 40 368—below the Rochdale record, but a big improvement on the previous year.

Receipts of more than £5000 were satisfactory, and eased the Council's problems a little.

Teams were:

Halifax: R. Davies; Higgins, Higgs, Haigh, F. Adams; I. Davies, Harrison; Renton, Rawnsley, Bland, Rees, Norcliffe, Atkinson.

York: Owen; H. Thomas, Rosser, W. J. Davies, W. Davies; Lloyd, W. Thomas; Pascoe, Myers, W. Davis, H. Davies, Johnson, Layhe.

Referee: Mr J. Edden (Swinton).

In the first 30 minutes York produced all the good football, while Halifax fumbled and showed 'Wembley nerves'. Pascoe kicked a goal for York, and Lloyd made a try for Harry Thomas. Then Halifax broke away for a gift try. The two Davieses on the York left wing fumbled between them and Bland scored a try converted by Adams. Harry Thomas restored York's lead with a try, but in the second half Halifax found their confidence and it was York who disintegrated. Adams kicked a goal, Dick Davies dropped a goal and Ivor Davies and Higgins (2) scored tries, Thomas converting two to give Halifax the cup by 22 points to 8.

Swinton won the championship for the third time in five years by beating Leeds 14—7 in the final at Wigan on 9 May. A crowd of 31 000 paid £2100 to see Swinton win an interesting struggle. Butters and Whittaker scored Swinton tries and Hodgson four goals, while Granger scored a try for Leeds and Thompson kicked two goals.

At the summer conference of the Council in 1931 a genuine attempt was made to meet Australia half-way on the alleged poaching of players. The Council, under chairman Mr Edward Brown of the Cumberland Commission, agreed that when a player was signed by an English club a fee of between £100 and £200 should be paid to the player's club. Reaction in Australia was mixed, for a few hundred pounds was regarded as poor recompense for a star player.

The Australians' willingness to invite Britain in 1932 unwittingly created a big problem for the Rugby League. To enable the tourists to make an early departure, the Challenge Cup final was brought forward to 9 April. This brought it too close to the

Association Football Cup final, and the Wembley authorities would not allow Rugby League use of the stadium. For one year at least the Wembley experiment was suspended. When Swinton and Leeds qualified for the final the chosen venue was Central Park, Wigan, for Swinton and Headingley were obviously ruled out.

A 45 000 crowd was expected at Wigan, but only 29 000 turned up, probably because a big crush at the turnstiles had been forecast. Receipts of £2450 were only half the previous year's total at Wembley, a big propaganda weapon for pro-Wembley officials. Teams were:

Leeds: Brough; Harris, Moores, O'Rourke, Goulthorpe; E. Williams, Adams; Lowe, Thompson, Smith, Cox, Douglas, Glossop.

Swinton: Scott; Buckingham, Green, H. Evans, Kenney; B. Evans, Rees; Armitt, Strong, Wright, Hodgson, Beswick, Butters.

Referee: Mr F. Peel (Bradford).

The match proved the tough struggle everyone had anticipated, with Leeds attempting to become the first team to score a try against Swinton in the 1931–2 cup competition. With Australians Moores and Eric Harris in great form on the right wing, there was every prospect of achieving this object, but the first half saw the Swinton defence keep its blank score sheet of 'tries against'. However, Leeds forward Joe Thompson was in kicking mood, and his four goals against one from Hodgson gave Leeds an 8—2 interval lead. A second Hodgeson goal made it 8—4, and the masterful Swinton pack stormed ahead for a great rally. They hammered away at the Leeds line, but Leeds defended courageously. Suddenly a Swinton attack broke down when a Rees pass to Green went astra. Moores pounced on it, gave it to O'Rourke, another Australian, who whipped it out to Eric Harris.

The tall 'Toowoomba Ghost' seized his chance in typical style, streaking past the cover and accelerating past full-back Scott for a great try. Swinton made another great effort, and Hodgson kicked two more goals, but Leeds held on to win 11—8.

Huddersfield, those great title-chasers, met St Helens in the championship final at Wakefield on 7 May, before 20 000 people Winnard scored a try and Lewis two goals to put St Helens ahead

7—0 against a lethargic and uninspired Huddersfield. Both sides were minus tourists, but St Helens seemed less affected, and although Walker scored a try for Huddersfield and Bowkett a goal, a Lewis goal gave St Helens the championship with a score of 9—5.

The 1932 tourists, managed by Messrs G. F. Hutchins (Oldham) and R. F. Anderton (Warrington), and captained by Jim Sullivan (Wigan), arrived in Australia at the end of May. The 26 players were *Backs:* J. Sullivan (Wigan), A. Ellaby (St Helens), A. J. Risman, B. Hudson (Salford), S. Smith, L. Adams (Leeds), J. Woods (Barrow), A. Atkinson (Castleford), S. Brogden (Huddersfield), W. Dingsdale (Warrington), G. Robinson, E. Pollard (Wakefield T.), I. J. Davies (Halifax), B. Evans (Swinton); *Forwards:* N. Silcock (Widnes), J. F. Thompson, J. Lowe (Leeds), W. A. Williams, J. Feetham (Salford), J. Wright, M. Hodgson, F. Butters (Swinton), L. White (Hunslet), N. Fender (York), A. E. Fildes (St Helens Recs.) and W. Horton (Wakefield T.).

After a series of good wins by the tourists the first Test at Sydney Cricket Ground on Monday, 6 June, an Australian holiday, aroused phenomenal interest. Huge queues formed hours before the game, and eventually the gates were closed with a world-record attendance of more than 70 000 in the ground. The teams for this match, played in an electric atmosphere, were:

Australia: McMillan; C. Pearce, Norman, Laws, Wilson; Weissell, Gee; Steinohrt, O'Dempsey, Madsen, T. Pearce, Little, Prigg.

Great Britain: Sullivan; Ellaby, Atkinson, Brogden, Smith; Pollard, Evans; Silcock, White, Thompson, Hodgson, Horton Feetham.

Both sides buckled down to the job with determination, and although fast, open moves were rare, the tension was maintained, as first one side then the other piled on pressure. Ellaby made a brilliant interception to race away and touch down for Britain, but two penalty goals from Weissell, one a beauty from half-way, gave Australia a 4—3 lead. Then Ellaby made another good run and gave Atkinson a try, converted by Sullivan. In the second half there was no further scoring, despite a big rally by Australia in the closing quarter, and Britain were one game up in the series.

The second Test at Brisbane on 18 June was vital for Australia, who needed to tie the series, and 27 000 attended.

Australia were quickly in the lead, for when Smith misfielded O'Dempsey sent Gee over for Weissell to convert. This quick lead gave Australia a spirit and confidence they never lost, and although at one stage Australia had only 11 men on the field, due to injuries, they kept well on top, and they won the game and tied the series with a 15—6 victory.

There big victories revived the confidence of the tourists in time for the vital third Test at Sydney on 16 July 1932, and although the Sydney crowd was not a record, a total of over 50 000 people saw the match. Britain had Risman, Horton, Fildes and Williams for the injured Pollard, Feetham, Fender and Butters, while Australia brought in Neaumann on the left wing.

Australia made all the running at first, and after Weissell had kicked two goals, Pearce beat Ellaby and gave O'Connor a try converted by Weissell. At 9—0 Australia seemed hot-foot after the Ashes, but Britain hit back and Risman made a try for Smith at the corner.

In the opening minutes of the second half Weissell kicked his fourth goal, but then Britain made a tactical switch, standoff Risman and centre Brogden changing places. Almost immediately Evans and Ellaby combined to put Brogden over, and then a terrific break by Horton sent Smith through. Sullivan's goal made it 11—11, and goals from Sullivan and Weissell tied the scores again at 13 points each.

The crowd was on its toes with excitement, roaring for a home try. When a try came, however, it was to Britain. Risman made the break and passed to Smith, and the winger's fine burst of speed sent him down the wing and in at the corner for his hat-trick and the winning try. Sullivan crowned yet another Ashes-retaining victory with a goal from the touchline. Great Britain had held the Ashes once again, and Australia had to look back to 1920 for their last series victory.

Great Britain went on to New Zealand in high spirits, and this time there were no slips. The first Test at Auckland was won by 24 points to 9 and the second at Christchurch by 25 points to 14. A third Test victory by 20—18 at Auckland gave the 1932 tourists a playing record of 23 wins and one draw in 26 games, a fine achievement.

It had been another great tour. A big profit had once again been made, both Test series handsomely won, and several points-scoring records had been broken. Sullivan recorded 223 points and Ellaby, Smith and Brogden led the try-scorers. It was a happy and successful party which returned to Britain on 22 September 1932.

11

France Enters the Field

THE mid-thirties were undoubtedly great and interesting years for Rugby League, years which brought alternating triumph and disaster and at least one massive new development of the game, the entry of France. These dramatic years began in 1932–3 with further storms of correspondence between Britain and Australia when J. Wilson and H. Gee, two prominent Australian players, were signed up by Wigan. After the usual flare-up it was agreed that when British teams toured Australia managers would ensure that no approaches were made to players during the tour.

It was when the Rugby League sat down to prepare the intinerary for this tour that an exciting new development took place in a country hitherto unconsidered as a potential Rugby League convert. Several French Rugby Union clubs had been warring with the French Union in a manner similar to the historic disputes in Britain and Australia. In April 1933, a delegation from France met Rugby League officials in London, and many pointed questions were asked by the French party, who made a request for the Australian tourists to play a game in France.

There were no immediate developments following this, but in the season which followed, 1933–4, the arrival of the Australian tourists set the ball rolling in France and paved the way for full-scale Rugby League in that country.

Meanwhile, at home, the Rugby League prepared for the return to Wembley after the 1932 break, and the 1933 final could hardly have been bettered as an outstanding attraction. Huddersfield and Warrington, two fine footballing teams, reached the final, and the Prince of Wales gave the event royal patronage. The return to the fine stadium, the interest aroused by this great inter-county clash and the attendance of royalty boded well, but in the end a crowd of 42 000, slightly below expectations, saw the 1933 Challenge Cup final. Receipts of £6500 were a home record. The atmosphere was electric, and the game proved a fitting one for a great occasion. Teams were:

Huddersfield: Scourfield; Mills, Brogden, Bowkett, Markham; Richards, Adams; Sherwood, Halliday, Banks, Tiffany, Talbot, Brindle.

Warrington: Holding; Thompson, Dingsdale, Shankland, Blinkhorn; Oster, Davies; Hardman, Bentham, Miller, Evans, Smith, Seeling.

Referee: Mr F. Fairhurst (Wigan).

The game was evenly balanced and keen from the start, with Warrington's heavier pack controlling the scrums, but Huddersfield's speed and alertness giving them the advantage in the loose. For the first 16 minutes Warrington attacked, but two breakaways by Huddersfield led to penalty goals from Bowkett. Then, when Huddersfield heeled from a scrum near the Warrington line, half-back Adams cut through and Brindle scored, Bowkett improving. Nine points down, Warrington fought back, and Dingsdale tore through for a try, Holding converting. Just before half-time Davies nipped through from a scrum, and Holding's goal put Warrington ahead 10—9.

It was touch-and-go, end-to-end stuff and a Bowkett goal, followed by a Brindle try converted by Bowkett, made it 16—10. Holding kicked a goal, but Huddersfield came back, and a Richards try goaled by Bowkett seemed to put Huddersfield beyond challenge. But Warrington had not finished, and Davies dummied his way over, Holding again landing the goal. It was just too late, however, and Huddersfield won one of the finest cup finals ever by 21—17.

The championship final was as disappointing as the cup final had been thrilling. Swinton and Salford met in a 'derby' match at Wigan before 18 000 people, and Salford won a moderate game 15—5. Brown, Jenkins and Feetham scored tries, Risman kicking three goals for Salford, while Shaw scored a try and Scott a goal for Swinton.

The 1933 annual meeting had plenty to discuss: the movement in France, another abortive plan to reintroduce two divisions to revive interest among struggling clubs and a novel and intriguing suggestion from London. From London White City, a greyhound stadium, came the suggestion that Rugby League should be played as one of the stadium's attractions. The team named was Wigan Highfield, who were on their last legs, and Brigadier A. C. Critchley, of White City, offered to pay travelling and broken-time expenses. The annual meeting set up a committee to consider the proposal, the committee approved and in 1933–4 London Highfield replaced Wigan Highfield and yet another experiment was born.

Like so many outpost experiments, this London gamble failed, and in 1934–5 the White City authorities gave up in face of increasing costs and apathy.

The Australian tourists arrived on 14 August 1933, and after a reception at Wembley again made their headquarters at Ilkley. The managers were Mr Harry Sunderland, on his second tour, and Mr W. W. Webb, and the captain Frank McMillan at full-back.

The players were F. McMillan, W. Smith, F. Laws, D. Brown, A. Ridley, F. Neaumann, J. Why, S. Gardner, F. Gilbert, V. Hey, C. Pearce, V. Thicknesse, F. Doonar, L. Mead, M. Madsen, S. Pearce, W. Prigg, A. Folwell, M. Glasheen, R. Stehr, D. O'Dempsey, F. O'Connor, F. Curran, J. Doyle, J. Gibbs, H. Denny, J. Little.

The tourists opened their tour with the longest winning spell of any Australian touring side in Britain. They won all 11 games before the first Test, and rattled up scores of 53 against Bramley, 33 against Lancashire and 38 at Oldham. The first Test was played at a new venue, Belle Vue Stadium, new home of Broughton Rangers, and a 30 000 crowd attended. The match was played on Saturday, 7 October, and the sides were:

Great Britain: J. Sullivan (Wigan); A. Ellaby (St Helens), A. J. Risman (Salford), S. Brogden (Huddersfield), S. Smith (Leeds); W. J. Davies (Castleford), B. Evans (Swinton); N. Silcock (Widnes), L. White (Hunslet), J. Miller (Warrington), M. Hodgson (Swinton), M. Horton (Wakefield T.), J. Feetham (Salford).

Australia: McMillan; Ridley, Brown, C. Pearce, Why; Hey, Thicknesse; Madsen, O'Dempsey, Stehr, O'Connor, S. Pearce, Prigg.

After the tourists' magnificent football in club games their performance in the Test was disappointing. The match developed into a tough contest of forward strength, with Britain as dour and determined as Australia, and the only scores consisted of two late penalties by Sullivan for Britain to win 4—0.

After the first Test the Aussies' club form slumped, and six out of ten games were lost between the first and second Tests. The second Test was played at Leeds on 12 November, and Australia brought in Smith, Gardner, Folwell, Gibbs and Doyle, while Britain had Hudson (Salford), Dingsdale (Warrington) and Woods (Barrow) replacing Ellaby, Brogden and Smith. Brogden replaced Davies at out-half. The attendance was 29 618, receipts £3873.

The match was almost a carbon copy of the first Test. Strong tackling and destructive forward play killed open football, and fast, exhilarating moves were rarely seen. Sullivan gave Britain the lead with a goal, but in a sudden flash of brilliance Ridley started an Australian movement for Brown to dash over for a try which he himself improved.

In the second half a Sullivan goal made the score 5—4, and amid terrific tension Britain struggled for the winning try. It came only two minutes from the end, when Bryn Evans broke away and Woods crashed over. Britain had once again held the Tests, but by the narrowest of margins.

Interest in the remainder of the tour was now academic, and when the third Test was played at Swinton, on 16 December, fog and rain kept the attendance down to 10 000. Ironically, this match was the best of the three! Britain brought in Atkinson (Castleford), Smith (Leeds), Jenkins and Watkins (Salford) and Armitt (Swinton) for Dingsdale, Woods, Brogden, Evans and White.

Australia also made changes, McMillan, White, Laws and Mead returning in the backs and S. Pearce in the forwards. With the Ashes problem out of the way, both sides played in attractive fashion, and the result was in doubt until the final whistle. Britain, who led 12—9 at the interval, finally won 19—16, but it was touch-and-go until a late penalty goal by Sullivan, who kicked five goals in all. Britain's tries came from Hodgson, Feetham and Smith, while Australia's points came from Hey and Prigg (tries) and Brown (five goals). Britain's victory meant a clean sweep in the 1933 Tests, yet by a mere handful of points each time.

The end of the Australian tour in Britain was the prelude to more developments in France. After negotiations between a Rugby League delegation, including Australian manager Harry Sunderland, and the French officials, a Sunday exhibition game between Australia and a Great Britain XIII captained by Jim Sullivan was played at Stade Pershing, Paris, a ground not under the control of the French Rugby Union, on 31 December 1933, the first time the Rugby League had sanctioned a game on a Sunday.

A good crowd saw the game, and on his return to Britain Mr John Wilson, Rugby League secretary, reported that a French side, under the leadership of Jean Galia, would tour Britain in the spring of 1934. This tour began on 5 March with a civic reception to the French players and officials at Leeds, and two English Test players, Jonty Parkin and Joe Thompson, were engaged to 'advise' the 18 players.

The French players included many Rugby Union internationals, with Jean Galia a tower of strength on and off the field. They played matches at Wigan, Leeds, Hull, London Highfield and Salford, and against a Rugby League side. They won only one, at Hull, but their enthusiasm and open play won them the applause of British crowds and at least one standing ovation, at Wigan. The tour made a slight profit, and the small band of tourists went back to France to launch Rugby League officially in their home country.

An 'international' match between France and Great Britain was played at the Buffalo Velodrome, Paris, on 15 April, before 20 000 spectators, and Britain won 32—21, and after this match discussions took place between Rugby League officials and MM Galia, Charles Benat and M. Blein to organize the appointment of a French Rugby League management committee. The next step in building up the French bridgehead was an April tour of French clubs by Leeds, an outstanding success, and in August 1934, under assurance of support from Britain, the French Rugby League came into being at a meeting at Toulouse. It was to be known as 'La Ligue Française de Rugby à Treize' and 12 founder members were Paris Celtic, Bordeaux, Côte Basque, Grenoble,

Sport Olympique de Paris, La Rochelle, Pau, Albi, Roanne, S.O. Beziers, Lyons and Villeneuve. The first full season began in October.

While the game spread apace in France, the Rugby League's domestic season brought a bumper championship-final attendance and another Wembley cup final. The championship final between Salford and Wigan was played first, on 28 April 1934, and 31 565 (£2113) saw Wigan beat the league leaders Salford by 15 points to 3, the 10th time in 15 seasons that the top-of-the-table club had failed in the play-off. Gwyn Davies, Morley and Targett (tries) and Sullivan (three goals) scored for Wigan, while Jenkins scored an unimproved try for Salford.

The 1934 Wembley final brought another inter-county duel between Hunslet and Widnes, and although the attendance of 41 280 was 600 below the 1933 figure, it was still good enough to confirm the value of the great stadium as a 'prestige' venue for the final. The referee was Mr A. Holbrook (Warrington) and the teams were:

Hunslet: Walkington; Dennis, Morrell, Winter, Broughton; Thornton, Todd; Smith, White, Tolson, Crowther, Dawson, Beverley.

Widnes: Bradley; Owen, Topping, Jacks, Gallimore; Shannon, McCue; Silcock, Jones, Higgins, McDowell, Ratcliffe, Millington.

Strong wind and sun gave the advantage to each side in turn, and Widnes, who had to face them first, led 3—2 at one stage, McDowell charging down a Hunslet kick to score a try for Widnes, and Tolson landing a goal for Hunslet.

Just on the interval Morrell, the Hunslet centre, broke through the middle gloriously and crashed over for an unconverted try.

Hunslet led 5—3 at half-time, but they had the elements to face in the second half, and Morrell was unable to resume because of a shoulder injury sustained crashing over for his try. Despite these odds, Hunslet put up a tremendous fight, and, surprisingly, got on top. Ratcliffe kicked a goal for Widnes, but Hunslet pounded the Widnes line and Beverley and Smith scored unconverted tries to win the game for the Yorkshire club by 11 points to 5 in a hard-fought final.

The annual meeting of the Rugby League at Leeds in June

made two more rule changes designed at tidying up the game. The newest play-the-ball rule stated that there should be only one acting half-back on each side, with other players within a radius of 10 yards and at least three yards behind the play-the-ball. In another attempt to sort out scrummaging, it was ruled that the ball should not be hooked until it had reached the foot of the hooker furthest away from the entry of the ball. This was to stop premature striking by props and hookers.

The other item of note in the 1934 close season was the winding-up of London Highfield, whose remnant of players and officials came north again to set up as Liverpool Stanley, hoping for a better fate than had befallen Liverpool City many years before.

Season 1934–5 was looked forward to eagerly as the testing time for the game in France. Anxious to keep enthusiasm on the boil, the Rugby League invited another Jean Galia team to Britain, while Salford and Hunslet made short tours in France.

Galia brought 20 players of the Villeneuve club, and they played free-scoring exhibition matches at Warrington, Broughton, Hull, Oldham and Leeds, losing the matches but gaining numerous friends. Again they made a small profit on the tour. So great was the newborn enthusiasm in France that leaders of the game in that country suggested that a World Cup competition should be organized for 1935! The idea was discussed for a time, but the first World Cup series was still some way ahead.

A terrific boost for French morale was a victory over Wales at Bordeaux on Tuesday, 1 January 1935, the score being 18—11 before 15 000 spectators. This was followed by a short tour by a Rugby League representative party, and then the Rugby League presented a trophy to be competed for as the French Challenge Cup. This event took place for the first time on 5 May, 1935, the day after the Wembley final. France went on from strength to strength, and before 20 000 at the Buffalo Velodrome on 28 March they drew 15—15 with a strong English side. The star of the French team was Rousie, who kicked three goals and scored a brilliant 85-yard try. Jean Galia also had the pleasure of scoring a try.

The first Rugby League *v.* France representative game in Britain took place as a Jubilee international at Headingley during the celebrations for King George V and Queen Mary. It was played on 6 May and 15 000 saw the Rugby League win an entertaining game 25—18.

It was a great season in France, and when the second season began four more teams joined the French League.

The Jubilee celebrations of 1935 were used by the Rugby League to publicize a 'Jubilee Wembley' for the 1935 cup final, but the publicity campaign did not pay off, for the crowd for the all-Yorkshire final between Castleford and Huddersfield was just below 40 000, paying £5800. The teams were well matched on paper, and Les Adams, the Castleford scrum-half, was appearing in his third final in four years, on different sides each time. He had won with Leeds and Huddersfield, and Castleford looked to him as their talisman. On the Huddersfield side Adams's opposite number was D. M. Davies, who had played against Adams while with Warrington in 1933. Teams were:

Castleford: Lewis; Cunniffe, Atkinson, Croston, Askin; W. J. Davies, Adams; McManus, Haley, Taylor, F. Smith, Crossley, Sadler.

Huddersfield: Scourfield; Mountain, Towill, Fiddes, Markham; Richards, D. M. Davies; Roberts, Watson, Sherwood, Tiffany, Fuller, Talbot.

Referee: Mr A. E. Harding (Broughton).

The match was not one of the greatest seen at Wembley, Huddersfield's performance was below the great 1933 display. Castleford were the more aggressive and polished side, but when the score stood at 11—8, with only minutes remaining, Huddersfield nearly pulled off an undeserved win.

Castleford's tries had come from Askin, Adams and Cunniffe, and Atkinson had kicked a goal. Huddersfield had scored through Towill and Fiddes (tries) and Sherwood (goal) but had never looked like winning. Then Tiffany, the Huddersfield forward, broke through with a superhuman burst, and had he seen support behind him it might have been a try. However, he tried to 'go it alone' and Atkinson tackled him brilliantly. Castleford's win gave Adams the remarkable record of three Wembley appearances with three clubs, and three winning medals.

The championship final at Wigan on 11 May saw Swinton

beat Warrington by 14 points to 3 before a 27 000 crowd (£1710). McGregor made a try for Green, and Hodgson kicked two goals to give Swinton a 7—0 interval lead. Garrett sent Dingsdale over for Warrington, but Sullivan (try) and Hodgson (two more goals) rounded off Swinton's comfortable win.

The annual meeting at Manchester on 12 June 1935, brought two more surprise entries into the League. Undismayed by the failure of London Highfield and White City, sport-minded business men in the Metropolis launched sides named Acton and Willesden, and Streatham and Mitcham.

The emphasis was entirely on the new entries to Rugby League during the early part of 1935–6. In France Swinton and a Rugby League XIII made successful tours, and France entered the international championship tournament, losing both their games to Wales at Llanelly and England at the Buffalo Velodrome. Receipts for the Paris match were £2510, an extremely good figure and a happy augury.

The two new clubs in London had fairly successful openings. Crowds were not large, but the two teams, stiffened with players of experience, won several impressive victories, and Streatham and Mitcham showed initiative by signing five New Zealanders, including a famous Maori full-back, George Nepia. Elsewhere there were rumblings of further expansion. In the North-East a group of Newcastle sportsmen banded together to finance and support a club, and after a public meeting in November 1935, it was decided that application for admission to the League would be made in the 1936–7 season.

As the season progressed, emphasis turned to the 1936 Australasian tour, and managers appointed were Messrs R. F. Anderton (Warrington) and W. Popplewell (Bramley). In March 26 players were named after two trial matches.

Making his fourth trip, a record, was Wigan full-back Jim Sullivan, who was appointed captain. The party comprised *Backs:* J. Sullivan, J. Morley (Wigan), J. Brough, S. Smith, F. Harris, S. Brogden (Leeds), B. Hudson, A. Edwards, A. J. Risman, E. Jenkins, W. Watkins (Salford), A. Atkinson (Castleford), W. Belshaw (Liverpool Stanley), T. McCue (Widnes); *Forwards:* N. Silcock (Widnes), H. Woods (Liverpool Stanley), H. Field (York),

T. Armitt, M. Hodgson (Swinton), J. Miller, J. Arkwright (Warrington), H. Jones (Keighley), L. A. Troup (Barrow), G. H. Exley (Wakefield T.), H. Beverley (Hunslet), H. Ellerington (Hull). To this party fell the responsibility of maintaining Britain's remarkable 16-year spell of immunity from defeat in a Test series with Australia.

The first party of tourists left on 17 April, and the following day Leeds and Warrington met for the 1936 Challenge Cup final at Wembley. The attendance was a good one, 51 250, and the receipts of £7200 were a record. Leeds sought to equal Huddersfield's record of four Challenge Cup wins, while Warrington were out for consolation for their 1933 defeat.

Teams were:

Leeds: Brough; E. Harris, F. Harris, Parker, Brogden; Ralph, Williams; Hall, Satterthwaite, Dyer, Jubb, Casewell, Isaac.

Warrington: Shankland; Garrett, Hawker, Dingsdale, G. Jenkins; Newcombe, Goodall; Hardman, Cotton, Miller, Flannery, Arkwright, Chadwick.

Referee: Mr A. S. Dobson (Featherstone).

Despite the large crowd and tense Wembley atmosphere, the game was not a great one, and scrummaging faults, dropped passes and 'incidents' between players spoiled the match. Leeds were well beaten in the scrums, but of the two sides they showed the greatest craft in attack, and they scored in their first real move when Eric Harris cross-kicked for Isaac to score. Williams kicked the goal and Leeds were 5—0. Warrington, who protested vainly that Isaac was offside, were badly shaken, and after Shankland had reduced the arrears with a penalty goal they fell further behind. It was a brilliant try scored by Leeds' 'other Harris', centre Fred, who had been signed from Leigh. He dummied to flying winger Eric Harris, kicked the ball over Shankland's head, gathered and touched down for one of the best tries ever seen at Wembley. Williams added a penalty goal and Leeds led 10—2 at half-time. The second half saw Leeds still on top in a disappointing game, and Eric Harris and Parker scored further tries, Williams kicking another goal. Leeds won 18—2, equalling Huddersfield's record of four cup victories.

The championship final at Fartown, Huddersfield, was fought out between Hull and Widnes, and once again Yorkshire provided the winner. Scores were tied 2—2 at the interval with goals from Oliver and Jacks, but in the second half Widnes collapsed in staggering fashion. Hull swept through time and again to win 21—2, and Joe Oliver, the Hull captain, had a personal tally of two tries and five goals, 16 points. L. Barlow scored a third try and Miller dropped a goal.

12

Record Crowds; War-clouds Again

AFTER 16 years of British domination the Australian Test team were desperately anxious to regain the Ashes in 1936. The tourists knew what they were up against, and when they played their first game only a few days after their arrival they fought hard for a 15—13 win against a strong Sydney Combined XIII. Defeat by 18—13 against a powerful New South Wales side was redeemed by victories over Queensland and Western Districts.

The first Test was played on Monday, 29 June 1936, at Sydney Cricket Ground, before a crowd topping 40 000, and Australia's determination to win was obvious from the start. They constantly won possession from the scrums, and pounded and harried the British line. Despite this, Britain scored the first try. Brown had kicked a penalty goal to give Australia the lead when forward Harry Beverley forced his way over the home line. Australia surged back, but their only tangible reward was another Brown penalty, giving them a 4—3 lead at half-time.

In the second half the green-and-gold jerseys found the attacking form that had always threatened. A brilliant combination between seven players saw Ridley run over for a great try, and Brown goaled. Britain caved in after this, and Brown, Pearce and Brown again ran in fine tries, Beaton kicking three goals. In a belated and formal British ralley Beverley got a second try, improved by Hodgson to make the final score 24—8.

Australia had shown they meant business, and Britain buckled down for the second Test at Brisbane the following Saturday. A crowd of 30 000 saw the game, and Britain brought in Brough, Arkwright, Risman, Watkins and Armitt to strengthen the side conclusively beaten in the first Test. Britain showed better form in this game, and after Edwards had scored a try Risman landed a penalty goal. The tourists threw the ball about in enterprising style, but this adventurous spirit proved disastrous when Risman dropped a pass and Crippin, the speedy Aussie winger, picked it up, raced away at top speed and swerved past full-back Brough for a spectacular try converted by Beaton.

The scores were level as the second half began, and the match became a tremendous end-to-end struggle, with first Ridley and then Edwards pulled down just short. Britain went into the lead when Edwards took Jenkins's cross-kick to score, and Risman goaled from touch. Brown kicked a penalty goal to reduce the lead, but a penalty from Hodgson made it 12—7 and Britain held on to square the series.

The Ashes were at stake when the third Test was played at Sydney on 18 July 1936, and a crowd of 53 000 paid £4299 to see the decider. Australia were on top in the early stages, and Brown kicked a goal, but Hudson swept through for a try and Hodgson converted, and Britain led 5—2 at half-time.

The first half was marred by some rough and rowdy exchanges between the forwards, and Stehr (Australia) and Arkwright (Great Britain) were sent off following a personal vendetta. In the second half Australia fought magnificently to get on terms, and Risman and Belshaw distinguished themselves with some mighty tackling. Then, after a long period of desperate defence, Britain broke away to score. Jenkins came away, fed Brogden on the burst and the Huddersfield man went through to score. Hodgson converted, then kicked a penalty goal and Britain led 12—2.

In the closing minutes Australia made a last, despairing effort. Prigg made a wonderful run, beating half the British team with great spirit and determination before sending Hey over the line. Brown converted, but it was too late, and Britain had once again held the Ashes with an identical score to that recorded in the second Test.

The tourists had won 13 out of 16 games, and could look forward to another good profit from gate receipts. The next stop was New Zealand, which began with a sequence of victories in 'minor' matches, including a match against South Auckland in which the tourists won with nine men on the field. Ellerington and Exley being injured, Hodgson ordered off and Beverley retiring hurt near the end. Because of a spate of injuries, Britain fielded both hookers, Field and Armitt, in the first Kiwi Test on 8 August, and Troup came in at loose forward.

The referee in this game penalized Britain incessantly, and had Hemi and Watene been in goal-kicking form Britain would have lost. Edwards and Jenkins scored tries for the tourists, and Hodgson two fine penalty goals, and these 10 points gave Britain a two-point victory, New Zealand's points coming from goals by Watene (3) and Trevarthen.

In the second Test at Auckland on 15 August the tourists had five Salford men, Risman, Watkins, Jenkins, Hudson and Edwards, in the backs, and the understanding of this quintet proved a vital factor in victory. Great Britain won 23—11, despite losing Arkwright, Belshaw and Jenkins for various periods during the game.

The 1936 tour had ended successfully, with a profit of over £8000.

The 1936–7 season in Britain began with the end of the experiment and the launching of another. The Acton and Willesden club disbanded after an indifferent season, and into their place came North-Eastern club Newcastle. The two outpost teams of the League had varying fortunes in the early stages, Streatham and Mitcham reeling off some fine victories, while Newcastle staggered from defeat to defeat.

Newcastle lost their first 13 games, and then astounded the Rugby League world by beating the reigning champions Hull by 5 points to 0! Soon both outpost clubs were flying distress signals, and midway through the season Mr Ivor Halstead, general manager of Streatham and Mitcham, announced his club's retirement from the League because they could no longer pay their way.

While home ventures foundered, the game in France continued to expand. Côte Basque made a short and successful 1937 tour in Britain under coach Tom Parker, former Wigan centre, and a big fillip for the game in France was its admission to the Fédération National des Sports, giving equality of status with other French sports. The Rugby League sent a representative touring team to

France, and a triangular international tournament was again held. Both Wales and England beat France, but the games were well supported, and the sprightly French team showed continued improvement.

The Challenge Cup final of 1937 brought together Widnes, playing their third final in eight seasons, and Keighley, who reached the final for the first time. The championship final brought together Salford and Warrington, and the championship play-off took place first, on Saturday, 1 May 1937.

The match was played at Wigan, attracting gate receipts of £1945, and was a disappointing affair. The star-studded back division of Salford did not 'click' as usual, and Warrington were equally uninspired. The first try came after 70 minutes, when the scores were tied 8—8 from four goals each. The Warrington hooker, Cotton, surprised Salford when he slipped over for an unconverted try, but Salford snatched a dramatic victory in the closing minutes when Hudson flashed over in the corner and Risman kicked a magnificent goal.

The following Saturday brought the great trek to Wembley for supporters of Widnes and Keighley. Neither club commanded big gates at home, but nevertheless a fair-sized crowd of 48 000 paid £6800 to see the game. Widnes had seven men from their 1934 side, while Keighley were led by half-back D. M. Davies, beaten finalist with Huddersfield and Warrington. The teams were:

Keighley: Herbert; Sherburn, Towill, Parker, Lloyd; Bevan, Davies; Traill, Halliday, H. Jones, Talbot, Dixon Gill.

Widnes: Bradley; Whyte, Topping, Barber, Evans; Shannon, McCue; Silcock, J. Jones, Higgins, McDowell, Roberts, Millington.

Referee: Mr P. Cowell (Warrington).

Widnes were ahead in 10 minutes when McCue made a break and his partner Shannon went over, Topping converting. Sherburn missed two penalties for Keighley, and the brilliant McCue jinked through again for a great try before a successful kick by Sherburn made it 8—2 for Widnes at half-time.

In the first 10 minutes of the second half Keighley battered the Widnes lines, and twice Parker was brought down inches from the line. Then Widnes raised the siege in decisive fashion. A pass between Bevan and Towill was intercepted by Barber who went through for a try. Topping's conversion finished Keighley, and a fourth Widnes try came from front-row forward Silcock. Topping added a penalty goal and Lloyd got a late try for beaten Keighley.

The Australian tourists arrived at Southampton on 15 September 1937. One big name was missing, for half-back Vic Hey had joined the Leeds Australian clan. Managers of the party were Mr Harry Sunderland, making his third trip as manager, and Mr R. E. Savage. There were many new faces among the players, for of the 26 only F. Gilbert, Stehr, Curran, Gibbs and Prigg were experienced tourists.

The full party was *Backs:* L. Ward, H. Robison, C. Hazelton, L. Dawson, J. Beaton, B. Williams, R. McKinnon, E. Norman, P. Williams, L. Thompson, G. Whittle, D. McLean, J. Reardon, F. Gilbert: *Forwards:* F. Nolan, P. Fairall, R. Stehr, F. Curran, J. Gibbs, H. Narvo, E. Lewis, W. Prigg, A. Norval, R. McLennan, H. Pierce, F. Griffiths, L. Heidke, E. Collins.

The Australians began their tour with wins at Leigh, York and Newcastle, but Lancashire, at Warrington, and Halifax beat the tourists. Wins were needed to boost Aussie morale, and they came against Yorkshire at Bradford, at Wakefield and at Rochdale. The first Test was played at Leeds on Saturday, 16 October, before a 32 000 crowd paying £3942. The Great Britain selectors had sprung a surprise by choosing the Castleford wing pair of Cunniffe and Croston to make their Test baptism following fine performances for their club. The teams were:

Great Britain: W. Belshaw (Liverpool S.); C. Cunniffe, A. J. Croston (Castleford), A. J. Risman (Salford), J. Morley (Wigan); E. Jenkins (Salford), T. McCue (Widnes); N. Silcock (Widnes), T. Armitt (Swinton), H. Woods (Leeds), J. Arkwright (Warrington), M. Hodgson (Swinton), H. Beverley (Hunslet).

Australia: Ward; Reardon, Beaton, McKinnon, B. Williams; Norman, P. Williams; Curran, Pierce, Stehr, Gibbs, Lewis, Prigg.

Great Britain's defence of the Ashes made a bad start. The home side plodded in workmanlike but dreary fashion, while Australia launched delightful attacks which failed only at the last minute through over-eagerness or handling mistakes. It was rank injustice that Australia's lead was only 4—2 at the interval, two goals from Beaton against one from Hodgson.

The true cost of those first-half missed chances became apparent in the second half. Australia still mounted impressive attacks without finishing them off, and it was a severe blow when midway through the half Jenkins found a gap in the tourists' defence to nip through for a try. In the last 10 minutes Britain lost Cunniffe with a leg injury, but the home defence weathered attack after attack, and Jenkins's try gave Britain a lucky 5—4 win.

Great Britain's Ashes defence had made a winning but streaky start, and there were changes for the second Test at Swinton on Saturday, 20 November 1937. In the interim the Australians had beaten Hull, Wigan and Oldham and been held by Salford to a draw, so interest in the second Test was high. In the Britain side Hudson, Watkins, Brogden and Edwards replaced Cunniffe, McCue, Croston and Morley in the backs, while Higgins (Widnes) and Jubb (Leeds) replaced Woods and Hodgson in the pack. The Australians had to find replacements for the injured Stehr and McKinnon. Dawson came into a reshuffled back division and Narvo and Heidke replaced Curran and Stehr.

Britain made no mistake in the second Test, having learnt clearly the bitter lesson of the first. In the first half Britain were rarely out of the Australian half, but, ironically, they had managed only an Edwards try at the interval. In the second half Britain were still on top, and after Brogden had dropped the ball over the Australian line Risman kicked a goal. When Australia launched a rare attack Dawson got an unimproved try, but Britain roused themselves and crisp passing put Edwards over again, Risman goaling. Near the end of the game Norman dropped the ball and Hudson dribbled ahead for a touchdown. Risman kicked another goal, and with Salford players getting all the points, Britain had held the Ashes yet again, for the eighth successive series. Worse was to come for the Kangaroos, who lost five consecutive club games, and the third Test at Huddersfield on 18 December 1937, attracted fewer than 10 000 spectators in poor weather.

The last Test brought belated consolation for the tourists, who won by 13 points to 3. The home team, resting too much on their laurels, were well beaten. Norval, Reardon and Narvo scored tries for Australia, Beaton placing two goals, while Hudson scored Britain's sole try. The victory had come too late to save either the Ashes or Australia's tour finances. Takings were nearly £10 000 below the 1933 figure, due to a shorter tour and the loss of the first two Tests, and the tourists were hard pressed to break even. Their record of 13 wins, 11 defeats and a draw contained the highest number of defeats since 1908–9. The weakness in attack was underlined by the fact that loose forward Prigg was highest try-scorer with eight. Beaton kicked 28 goals.

The home competitions of 1937–8 brought an unusual decision from the League in allocating the championship-final venue. The two Leeds clubs, Hunslet and Leeds, reached the play-off, and although the match was scheduled for Wakefield, both clubs made representations to the League to allocate the match to the spacious Elland Road soccer ground, home of Leeds United, in view of public interest in the city. The League authorities agreed, and must have thanked their lucky stars for the wisdom of the decision. When the match was played on 30 April 1938, the crowd was more than 54 000, a record for any Rugby League game in England.

The game was a hard-fought local 'derby', but Leeds were handicapped by injuries which reduced the power of internationals Smith and Hey. Morrell, the Hunslet centre, had a great game, while Walkington's kicking was another trump card. Hunslet won the game and the title by 8 points to 2, Winter and O'Sullivan scoring tries and Walkington dropping a goal against a goal from Tattersfield.

The following Saturday was Wembley day, with Barrow and Salford fighting out the Challenge Cup final before a crowd of 53 000 (£7200). Here was a match which was to produce one of those sensational finishes that keep crowds talking for years afterwards.

Teams were:

Barrow: French; Cumberbatch, Higgins, McDonnell, Thornburrow; Lloyd, Little; Rawlings, McKeating, Skelly, Troup, Ayres, Marklew.

Salford: Osbaldestin; Hudson, Brown, Gear, Edwards; Risman, Watkins; Williams, Day, Davies, Thomas, Dalton, Feetham.

Referee: Mr F. Peel (Bradford).

As the two teams became locked in a titanic defensive struggle, it was obvious that few tries would be scored, with Salford having conceded only one try in their Challenge Cup run and Barrow in equally tenacious 'they shall not pass' mood.

French gave Barrow the lead with a penalty, but Risman dropped a fine goal and then kicked a penalty goal to give Salford a 4—2 lead after a dour first half. The second half followed a similar pattern, and Salford's rugged defence seemed likely to hold out until Little dropped a wonderful goal to equalize the scores. As the last seconds ticked out, Barrow held the ball tightly on their own line, and the crowds streamed for the exits ready for the replay at Wigan. Suddenly there came tragedy for Barrow, triumph for Salford. Barrow were hanging on for the whistle when Troup, harassed in possession, rolled out a pass. Gear, the Salford centre, swooped on it and touched down with half the Barrow team clinging to him. The Barrow side protested that Gear had not grounded properly, but Mr Peel ruled a try, and Salford won the cup 7—4.

The 1938 annual meeting at Leeds on 8 June ended the brief and unhappy career of Newcastle.

Season 1938–9, the last season before the Second World War, brought the 'arrival' of France as an international Rugby League force. France beat England 12—9 at Swinton, and then beat Wales 16—10 at Bordeaux to win the international championship an achievement hailed with delight in France and applauded in Britain.

The early part of the season brought a new Rugby League headquarters in Australia. A magnificent, palatial building, costing in the vicinity of £85,000, was opened in Sydney as the new H.Q. of the Australian Board of Control, and the new building, brainchild of Mr H. R. Miller, secretary of the Board, was immediately classed as one of the finest sporting clubs in the world. Another landmark of a more individual kind occurred in Britain, where Jim Sullivan of Wigan topped 100 goals in the season, a feat he had attained every year since 1921.

Consistency was also the hallmark of Salford, who reached Wembley for the second successive year in 1939, with Halifax as their opponents. They also reached the championship final, with Castleford their challengers.

The last pre-war Wembley final brought a new record for Britain, the attendance of 55 543 proving the largest ever. The match was played on Saturday, 6 May, with Mr G. S. Phillips (Widnes) as referee, and the teams were:

Halifax: Lockwood; Bevan, Smith, Treen, Bassett; Todd, Goodall; Baynham, Field, Irvin, Cox, Chadwick, Beverley.

Salford: Osbaldestin; Hudson, Miller, Risman, Edwards; Kenny, Watkins; Davies, Day, Bradbury, Thomas, Dalton, Feetham.

If Halifax were impressed by Salford's reputation they showed no signs of it as they took charge of the game. Risman seemed out of form, and Salford were without Osbaldestin for the last 30 minutes, but these drawbacks apart, Salford were second best. After 16 minutes a fine passing movement gave Smith a try, and another cultured move sent Treen over. Lockwood kicked both goals and Halifax led 10—0 at half-time. In the second half Risman showed a flash of form to score a try, but after Osbaldestin's retirement Halifax took control again and Todd and Bevan added tries, both converted by the accurate Lockwood. Mr Phillips's final whistle rang down the curtain at Wembley for seven years.

It seems bitterly ironical that this last pre-war season ended on the crest of a wave of mounting popularity. The championship final was again played on a soccer ground at Maine Road, Manchester, and drew a superb attendance of just under 70 000 a new record.

The game, however, did not reach heights worthy of the attendance, and until eight minutes from time Castleford, hanging on grimly to a one-point lead, seemed likely to disappoint Salford once again. Salford were patchy, and Adams made a try for Brindle to put Castleford ahead. Watkins made a similar opening for Kenny to equalize, but Castleford broke away again and Robinson scored. A Risman goal made it 6—5 and Castleford held on until the 72nd minute, when swift Salford handling for the first time created an opening and Edwards scored a fine try.

The 1939 summer brought the passing of a fine club and a great

Rugby League immortal. The St Helens Recreation team, the 'works team' from Pilkington Bros. Ltd., disbanded after a season of heavy financial losses, and a side which had won several honours went out of existence. July 1939, brought the passing of Harold Wagstaff, the great Huddersfield and Britain centre, hero of 'Rorke's Drift' and one of the greatest players the game has known. 'Waggy', a great Rugby artist, was widely mourned.

The 1939 annual meeting made two important rule changes. The hooker was allowed to strike with either foot, and a proposal that scrums be formed 10 yards from touch was accepted. In common with other sporting and civic authorities, the Rugby League hoped against hope that the threat of another war with Germany would not blow up, and arrangements were made for the arrival of a New Zealand touring team in 1939–40. This Kiwi tour was destined to be the shortest in history. The outbreak of war reduced it to two games.

13

The 1939–45 War Years

THE Second World War shattered and disrupted organized sport, just as the first had done 25 years before.

Soccer and Rugby League programmes, which had hardly begun, were cancelled and replaced by 'friendlies'. The 26 New Zealand players arrived in Britain on 29 August with their managers, Messrs R. Doble and J. A. Redwood, played two matches, at Dewsbury and St Helens, and then left for home. The tourists had travelled 24 000 miles to play two matches, and the outbreak of war cost them £8000.

The inevitable soon happened as teams disintegrated and players went off to join the forces.

Once again the long years of war hit the Rugby League hard. Great teams disbanded, great players went away to fight and serve and young players who might have made international status lost the best years of their lives at the front.

The Rugby Union made a welcome gesture to Rugby League. The ban on Union players appearing alongside League players was lifted for the duration of the war, and services' teams soon testified to the value of this magnanimous decision.

In view of the fact that military service and special munitions work were robbing teams of players, the League decided to allow 'guesting' in wartime matches. This permitted players to 'guest with teams near their place of posting, and one side who benefited greatly from the 'guest' system was Dewsbury, who built up a powerful side during the war years.

There were no Challenge Cup or championship matches in 1939–40, but county cups were held. Swinton beat Widnes in a home-and-away Lancashire Cup final, and Featherstone Rovers won the Yorkshire trophy by beating Wakefield Trinity 12—9 at Odsal. In a wartime emergency championship match Yorkshire competition winners Bradford Northern beat their Lancashire counterparts Swinton in home and away games.

The first wartime annual meeting of the League was held at Leeds on 12 June 1940, and inevitably a slight loss was reported. The meeting was very short, and at the end the officials expressed the hope that clubs would 'do their best to provide regular football'. When clubs lined up for the second wartime season there were nine in the Lancashire League and 14 in Yorkshire. Clubs who had withdrawn included Barrow, Widnes, Rochdale Hornets and Hull K.R., and others were soon doubting the wisdom of continuing when gates at early matches dwindled to between 1000 and 2000.

Season 1940–1 was not a very long one, and Salford and Warrington withdrew midway during the season. No Lanchashire Cup was played for, but Oldham and Wigan were accepted as competitors in the Yorkshire Cup, which was won by Bradford Northern, who beat Dewsbury 15—5. The depleted Lancashire competition was won by Wigan, and the Yorkshire title by Bradford Northern, who rounded off a successful season by beating Wigan home and away to take the wartime championship title once again. The Challenge Cup was revived in 1941, and a pointer to the popularity of the final even under wartime conditions was the crowd of 29 000 at Odsal on 19 May to see Leeds beat Halifax 19—2.

When the Rugby League Council met on Thursday, 30 July the situation was serious, with more clubs indicating their inability to carry on under wartime restrictions. The Council decided that the separate county competitions would be fused into one in 1941–2.

Rugby League suffered a severe international blow, however, when in November 1941, the French puppet Government, which had capitulated to the Germans under Pétain, banned Rugby League in France and transferred all the League's property and funds to the National Committee of Sports. During the remainder of the war years the game was kept alive in France by village teams playing furtively in areas of lax German rule.

One of the great features of the war years was the quality of services football, with the finest players from both rugby codes playing side by side in representative matches. In an RAF *v.* Army game at Rosslyn Park in January 1942, the RAF team included Edwards (Salford), W. T. H. Davies (Bradford N.) and E. Watkins (Wigan), while the Army included S. Brogden (Hull), A. J. Risman (Salford), T. Foster and E. Hodgson (Bradford Northern), K. Jubb (Leeds) and G. Williams (Wigan). There were matches between England and Wales in services RU internationals, and between Lancashire Services and Yorkshire Services, and names like Cox (Bradford Northern), Prosser, Jubb and Tattersfield (Leeds) and Mills (York) joined other Rugby League players in the teams.

A particularly interesting wartime game was the Rugby League XIII *v.* Northern Command match at Thrum Hall, Halifax, in March 1942. The Command team was composed entirely of Rugby League players, and before 7000 spectators they beat the Rugby League XIII by 22 points to 18. Ernest Ward Bradford N.) kicked five goals for Northern Command, and Francis, Pepperell, Case and Walsh scored tries. Chapman (2) and Lawrenson (2) scored for the Rugby League and Lockwood kicked three goals.

Severe weather during 1941–2 caused the extension of the third wartime season until 6 June, when the Challenge Cup final was played. Previously, in April, Dewsbury's cosmopolitan side beat Bradford Northern at Headingley to win the emergency championship.

The Challenge Cup final at Odsal, before a crowd of 15 250 paying £1276, was a repeat of the previous year's final between Leeds and Halifax, and once again Leeds did the trick. The score was 15—10, Edwards (2) and Morris scoring tries and Risman three goals against five goals from Lockwood. A wartime oddity was the appearance of Edwards and Risman for Leeds. In April they were in Dewsbury's championship side as guests!

Clubs had again scratched and scraped their way through their season with tiny attendances, and in 1942–3 Castleford, Bramley and Hunslet and Broughton Rangers decided not to continue, reducing the total in the emergency league competition to 14.

An even more interesting game was a League *v.* Union clash at Headingley on 23 January 1943, before 8000 spectators. The

Northern Command Rugby Union side met the Command League side under Rugby Union rules, and after a great game the League won 18—11, after being eight points down. The League team scored six unconverted tries through Mills (2), Jubb (2), Tattersfield and Chapman.

Dewsbury won the two-leg Yorkshire Cup in 1942–3, and when the Challenge Cup final was played under the two-leg system for the first time Dewsbury were again finalists. They met their doughty rivals Leeds in a 'derby' game, and in the first leg at Dewsbury, on 24 April 1943, they won 16—9 before 12 000 spectators. Edwards, Seeling, Kenny and Robinson scored Dewsbury's tries, and Seeling landed two goals. Eaton scored all the Leeds points with a try and three goals. In the return game at Headingley two days later the battle was dour and unrelenting. A goal each from Eaton, D. Jenkins and Walkington (Hunslet) gave Leeds a 6—0 lead, one point behind on aggregate, but strive as they could Leeds could not get the point, and Dewsbury held out to win the cup on aggregate 16—15. Leeds' unbeaten Challenge Cup run was over.

Dewsbury, a superb collection of stars from the pick of the League's clubs, made a clean sweep of the honours by beating Halifax home and away in the championship final.

Dewsbury's elation at a great season turned to consternation at a meeting of the League's war emergency committee at Leeds on 7 July 1943. Bradford Northern complained that Dewsbury had played an ineligible player, Smith (Castleford), in their semi-final championship game with Northern, and the committee declared the championship null and void. In addition Dewsbury were fined £100.

Season 1943–4, for the second year under the chairmanship of Mr R. F. Anderton (Warrington), began with 16 teams, Barrow returning in Lancashire and Hunslet in Yorkshire. During this season Britain's military position in Europe and Africa was improving and the League made tentative decisions to hold post-war Challenge Cup finals at Wembley.

Another affluent club despite wartime restrictions was Bradford Northern, and they continued their quest for honours by beating

Keighley in the Yorkshire Cup final. Northern reached the two-leg Challenge Cup final, in which they met Wigan home and away Wigan won 3—0 at Central Park, Featherstone getting the try, but powerful Northern won 8—0 at Odsal, Batten and huge forward Frank Whitcombe scoring tries and Carmichael a goal.

Undaunted, Wigan again challenged the Yorkshire monopoly in the championship final. They beat Dewsbury 13—9 at Central Park, and in the return game at Crown Flatt won by 12 points to 5 to become the first Lancashire club to win a wartime title. The most notable feature of Wigan's performance was the appearance at fullback of Jim Sullivan, who had first played for Wigan 23 years before. Sullivan kicked three goals in the second leg to help his side to victory against a team for whom he had 'guested' in wartime football.

The season ended on a note of increasing optimism as news from the war fronts improved, and the League sent out a circular asking all clubs to resume, if possible, ready for peacetime football. M. Jean Galia in France wrote to say, early in 1945, that the diehard French teams would resume once the war had ended, and Australia was so optimistic that an invitation was sent for a British touring team to travel in 1946!

A new team was admitted in 1945, that great breeding ground of Cumberland providing its own club, Workington Town, with good potential support and ample backing under the chairmanship of Mr F. Meageen.

Season 1944–5 proved, as expected, the last in wartime. Halifax beat Hunslet in the Yorkshire Cup, Huddersfield beat Bradford Northern in the two-leg Challenge Cup, with Bawden the Huddersfield scoring hero, and Bradford Northern beat Halifax in the championship after losing the first leg.

14

Another Post-war Boom

On Monday, 30 May 1945, club representatives met at Leeds and recommended that full activity should be resumed in 1945–6.

The first League games were played on 25 August, and, happily crowds were good to welcome the resumption of full-scale Rugby League. Two clubs, Wigan and Hunslet, appointed former players as coaches, Jim Sullivan taking over at Wigan and Jack Walkington at Hunslet. These appointments, together with the return from the forces of great players, gave added punch and interest to the opening League games, and in the early weeks there were crowds of 16 000 at Wigan, 12 000 at Odsal, 10 000 at Barrow and typically big crowds at Headingley. The county cups pulled in attendances equal to and in many cases bigger than pre-war crowds. In Australia too there was fantastic evidence of revival, with 50 000 watching New South Wales and Queensland at Sydney. In France the indefatigable Jean Galia arranged for a short tour by English club Castleford.

The Australians pressed for the visit of a touring team from Britain in 1946. The Rugby League Council delayed its reply for the very important reason that all shipping space in the hectic aftermath of war was fully booked or requisitioned for transport of returning and repatriated troops. Dr H. V. Evatt, Australian Minister for External Affairs, pressed Australia's case in Britain, and the sequel was Britain's decision to make the tour—which later meant transporting the British team by aircraft-carrier!

In view of the projected tour, the England *v.* Wales game on 24 November 1945, became a Test trial. It was played in Wales at St Helens Rugby Union ground, Swansea, and before a crowd of 30 000 Wales won 11—3, G. Price (2) and D. Phillips scoring tries and Risman a goal, against a try by Nicholson.

Event followed event with rapidity. Mr John Wilson, secretary of the League, retired after a quarter of a century of fine service, and the new secretary, Mr William Fallowfield took over, to become only the third secretary in the history of the Northern Union and Rugby League. England beat France in Paris and at Swinton before good crowds, and a new pattern in overseas signings was set by Wigan, who brought over Brian Nordgren, a winger, and Cecil Mountford, a stand-off half, from New Zealand.

After two more Test trials at Wigan and Leeds the tour managers were appointed. They were Messrs. W. M. Gabbatt (Barrow) and W. Popplewell (Bramley), and they were told that they and their party of 26 players would be taken to Australia on HM Aircraft Carrier *Indomitable*, together with returning Australian servicemen. This was all the shipping space available!

The players chosen to make the first tour since 1936 were *Backs:* M. Ryan, Ted Ward (Wigan), J. Jones, W. Horne, J. Lewthwaite, B. Knowelden (Barrow), E. Batten, J. Kitching, E. Ward (Bradford Northern), A. J. Risman (Salford, captain), A. Bassett (Halifax), A. Johnson (Warrington), T. McCue (Widnes), D. Jenkins (Leeds), W. H. T. Davies (Bradford Northern); *Forwards:* K. Gee, J. Egan (Wigan), G. Curran (Salford), F. Whitcombe, T. Foster (Bradford Northern), F. Hughes (Workington T.), D. Phillips (Oldham), R. Nicholson (Huddersfield), L. White (York), I. Owens (Leeds), H. Murphy (Wakefield T.).

The 'Indomitables' sailed in April, creating problems for clubs who were still engaged in Challenge Cup and championship battles. Worst hit were Wigan, who fought their way through to finals of both trophies minus four players on tour. Yet such was Wigan's reserve strength that they put powerful sides in the field for the Wembley cup final against Wakefield Trinity and the championship final against Huddersfield at Maine Road soccer ground, Manchester.

The Challenge Cup final returned to Wembley on 4 May 1946, and a crowd of 54 730 paid world-record receipts of £11 995. The teams were:

Wakefield Trinity: Teall; Rylance, Stott, Croston, Baddeley; Jones, Goodfellow; Wilkinson, Marson, Higgins, Exley, Howes, Bratley.

Wigan: Cunliffe; Nordgren, Ratcliffe, Ashcroft, Jolley; Lowry, Bradshaw; Banks, J. Blan, Barton, Watkins, Atkinson, W. Blan.

Referee: Mr A. Hill (Leeds).

The match provided 80 minutes of excitement and fluctuating fortunes, and one of the best finishes ever recorded in a Challenge Cup final. Wigan secured a one-point lead at half-time, Nordgren and J. Blan running in unconverted tries against a try and goal scored by Billy Stott, the centre Wakefield had secured from Oldham at the 'give-away' fee of £90. As play swung from end to end, both sides added two unconverted tries, Jolley and Nordgren again for Wigan, and Croston and Rylance for Trinity. With only 90 seconds left for play there came drama. Referee Hill awarded Wakefield a penalty kick some distance out and at an angle. Wigan led 12—11, and every spectator held his breath as Stott shaped for the difficult kick. Stott took careful aim, walked slowly back, ran up to the ball and sent it high and true through the middle. Wakefield supporters went mad, but the drama had not finished, for Nordgren made a desperate effort to land a long-range penalty for Wigan and failed. Trinity had won 13—12 through Stott's match-winning kick.

Stott's reward for a great performance was the award of the Lance Todd Trophy, a new trophy to be granted each year to the outstanding player in the Challenge Cup final. The trophy commemorated and was named after the great New Zealand player, Salford manager and BBC commentator who was killed in a car crash in 1941.

Wigan sought consolation in the championship final at Maine Road on 18 May. A crowd of 67 136 paid £8386 to see the game, in which Wigan obtained their consolation prize with a 13—4 win. Hero was Jack Cunliffe, the Wigan full-back, who was dazed in a tackle, went to half-back and scored a great try. Ashcroft got two tries and Nordgren two goals, while Bawden landed two goals for Huddersfield.

Interest turned to the first post-war tour of Australia. The 'Indomitables' lost two of their 'pipe-openers', at Wollongong and Newcastle, but won important state matches before massive and enthusiastic crowds.

The first Test was at Sydney on Monday, 17 June 1946, and

Britain were without both full-backs, Ryan and Jones, because of injury. Risman played No. 1, and the teams were:

Australia: Parkinson; Newham, Cooper, Jorgenson, Bailey; Devery, Grice; Westaway, Watt, Farrell, Clues, Kay, Mulligan.

Great Britain: Risman; Batten, Ernest Ward, Kitching, Johnson; Horne, McCue; Gee, Egan, Whitcombe, Phillips, White, Owens.

The game attracted 64 000 spectators, and resulted in a draw, eight points each. Britain should have won, but Risman missed eight out of nine shots at goal. Britain led 6—2 at half-time. Horne shooting over the line for a scrum and Whitcombe ploughing his massive bulk over, while Jorgenson kicked a goal for Australia.

Britain played the second half with 12 men, Jack Kitching having been sent off the field after an incident involving Jorgenson. Australia set up a powerful attack, and Bailey sidestepped his way over for a try. Risman's only goal made it 8—5 for Britain, but Cooper brought the house down for the Kangaroos when he outpaced the defence from inside his own half and beat Risman for a try. Jorgenson missed the kick, and Britain had a big let-off when the same player missed a kick under the posts.

At this stage the tourists were badly hit by injuries, but transport difficulties ruled out replacements. Britain had Ernest Ward at full-back for the second Test at Brisbane on Saturday, 6 July, and Ted Ward and Bassett came into the backs. The attendance was 45 000, with thousands more locked outside, and the big Brisbane crowd saw the injury-hit British side rise to the occasion brilliantly, with magnificent defence and speedy attack. Bassett, the big Halifax policeman, ran in a stunning hat-trick, and Johnson a great try from half-way, Ernest Ward landing one goal. Cooper got a try for Australia and Jorgenson a goal, and Britain's 14—5 win put them one up with one to play.

The 'Indomitables' were setting up new records in scoring and in tour proceeds. As they continued their run of success with wins over Brisbane, Toowoomba and Northern Districts, it was reported that the 1946 tourists had topped £21 000 in receipts. All that was needed to complete the picture was victory in the final Test at Sydney, and it duly came by 20 points to 7. The Australians took the lead with two Jorgenson goals and a Kennedy try, and when Risman kicked a penalty Britain trailed 7—2 at half-time. The second half saw a transformation. Britain played brilliantly and tries flowed from Bassett (2), Curran and Owens, Risman landing three goals.

After their storming finish to the Test series in which they created a new record by emerging unbeaten in Australia, the 'Indomitables' went to New Zealand for an ego-deflating shock. They lost against West Coast, and although they beat the Maoris at Wellington, Auckland and South Auckland, they were stunned and surprised in the only Test match. The Auckland ground was in poor condition, hampering Britain's back play, and the referee penalized Britain so often that New Zealand's 13—8 victory came entirely from penalties. Clarke kicked four penalty goals, and converted a try by Graham after the touchdown had been made from a penalty which hit a post and rebounded. Ernest Ward and Batten scored tries for Britain, and Ward kicked a goal.

The tour over, the party left Wellington on the S.S. *Rangitiki* on 14 August. Top scorer was Ernest Ward, with 43 goals and five tries, with his namesake Ted second with 79 points. Jim Lewthwaite, who did not play in a Test, had 33 tries, while, oddly enough, vice-captain Tommy McCue did not score a single try!

The tour saw the end of Gus Risman's connection with Salford for after his return he signed as player-manager for the new Workington Town club. The 1946–7 season opened with more Australasian signings, Leeds securing Arthur Clues, a forward, and Bert Cook, a full-back, while Huddersfield signed up Johnny Hunter, full-back, and Pat Devery, half-back. The Aussies received a rude welcome from the British climate, which chose the 1946–7 season for one of Britain's worst winters. Snowbound and frozen grounds throughout the League caused postponement week after week, and the season was finally extended to midsummer, 21 June, when the championship final took place.

Challenge Cup ties were played off as and when grounds were available, but the competition rounded off in time for the Wembley final on 3 May 1947. Interest in the event was higher than ever, and a magnificent crowd of almost 80 000 paid record receipts of £17 050 to see the Bradford Northern *v.* Leeds battle.

Referee was Mr Paul Cowell (Warrington) and the teams were:

Bradford Northern: Carmichael; Batten, E. Ward, Kitching,

Walters; Davies, D. Ward; Whitcombe, Darlison, Smith, Tyler, Foster, Evans.

Leeds: Cook; Cornelius, Price, T. Williams, Whitehead; R. Williams, Jenkins; Prosser, Murphy, Brereton, Watson, Clues, Owens.

The final was a disappointing affair, with Leeds in particular below their best. Willie Davies, the Northern half-back, performed untiringly, and his efforts paved the way for Northern's 8—4 win. Walters and Foster scored the tries for Northern, Ernest Ward landing a goal, while Leeds' points came from two goals from full-back Bert Cook. After his great performance Willie Davies became the second holder of the Lance Todd Trophy.

The backlog of League fixtures was concluded with the championship final at Maine Road on 21 June. Wigan and Dewsbury were the finalists, and again the match proved a disappointment. A Ledgard goal against an unusually lustreless Wigan gave Dewsbury an interval lead, but in the second half Wigan hit their best form. Ted Ward snapped up a loose ball to send Nordgren over, and Ward goaled. Wigan, in full cry, scored further tries through Lawrenson and Bradshaw, Ward placing one goal. A dropped goal from Holt for Dewsbury made the final score 13—4 to Wigan.

The 1947 close season brought more activity in the overseas market. A stream of incoming players included Harry Bath, who joined Barrow and later Warrington, Duncan Jackson, half-back and Bruce Ryan, winger, who joined Hull, Don Graham, back, who came to Hunslet, Dinny Boocker, back, to Wakefield Trinity, and Len Kenny and Ted Verrenkamp, who were brought over by Leeds.

Following the new flood of overseas players into Britain, there had been renewed protests from Australia and New Zealand, and the Council placed a five-year ban on overseas signings.

The 1947–8 season brought the visit to Britain of a New Zealand touring side, only the third full tour since 1907–8 by the Kiwis. The previous tour in 1939 had been cut to two matches by war. The tourists arrived on 23 September 1947, under managers Messrs J. Redwood and C. Hunter, with forward P. Smith as captain.

Former Great Britain full-back and centre Jim Brough was appointed adviser to the team during the tour.

The party consisted of P. Smith, D. Barchard, J. Haig, J. Hancox, R. Nuttall, W. S. Clarke, R. Clark, T. Hardwick, M. Robertson, J. Forrest, D. Anderson, A. McInnarney, R. Cunningham, L. Jordan, L. Pye, G. Davidson, G. Johnson, A. Gilman, J. Newton, K. Mountford, C. McBride, A. Graham, R. Aynsley, J. Johnson, A. W. McKenzie.

The tourists played their first match at St Helens two days after their arrival, and the first Test at Headingley after a fortnight. It was a tough, hard-fought game in which the Kiwis showed that their form at home in 1946 had been no fluke. Britain finally scraped through 11—10. A crowd of 28 445 attended, and they saw a drab performance by Britain, who were behind for most of the game. With 10 minutes left for play, New Zealand led deservedly by 10—8 McGregor and Forrest scoring tries and Clarke two goals against tries for Britain by Aston (St Helens) and Gwyther (Belle Vue Rangers) and a goal from Ernest Ward (Bradford N.). With the minutes ticking away, the Kiwis' luck ran out. Stott, the St Helens centre, appeared to knock on before kicking ahead, and Johnson, the Warrington winger, raced up to score a disputed touchdown which gave Britain a lucky win.

The New Zealanders continued their fine form, winning five matches in a row, but just before the second Test the tourists lost at Hunslet and Hull. However, the sprightly tourists ensured a third Test play-off when they beat Britain 10—7 at Swinton on Saturday, 8 November.

New Zealand won the game despite being out-hooked badly in the scrums. Forrest gave them the lead after a mix-up in the British defence, and although Britain took a lead through a try by Dai Jenkins (Leeds) and two goals from Ledgard (Dewsbury), they fought back with typical spirit and a try by Newton and two goals from Clarke gave them victory.

Interest was high for the third and final Test at Odsal on 20 December, and 45 000 paid £5800 to see it. The match, alas, proved an anticlimax, for Great Britain played superb football while the tourists drooped and faded. Britain won by 25 points to 9, five tries and five goals against a try and three goals. This was a big disappointment to the Kiwis, but consolation for them was a tour profit of more than £6000. The tourists made a short tour of France and then left for home from Tilbury on 29 January, leaving behind in Britain the impression of a good and sporting team.

A major step in international football was taken at a meeting in Bordeaux in 1948. This was the setting up of a Rugby League International Board consisting of representatives of Britain, Australia, New Zealand and France.

The 1948 Challenge Cup final brought the exciting prospect of a clash between the post-war 'giants', Wigan and Bradford Northern, with Northern making their second successive appearance.

Such an attraction was a 'natural' for Wembley and a tremendous crowd, topping 92 000, swarmed to Wembley Stadium in May. The teams were:

Bradford Northern: Leake; Batten, Case, E. Ward, Edwards; Davies, D. Ward; Whitcombe, Darlison, Smith, Foster, Tyler, Traill.

Wigan: Ryan; Ratcliffe, Ted Ward, Ashcroft, Hilton; Mountford, Bradshaw; Gee, Egan, Barton, White, W. Blan, Hudson.

Referee: Mr G. Phillips (Widnes).

Unfortunately, the match did not produce the brilliant game expected of two fine sides, for both defences were in great form. Wigan scored first when Egan cross-kicked, Batten fielded and attempted to kick clear and Hilton pulled down Batten's kick and scored. Ted Ward goaled from touch. Three minutes later a fumble by Ratcliffe saw Northern winger Edwards touch down, but Ernest Ward failed at goal. With Wigan leading 5—3, the game became a tenacious struggle with the emphasis on defence, and only a minute from the end Wigan made the game safe when their forwards ploughed upfield and Barton forced his way over for a try. It had been a tough game, and the Lance Todd Trophy went to giant Bradford front-row forward Frank Whitcombe.

Northern hopes of a championship-final consolation victory foundered at Maine Road when Warrington won 15—5. Warrington played smooth and speedy football against a Northern side still in the Wembley doldrums, and Bevan, Powell and Pimblett scored tries, Palin landing three goals. Case (try) and E. Ward (goal) scored for Northern.

The success of Workington's inclusion led to the foundation of another Cumberland club in May 1948, when Whitehaven were admitted under manager Jack Kitching, formerly of Bradford Northern and Great Britain.

The busy international programme continued almost breathlessly with another major tour in 1948, the Australians arriving for their first post-war tour. Managers were Messrs Bill Buckley and E. J. Simmonds, captain Colin Maxwell and the players were *Backs:* C. B. Churchill, V. J. Bulgin, R. Dimond, J. N. Graves, J. Horrigan, R. J. Lulham, C. M. Maxwell, P. McMahon, D. A. McRitchie, L. R. Pegg, W. H. Thompson, G. K. Froome, J. N. Hawke, B. Hopkins, W. P. O'Connell; *Forwards:* W. Tyquin, L. G. Cowie, E. Brosnan, F. L. DeBelin, A. Gibbs, D. Hall, N. R. Hand, R. F. Holland, F. E. Johnson, N. G. Mulligan, R. J. Rayner, K. B. Schubert.

The tourists lost their first game at Huddersfield, but beat Belle Vue, Hull, Wakefield, Leigh and Salford before the first Test at Headingley on 9 October. The crowd was more than 35 000 (£8400).

The match was a corker, a feast of football with 44 points scored. At one stage the Aussies, down 17—6, staged a magnificent rally which had Britain rocking and were finally narrowly beaten 23—21. Hall and Froome scored tries for Australia in the first quarter, then it was Britain's turn to show brilliant football, with tries from Foster (2) and McCormick, and one goal from Ward. In the second half McCormick and Valentine scored unconverted tries to make it 17—6. Australia came storming back, and despite two unconverted tries from Pimblett, they ran in tries from Froome, Graves and McMahon and two goals from Graves. With the score 23—21, Britain had to hang on grimly in the last 10 minutes to win the first Test.

The second Test was held at Swinton on 7 November. Britain had Ryan (Wigan) at full-back and Dicky Williams (Leeds) at out-half. The Australian captain, Maxwell, was unfit, and other changes brought in Horrigan, Thompson, Hand and Tyquin. A crowd of 37 000 saw Australia still out of form, and Britain clinched the series by a score of 16—7. Two fine tries by Pimblett and two goals from Ward, against a goal by Graves, made it 10—2 at half-time, and in the second half, after an Australian rally in which Horrigan scored a try converted by Graves, two unconverted tries by Lawrenson made certain the Ashes stayed in Britain.

The third Test at Bradford, scheduled for 18 December, was postponed because of fog until 29 January 1949, after the Kangaroo's tour of France, and by a cruel irony Colin Maxwell was again unfit. Britain made the expected clean sweep of the series by 23 points to 9, after trailing 6—5 at the interval. In the second half Britain went on a scoring spree against tiring opposition, and ran in four fine tries. Britain's try-scorers were Ernest Ward, Curran (2), McCormick and Dicky Williams, while Ward kicked four goals. It was a disappointing end to a disappointing tour after the brilliant promise of the first Test.

Yet, despite the tour fade-out, the post-war boom in Rugby League football was just reaching its peak. When the 1949 Challenge Cup final was played at Wembley on 7 May a new record attendance of 95 000, the maximum for a Rugby League match at the Stadium, attended the match between Bradford Northern and Halifax. The fine Northern side were playing in their third final in successive years, and teams were:

Bradford Northern: Leake; Batten, E. Ward, Kitching, Edwards; Davies, D. Ward; Whitcombe, Darlison, Greaves, Foster, Tyler, Traill.

Halifax: Chalkley; Daniels, Reid, Price, McDonald; Kenny, Kielty; Condon, Ackerley, Rothwell, Healy, Pansegrouw, Mawson.

Referee: Mr G. Phillips (Widnes).

The game was too one-sided to be termed great, with Northern constantly on the attack. Winger Eric Batten played for the better part of the game with a cracked shoulder-bone, but Northern kept this secret, gave Batten little of the ball and used their powerful pack magnificently.

Batten got Northern's first try early on when he took Ward's shrewd cross-kick, and forward Trevor Foster scored the second near the end. Ernest Ward kicked three goals in an easy 12—0 win.

The spectator interest in the Challenge Cup was rivalled by the championship final at Maine Road between Huddersfield and Warrington on Saturday, 14 May, the crowd of 75 194 paying receipts of £11 073.

The match itself proved a magnificent encounter, a fitting conclusion to the season. Huddersfield won by a solitary point, 13—12, after Warrington had made a breathtaking rally to pull back from 13—0. Tries by Daly, Cooper and Devery and two goals from Devery put Huddersfield well ahead, but in that tremendous finish Francis and Jackson scored tries and Bath (2) and Palin kicked goals for Warrington.

After the championship final St Helens and Huddersfield made a short tour of South Wales as a 'booster' for another Welsh venture, an eight-team Welsh League which was launched on a new wave of optimism in 1949–50. Yet another decision resulted in the revival of the Other Nationalities side in the home international tournament. The post-war boom was at its peak.

Alan Smith, Leeds and Great Britain winger, on his way to the posts for a try

Terry Clawson, the man whose kicking helped Leeds to a great Championship Final win in 1973

Above right: At the bottom of the pile, but triumphant, John Bevan gets his first try

Right: Superb action picture of John Bevan, Warrington's signing from Welsh Rugby Union. Bevan, a British Lion, soon settled down in Rugby League

Controversial but brilliant leader with St Helens, Leigh and Warrington, Alex Murphy boots the ball to touch

Oh, my aching head! Murphy and Stephens (St Helens) hold their heads after colliding with Gregory of Warrington

15

Towards the World Cup

THE launching of the Welsh League of eight teams coincided with a serious decline in interest in international matches played in Wales with an eye to propaganda. Wales *v.* France at Swansea made a loss of more than £200, and Wales *v.* Other Nationalities at Abertillery also made a loss. It was a grim omen for the newly born Welsh League, which was struggling from the start against entrenched interest in soccer and Rugby Union. However, clubs battled on during the season, and two of the Welsh clubs, Cardiff and Llanelly, were sufficiently successful to apply for membership of the Rugby League in 1950–1.

There was to be no respite from Tests and thought-of Tests in 1949–50. The second post-war tour of Australasia was scheduled for the summer of 1950, and in March the party was announced. Managers were Messrs. Tom Spedding (Belle Vue Rangers) and George Oldroyd (Dewsbury), and Ernest Ward of Bradford Northern was captain. The 26 players chosen were *Backs:* M. Ryan, J. Hilton, J. Cunliffe, E. J. Ashcroft, T. Bradshaw (Wigan), J. Ledgard (Leigh), A. H. Daniels (Halifax), R. Pollard (Dewsbury), L. Williams (Hunslet), E. Ward (Bradford Northern, capt.), T. Danby (Salford), W. Horne (Barrow), R. Williams (Leeds), A. J. Pepperell (Workington); *Forwards:* K. Gee, J. Egan (Wigan), D. Naughton, F. Higgins (Widnes), F. Osmond (Swinton), E. Gwyther, D. Phillips (Belle Vue R.), J. Featherstone, R. Ryan (Warrington), H. Street (Dewsbury), H. Murphy (Wakefield T.), K. Traill (Bradford N.).

Wigan, who had created a club record by providing seven players, made it eight when G. Ratcliffe replaced L. Williams (Hunslet), who withdrew for business reasons. With eight players on tour, Wigan proved their fantastic reserve strength by fighting through to, and winning, the 1949–50 championship—a truly magnificent performance.

The 1950 Challenge Cup final produced a 'derby' match between Lancashire rivals Warrington and Widnes, with Widnes shaking everyone by beating Bradford Northern 8—0 in the semi-finals. The great Wembley Stadium was agian packed with a crowd topping 90 000 when the teams trooped out with Mr A. S. Dobson (Featherstone) as referee. Teams were:

Warrington: L. Jones; Bevan, Ryder, A. Naughton, Johnson; Knowelden, Helme; Fisher, Fishwick, Derbyshire, Bath, Lowe, Palin.

Widnes: Bradley; Parks, Hutton, Sale, Malone; Fleming, Anderson; Rowbottom, Band, Leigh, J. Naughton, Wilcox, Reynolds.

The battle between these neighbouring clubs provided an interesting but unspectacular contest. Widnes played with spirit and enthusiasm, but the power came from Warrington, whose winning margin of 19—0 was exaggerated but decisive. Bath, Ryder and Knowelden scored tries against a gallant Widnes defence, and Palin, kicking extremely well, landed five goals. Widnes fought magnificently in the second half but were unlucky to find the Warrington defence in top form. The Lance Todd Trophy went to Gerry Helme (Warrington).

The championship final at Maine Road brought together Wigan and Huddersfield for the second successive season, and Wigan, after finding replacements for eight tourists, played superlative football to win by 20 points to 2—a resounding success, watched by a 65 000 crowd. Silcock, Nordgren, Broome and Blan scored tries and Ted Ward kicked four goals, while Bawden replied with a penalty goal.

The summer of 1950 brought two new teams into the Rugby League. Cardiff were admitted, and in Yorkshire a group of businessmen enthusiasts in Doncaster raised guaranteed capital of £10 000 and were granted admission.

The annual meeting at Leeds in June raised the gate 'levy' from five per cent to 10 per cent to help the poorer clubs.

In Australia the touring team began well by beating Canberra,

Newcastle, Riverina and New South Wales, and a typically huge Sydney crowd saw the first Test on Monday, 12 June.

Unfortunately for good football, the day was wet, dull and squally, and poor ground conditions ruled out open play. Britain, who received four penalties against 19 awarded to Australia, performed prodigious feats in defence to win by 6 points to 4. Stars were the Wigan pair Ashcroft and Hilton, who twice broke through for Hilton to supply the finishing touches. Pidding replied with two goals for Australia, who made desperate efforts in the closing minutes and several times should have scored. An Australian player dropped the ball over the British line and Pidding missed narrowly with two penalties.

The tourists prepared for the second Test with a successful tour of Queensland, in which they hammered Central Queensland by a record 88 points. This was useful training for the second Test at Brisbane on 1 July, but things did not quite work out as Britain expected. Australia again appeared to have the better of the referee's rulings, and in addition the British team were handicapped in the second half by injuries. Britain got the first try with a barnstorming touchline run by Danby, but Graves scored a try and kicked a penalty before half-time. In the second half Cowie and Holman ran in tries for Australia and Holland and Churchill landed goals. This victory was Australia's first in a Test against Britain for 13 years.

Britain's misfortunes in Queensland continued with torrid battles against Brisbane and Ipswich, both won at the cost of injuries and the sending-off of scrum-half Bradshaw and forward Gwyther. Both British players received suspensions, despite protests of unjust treatment by the British managers. The harassed tourists were left with only 14 fit men from whom to choose the team for the third Test at Sydney on Saturday, 22 July. This game ended Britain's 30 years' stranglehold on the Ashes, the Kangaroos winning 5—2 after a fiercely fought and gruelling battle on a heavy ground.

Both sides scored a penalty goal in the first half, Churchill for Australia and Ward for Britain. In the second half Britain held out against onslaught after onslaught from the green-and-gold jerseys, until, amid wild excitement, Roberts scored the winning try for

Australia. At the end of the match the Sydney crowd invaded the pitch and chaired the victorious Aussies.

The Test series had ended in defeat for the tourists, but they had the consolation of record receipts of £43 000 from the tour. To this would be added proceeds of the New Zealand tour, which began with a 40—15 victory over Wellington. The first Test at Christchurch provided another setback for Britain, who were beaten 16—10 and lost full-back Jim Ledgard with a spinal injury which ruled him out for the rest of the tour. After victories over Greymouth and Auckland the tourists' cup of woe was filled to overflowing when the Kiwis won the second Test at Auckland by 20 points to 15.

The New Zealand tour sparked off a flurry of overseas signings. Bradford Northern signed Wellington Rugby Union players J. Phillips, a full-back, and N. Hastings, a winger. Leigh paid £5000 for Australian Rugby Union centre Trevor Allan, and followed this by signing New Zealand Rugby Union half-back George Beatty. Bradford Northern and Huddersfield secured New Zealand Rugby Union wingers J. K. McLean and Peter Henderson respectively, and Huddersfield signed South African centre Ian Clark.

Rochdale Hornets, who had appointed former Australian Test centre Cec Fifield as manager, brought over five young Australians to try their luck. They were Reg and Ron Stanford, Duffy, Ellean and Kelly, whose registrations were disputed for some time because they had originally played junior Rugby League in Australia.

The 1950–1 season swelled the ranks of overseas players in Britain, and also brought the visit of an all-amateur Rugby League team from Italy.

The Wembley final on Saturday, 5 May 1951, featured Wigan and Barrow, and attracted another capacity attendance of 95 000. Mr Matt Coates (Pudsey) was referee, and the teams were:

Barrow: Stretch; Lewthwaite, Jackson, Goodwin, Castle; Horne, Toohey; Longman, McKinnell, Hartley, Grundy, Atkinson, McGregor.

Wigan: Cunliffe; Hilton, Broome, Roughley, Nordgren; Mountford, Bradshaw; Gee, Curran, Barton, Slevin, Silcock, W. Blan.

The turf was slippery after un-Wembleylike weather, and both sides were unable to move smoothly into the attack. Barrow, in particular, seemed unable to get their attack going, and it was Wigan who provided most constructive breaks. The only score of the first half was a Mountford penalty for Wigan, and the first try took 60 minutes to arrive. Then a Barrow defender slipped as he went to tackle Mountford, and the New Zealand stand-off accelerated clear and passed to Broome, who put Hilton over. Shortly afterwards another Mountford break gave heavyweight prop Gee a try, goaled by Mountford. It was not surprising that Mountford's part in a 10—0 Wigan victory earned him the Lance Todd Trophy.

In the championship final at Maine Road 'new' Cumbrian club Workington Town won their first major trophy by beating an unlucky Warrington side by 26 points to 11. The fates were with the Cumbrians, for Warrington winger Johnson broke his leg after eight minutes and front-row forward Derbyshire hurt an arm and could not tackle.

Season 1951–2 offered plenty of interest to spice the early part of the season. The New Zealand tourists arrived for their second post-war tour, and Doncaster and Cardiff, newly elected, played their first game in senior company. Doncaster, under Gareth Price, former Halifax, Leeds and Wales centre, had an impressive opening, with several good victories, but Cardiff, the lonely Welsh outpost club, took hiding after hiding and were obviously doomed from the outset.

The Kiwi touring party, carrying with them the newly won reputation of having beaten Britain twice in 1950, arrived in mid-September under the management of Messrs T. F. McKenzie and D. A. Wilkie.

The captain was M. Robertson, and with him were J. Forrest, J. Haig, D. Barchard, G. Davidson and C. McBride of the 1947 party. Others were D. White, A. Berryman, W. B. Hough, J. Edwards, C. Eastlake, T. Baxter, W. Sorenson, B. Robertson, A. Menzies, J. Good, C. Johnson, K. English, R. Crouch, W. McLennan, L. Blanchard, J. Curtain, G. J. Burgoyne, D. Richards-Jolley, A. J. Atkinson and M. Mulcare.

The tourists showed in-and-out form, beating Rochdale Hornets and the champions Workington, losing at Halifax and Oldham and then winning at Castleford. The first Test was played at Odsal on Saturday, 6 October, and Great Britain, who were out for revenge, won by 21 points to 15 after leading 8—5 at the interval. The star of the victory against tough opposition was Workington winger George Wilson, who ran in a sparkling hat-trick of tries.

The tourists hit top form after their first Test defeat, and rattled up six good wins in succession. They then made touring-team history by playing for the first time under newly installed flood-lights at Odsal Stadium, Bradford Northern winning the match 13—8 before a 30 000 crowd.

The Kiwis were in great heart for the second Test at Swinton, and it was rank bad luck that after scoring five tries to Britain's four they were beaten 20—19 by a last-minute penalty goal from Ledgard.

Although the Test series had been narrowly won and lost, with the Kiwis beaten by goal-kicks in the second Test, they kept interest alive with some fine performances in the remaining games, and the third Test at Headingley produced another close and exciting game before Britain won 16—12. When the 1951 New Zealanders left for home they had failed to win a single Test, but their performances had won renewed respect for the game of their home country and many British fans had awarded them the second Test as a moral victory.

The departure of the Kiwis did not end interest in Test and international rugby, for at an international conference at Lyons on 12 January 1952, an historic step was taken. The idea of a World Cup had been mooted for years, but snags of cost, organization and timing had held up progress. However, at the Lyons conference great enthusiasm was shown for a World Cup tournament, and members of the International Board agreed to take exploratory steps. These moves were to lead to the first World Cup tournament in 1954.

The Challenge Cup final of 1951 for once brought two completely new teams to Wembley. Gus Risman's Workington and gallant Featherstone Rovers from the Yorkshire mining town together entered the final for the first time.

Unfortunately the match, on Saturday, 19 April, saw the end of the post-war wave of capacity attendances, for the crowd totalled 73 000—still, however, a good crowd by any standard—and receipts were over £23 000. The teams were:

Featherstone Rovers: Miller; Batten, Tennant, Metcalfe, Mitchell; Cording, Evans; Welburn, Bradshaw, Daly, Hulme, Gant, Lambert.

Workington Town: Risman; Lawrenson, Paskins, Gibson, Wilson; Pepperell, Thomas; Hayton, McKeating, Wareing, Mudge, Wilson, Ivison.

Referee: Mr C. F. Appleton (Warrington).

Workington were favourites, but Rovers showed the grit and fighting qualities that had carried them through, and the only try of the first half was a disputed one by Lawrenson. The Workington winger was tackled on the line, played the ball quickly and touched down before anyone could get a clear idea of what was happening. Two goals from Risman against two from Miller made it 7—4 at half-time. In the second half Rovers' veteran winger Eric Batten made a great run for an equalizing try, but then Australian forward Johnny Mudge made a superb diagonal run to put Workington ahead. Workington pulled further away with tries by Lawrenson and Wilson, but courageous Rovers scored the last try through Evans. Town had won their first Challenge Cup 18—10, and the Lance Todd Trophy went to Billy Ivison (Workington T.).

In the championship final those two outstanding sides Bradford Northern and Wigan met at Huddersfield, and dazzling Wigan won their fourth success in seven seasons. It was 5—4 at half-time, a Silcock try and Gee goal against two goals from New Zealander Joe Phillips, and in the second half Phillips's third goal put Northern ahead. Then the speedy Wigan attack carved out some priceless openings and Cunliffe and Ryan ran in tries, Gee kicking a goal in a 13—6 win, watched by a 48 656 crowd.

The annual meeting saw the quick end of the sad Cardiff experiment. The Welsh side had been nothing more than a chopping-block, and clubs were tired of the long trip to South Wales.

Each season was now bringing its Test series with unfailing regularity, and in 1952–3 the Aussies were in Britain. Their managers were Messrs N. Robinson and D. MacLean, and players were *Backs:* C. Churchill, R. W. Willey, N. Pidding, B. Carlson, T. A. Ryan, D. J. McGovern, F. Stanmore, K. Holman, H. Wells, D. J. Flannery, R. Duncan, N. Hazzard, G. Hawick, D. Donoghue, C. S. Geelan, K. McCaffery; *Forwards:* D. Hall, T. L. Tyrrell, A. L. Collinson, A. Paul, K. Schubert, C. M. Gill, K. Kearney, J. Rooney, F. A. Ashton, B. Davies, A. Crocker, R. Bull.

The tourists began in great shape, walloping Keighley, Hull, Barrow, Halifax and Wigan, but defeats at Oldham and St Helens steadied them. In the Halifax match the Australian hooker, Ken Kearney, was sent off and became the first Australian to be suspended in Britain.

The first Test was held at Headingley on 4 October, and a crowd of 30 000 saw the contest.

The tourists' performance did not fulfil expectations after their scoring feats in the early games and Britain won comfortably 19—6. Winger Frank Castle put them on the way to victory with a wonderful try in which he raced past Pidding, Hawick and Churchill, and Ryder and Daniels quickly showed clean pairs of heels for the second and third tries. Horne kicked five goals in five shots to complete 19 points, and Australia's sole contributions came from three goals from winger Noel Pidding.

By a strange irony, the Australians swept right back into brilliant scoring form after the first Test. They beat Bradford, Warrington, Leigh, Swinton, Hunslet, Doncaster and Huddersfield in irresistible style to build up for the second Test at Swinton.

The Kangaroos made six changes, bringing in Flannery, Stanmore, Donohue, Geelan, Collinson and Gill into the side. Britain called up D. Greenall (St Helens), T. McKinney (Salford) and D. Valentine (Huddersfield) for the Swinton Test on 8 November, Greenall replacing Ryder in the centre, McKinney taking over as hooker from Ackerley and Valentine taking the No 13 jersey from Ryan.

Once again the brilliant scoring form of club games eluded the Aussies just when it was most needed, and Great Britain were well on top for most of the game. Fine teamwork stretched the Australian defence to the limit, and slick, passing and speedy running brought five tries to Castle (2), Greenall (2) and Ward, with Ward landing two goals to round off a real captain's game. Horne also dropped a goal for Britain, while a Geelan try and Carlson penalty goal were the only Australian replies in a British victory by 21 points to 5. The Ashes were back in Britain.

The Australians' Jekyll-and-Hyde form was remarkable. Their worst form seemed reserved for the Tests and the best for club games, for after the second Test Wakefield, Hull K.R., Lancashire, Leeds, Yorkshire and Dewsbury were slammed as the tourists hit up a record touring-team total of 771 points in Britain. Victory over Widnes by 18—7 was followed by the third Test at Odsal on 13 December, and at long last, with the series decided, the Kangaroos showed their real Test-match form.

Against the British team which showed only one change, D. Bevan (Wigan) for Daniels on the wing, the Australians won by 27 points to 7 in a great display of powerful running and handling. Unfortunately, the game was spoiled by outbursts of temper and frequent clashes which resulted in the sending off of Hall, the Australian vice-captain. Stanmore and Holman behind the scrum were in brilliant form, and sparked off the football display which won the match. Noel Pidding kicked six goals and scored a try, and other Australian tries came from Ryan (2), Davies and Holman. Horne scored a try and Evans two goals for Britain. The Aussies finished with 23 wins and one draw in 27 games, a record number of points scored and a record for the smallest number of points conceded, yet they had forfeited the Ashes with ease in the first two Tests. There was much head-shaking as the party set off on the return trip.

International football continued to steal most of the headlines, and the World Cup project came a step nearer when French business man M. Paul Barrière offered to raise a guaranteed sum of £25 000 to sponsor the competition. The way was being paved for the first World Cup in 1954.

The home season was a great one for St Helens, who went through 1952–3 without defeat away from home and reached the finals of the Challenge Cup and championship.

The cup final between St Helens and Huddersfield promised a fine open game at Wembley, and the crowd was back in the region of 90 000. Referee was Mr G. Phillips (Widnes) and the teams were:

Huddersfield: Hunter; Henderson, R. Pepperell, Devery, Cooper; Ramsden, Banks; Slevin, Curran, Bowden, Brown, Large, Valentine.

St Helens: Moses; Llewellyn, Greenall, Gullick, McCormick; Honey, Langfield; Prescott, Blakemore, Parr, Parsons, Bretherton, Cale.

The teams were closely matched, and both bristled with internationals, but it was a comparative unknown who stole the honours. Huddersfield stand-off Peter Ramsden celebrated his 19th birthday with a great performance which won him the Lance Todd Trophy. Early in the game he was awarded a controversial try when he beat two men and was awarded a sliding try when Prescott brought him down. Devery kicked the goal. St Helens drew level with a 60-yard try by Llewellyn, converted by Langfield before half-time, and then a fine combined move sent Langfield over for St Helens to lead 8—5. The game swung back and forward and a quick burst from the scrum by Banks brought a try converted by Cooper. A Langfield drop goal equalized at 10—10, but then Ramsden sealed his birthday performance by racing past three men for the winning try, converted by Cooper.

St Helens gained consolation in the championship. The week after Wembley they walloped Huddersfield 46—0 in the semi-final and went on to beat Halifax 24—14 in the Maine Road final.

Leigh made the sporting world sit up in 1953 when they signed a world-famous sprinter and installed floodlights. The signing of E. MacDonald Bailey, the West Indian flyer, was, to say the least, not a success. He was obviously not at home in Rugby League surroundings, played only one friendly game and suffered an injury. Both club and player quickly ended the ill-fated experiment. Leigh's bold decision to install floodlights was also unsuccessful, for other clubs showed reluctance to play under lights, and the Leigh lights became something of a white elephant—poor reward for the club's enterprise.

At a meeting of the Rugby League Council in May, 1953, a new club entered the League. Blackpool Borough, supported by £6000 in capital, joined the League with Mr Chris Brockbank, former Swinton player and Warrington manager, at the helm. At the same meeting two-leg Challenge Cup ties were finally abolished, and 'sudden-death' first-round ties were adopted, with their promise of giant-killing acts to spice the proceedings.

Two special Test trials were held at Swinton and Headingley before the touring party was announced under the management of Messrs Hector Rawson (Hunslet) and Tom Hesketh (Wigan). Dickie Williams (Hunslet) was captain of the following party. *Backs:* E. Cahill (Rochdale H.), J. Cunliffe (Wigan), W. J. Boston, E. Ashcroft (Wigan), P. Jackson, F. Castle (Barrow), L. Jones (Leeds), T. O'Grady (Oldham), R. Price, G. Helme (Warrington), R. Williams, A. Burnell (Hunslet); *Forwards:* J. Henderson (Workington), A. Prescott (St Helens), T. Harris (Hull), T. McKinney (Salford), J. Bowden, B. Briggs, D. Valentine (Huddersfield), J. Wilkinson (Halifax), G. Gunney (Hunslet), C. Pawsey (Leigh), D. Silcock (Wigan), K. Traill (Bradford N.).

Whatever their performances in the Tests, the 1954 tourists were destined to make history. They were the first touring team to travel to Australia by air, a League decision greeted with delight by clubs who would otherwise have been robbed of players at vital times.

16

The Invasion of Odsal

SATURDAY, 24 April 1954, was cup-final day. It was a fine afternoon, with a crowd well over 80 000, and Warrington starting favourites despite injuries which cost them the services of A. Naughton, Phillips and White. The teams were:

Halifax: Griffiths; Daniels, Lynch, Todd, Bevan; Dean, Kielty; Thorley, Ackerley, Wilkinson, Fearnley, Schofield, Clarkson.

Warrington: Frodsham; Bevan, Challinor, Stevens, McCormick; Price, Helme; D. Naughton, Wright, Lowe, Bath, Heathwood, Ryan.

Referee: Mr R. Gelder (Wakefield).

The final turned out to be one of the dreariest games in the history of the cup. No tries were scored, defences were on top throughout and match-winning wingers like Arthur Daniels and Brian Bevan saw little of the ball. Halifax at one stage led 4—0 through two goals from Griffiths, but two second-half goals from Bath levelled the scores and ensured a reply.

The replay was not held until Wednesday, 5 May, allowing the same two clubs, Warrington and Halifax, to win through to the championship final the previous Saturday. This fact increased the already great interest in the replay, but no one could possibly have foreseen the fantastic and almost frightening crowd scenes that resulted at Odsal. The match had an early-evening kick-off, and throughout the day vehicles of every shape and horsepower poured into Bradford from every point of the compass. Shortly before the kick-off, queues of vehicles stretched for miles, with more arriving, and inside the ground there were even more remarkable scenes.

Well over 100 000 people milled and swarmed inside the ground on the densely packed slopes of the Odsal bowl. Thousands more clamoured for admission outside, and those at the back of the high terraces were lucky if they could see more than a section of the playing surface below. Half an hour after the kick-off spectators still trying to get into the ground were meeting disgusted and battered spectators trying to get out. Police, officials and marshals did a great job in trying to cope with the crush, but the completely unexpected rush to Odsal had taken everyone by surprise.

Marvellously, the match was played without serious riots and accidents, and it was as closely fought, if a little more exciting, than the Wembley game. Challinor scored a try for Warrington early on, and a Griffiths goal made it 3—2 at half-time. A goal each to Bath and Griffiths made it 5—4, and then came the thrill of the match. Gerry Helme, the Warrington scrum-half, made a dazzling run from half-way, heading for the left-hand corner flag. He swerved and sidestepped past man after man before finally dummying to McCormick and diving under Griffith's arms for a spectacular try that won him the Lance Todd Trophy.

Three days later, at Maine Road, Warrington completed the double at the expense of luckless Halifax before a crowd of only 36 519, a reaction, possibly, against the Odsal crush. A try by Thorley and two goals from Griffiths gave Halifax the lead, but Bath landed four goals, including a late winner, to disappoint the Yorkshiremen again.

After flying to Australia the tourists did not open impressively. They lost at Bathurst on 19 May, then lost against Newcastle and Sydney and drew with Southern Districts, with a victory at Riverina the only bright spot. The touring party followed these setbacks by engaging former Australian Test player Ross McKinnon as coach, a move which aroused some criticism, but which helped towards victory over New South Wales at Sydney.

The first Test at Sydney Cricket Ground on Saturday, 12 June, brought more unpleasant shocks for Britain. A typically large and enthusiastic Sydney crowd roared its delight as a tremendous grandstand finish by the Kangaroos swept Britain aside. Twenty minutes from the end the scores were tied 12—12, then the Aussies surged into magnificent, all-out attack and the tourists' defence crumbled. The Australians rattled up 25 points in 20 minutes against a demoralized defence and won by a 37—12 score, the highest for Australia against Britain. Pidding scored a try and eight goals, and other tries came from McCaffery (2), Provan,

O'Shea, Hall and Carlson. For Britain Silcock and Jackson scored tries and Jones three goals.

The Test defeat wakened up Britain. They beat Queensland, Wide Bay, Brisbane, Mackay, Northern Zone and Northern Queensland as preparation for the Brisbane Test on 3 July. Great Britain made five changes—O'Grady, Williams, Bowden, Pawsey and Boston replacing Cunliffe, Castle, Price, Wilkinson and Traill.

The Queensland tour reached its climax at Brisbane, for Britain won a free-scoring and entertaining Test 38—21. Both sides placed the emphasis on attack, and the result was an exciting match, with Britain the better side. Boston scored two fine tries for Britain, and Lewis Jones set up a Test record with 10 goals. Other British try-scorers were Pawsey, Williams, Helme and Jackson, while for Australia Carlson (2), Holman, Hall and Hazzard scored tries and Pidding three goals.

The tourists seemed to have found their best form in the fight to retain the Ashes, and they beat Toowoomba and Northern New South Wales. But then came trouble. The pre-Test game with New South Wales got out of control, and the brawls and pile-ups between players got so completely out of hand that the referee abandoned the game as players fought wildly and uncontrollably.

It was not a happy augury for the third Test at Sydney on Saturday, 17 July, but fortunately this match was never allowed to flare up. Before a 60 000 crowd Britain took the lead at 8—0, but then Australia, urged on by a vociferous crowd, went ahead 10—8 at the interval. Britain fought back in the second half, and the game switched from end to end, but Australia held on to the lead and regained the Ashes 20—16. Wells, Watson, Pidding and Diversi scored tries for Australia, and Pidding four goals. Britain's tries came from Williams (2), Valentine and Ashcroft, with two goals from Jones.

The Australian series had ended in defeat for the tourists, and they left for New Zealand knowing that the previous team in 1950 had fared badly there. Three Tests were fixed in New Zealand, and in the first at Auckland the Lions set off in good style by winning 27—7. Boston swept his way through the Kiwi defence for four good tries, Ashcroft scored two, Harris one and Jones kicked three goals. The second Test was at Greymouth on 31 July, and the Kiwis squared the series by winning 20—14. The tourists built up a sevenpoint lead, but then faded, and the home side added two second-half tries by Butterfield and Mulcare to the seven goals kicked by White. O'Grady and Wilkinson scored the British tries, Jones kicking four goals.

The tourists tuned up for the third Test with some free-scoring performances against Canterbury and North Island. Then, at Auckland on 14 August, they erased the 1950 memory by beating New Zealand 12—6. Price and O'Grady got the tries and Jones kicked three goals. After the third Test came one of the roughest matches of a tour which had been marred by many incidents. Auckland beat the Lions 5—4, and in the heated exchanges Silcock and Wilkinson were sent off. A happy feature for Britain was Jones's success in passing 100 goals for the tour. The party returned to Australia for a match with Southern Districts at Canberra, and in a bumper 66—21 win Jones kicked 15 goals. He ended with 127 for the tour, beating Jim Sullivan's 1932 record of 110, and Boston's 37 was a new try-scoring record.

It was anticipated that players would fall over themselves for the honour of competing in this first World Cup tournament, and the Rugby League was shocked when this did not prove the case. Many players from the 1954 tour came home feeling jaded and football-weary, others were nursing injuries, among them Cahill, Castle, Williams, Ashcroft and Wilkinson, and some felt that the terms of payment were inadequate. Terms were £25 for three weeks of duty, in addition to tour expenses, and this was not regarded as enough, despite the prospect of winning bonuses. With all these problems, the League had the greatest difficulty in selecting a panel of 18 players to represent Britain in France, and when the team finally crossed the Channel in October 1954, it included many young players who were being 'blooded' into international football in the first World Cup. A seasoned player, Dave Valentine (Huddersfield), was skipper of a British team which, quite frankly, was given little hope of beating Australia, France and New Zealand. Late withdrawals, by Boston and Gunney through injury and Horne through business commitments, made matters worse.

The 18 players who made up Britain's 'scratch' party of seasoned players and untried young players were: D. Valentine (Huddersfield, captain), J. Ledgard, F. Kitchen (Leigh), D. Rose, G. Brown (Leeds), P. Jackson (Barrow), M. Sullivan, W. Banks, R. Rylance (Huddersfield), G. Helme, A. Naughton (Warrington), J. Thorley, A. Ackerley (Halifax), S. Smith (Hunslet), R. Coverdale, J. Whiteley (Hull), D. Robinson (Wakefield T.), B. Watts (York).

The competition began on 30 October 1954, and continued for a fortnight. France beat New Zealand 22—13 in Paris, and Great Britain surprisingly beat Australia 28—13 at Lyons in the first games. Great Britain and France drew 13—13 in Toulouse, while Australia beat New Zealand 35—15 in Marseilles. When France beat Australia 15—5 at Nantes and Great Britain beat New Zealand 26—6 at Bordeaux, a play-off for the title between Britain and France was fixed for 13 November at Paris. This was the great test for Valentine's 'scratch' team, and they came through it magnificently. With the 'old heads' of Helme in the backs and Valentine in the forwards inspiring the side, Britain beat France in a fine game by 16 points to 12. Helme set the seal on Britain's World Cup triumph by scoring a brilliant solo try when France had taken the lead, and stand-off half Gordon Brown scored two tries. Britain's other try came from David Rose, while Ledgard kicked two goals. For France Cantoni and Contrastin scored tries and Puig Aubert landed three goals.

The team that was given no chance came back to Britain with the first World Cup.

In 1954–5 Wales ceased to function in the home international tournament. The League decided to drop the team due to the reduction of Welsh players coming into the game, and also to allow Welshmen to be available for selection in the Other Nationalities team, which, ironically, was only destined to last for one more season.

The 1955 Challenge Cup final was a North-West 'derby' between Barrow and Workington Town, and the final between two outpost sides at Wembley on 30 April attracted a 67 000 crowd, a fair one considering the 'parochial' nature of the game. Teams were:

Barrow: Best; Lewthwaite, Jackson, Goodwin, Castle; Horne, Toohey; Belshaw, McKeating, Barton, Grundy, Parker, Healey.

Workington Town: Vickers; Southward, Paskins, Gibson, Faulder; Wookey, Roper; Hayton, Lymer, Key, Mudge, Edgar, Ivison.

Referee: Mr R. Gelder (Wakefield).

The first half of the game was well below expectations. Both sides seemed affected by the occasion, and the half-time score was only 4—2 for Barrow, two goals by Horne against one from Paskins. Then, in the second half, Barrow went into the attack, Horne dropped a goal and Barrow came out of their shell. Jack Grundy, a forward whose storming display won the Lance Todd Trophy, made a try for McKeating converted by Horne. Then Grundy started two more moves which brought tries to Castle and Goodwin. Workington, although handicapped by an injury to Roper, fought back, and Faulder and Gibson scored tries. Paskins kicked three goals for Workington and Horne completed six goals for Barrow, who won 21—12. It was Barrow's first-ever win in the Challenge Cup.

The championship final at Maine Road on Saturday, 15 May, produced a clash between Warrington and Oldham. Heavy rain reduced the attendance, and made conditions slushy and difficult. What might have been a fast open game became a mud-soaked battle. Bevan scored a try for Warrington, and Pitchford produced an individual burst to equalize, before the trusty boot of Australian Harry Bath won the game for Warrington with two penalties.

The 1955 annual meeting at Leeds in June saw yet another attempt to reintroduce two divisions fall by the wayside, and season 1955–6 began with the loss of one of the oldest teams in the League, Belle Vue, formerly Broughton Rangers.

The touring team merry-go-round continued in 1955 with a visit from the New Zealanders under the managership of Messrs H. Tetley and C. Siddle. The 1955 Kiwis began their tour disastrously, being held to a draw by the Babes of the League, Blackpool Borough, and losing to York and Halifax. Before the first Test at Swinton on 8 October they won two games, against Yorkshire and Hull, but lost four and drew two.

Britain had an early casualty in the Swinton Test, Robinson, who left the field injured, but they were the better side, their five-man pack, containing the Kiwis.

With 10 minutes to go, Britain led 10—6, after keeping in front for most of the game, then the tourists' defence suddenly crumpled and in a devastating finish Britain ran in 15 points to win 25—6. Boston, Sullivan (2), Grundy and Wilkinson scored tries and Jones kicked five goals, while for New Zealand Robertson and Maxwell scored tries.

The patchy form of the Kiwis continued, with heartening victories soon followed by crushing defeats. For the second Test at Odsal on 12 November the New Zealanders brought in Haggie, Hawes, McKay, Roberts, Butterfield and Percy for Moore, Robertson, Sorenson, Creedy, Kilkelly and Grey. For Britain, as Price and Robinson were injured, G. Brown (Leeds) and B. Watts (York) were included.

The second Test was won by Britain as easily as the first, the tourists fading away after their speedy winger Bakalich had nearly scored in the opening minutes. Stevenson, the British scrum-half, was in brilliant form, and the Leeds half-backs spearheaded a fine attacking performance. Stevenson got one try following a 75-yard run, Sullivan got a hat-trick and Prescott, Wilkinson and Watts also touched down, Jones kicking three goals. For a chastened New Zealand, Roberts and Menzies scored late tries and Haggie kicked three goals.

The third Test at Leeds on 11 December appeared a formality, and Britain dispensed with special training. In the home side Jones was at full-back, T. Hollindrake (Keighley) on the wing, A. Davies (Oldham) in the centre and D. Schofield (Halifax) in the forwards. The Kiwis had Creedy as their third Test full-back, McNicol and Sorenson for Hawes and Menzies, and Bond and Blandchard for Atkinson and McLennan.

The British decision not to have special training had unexpected repercussions. The tourists at long last found Test form, and against an England team prepared to rest on their laurels they won a brilliant victory by 28 points to 13. The quality of the Kiwis' teamwork was a revelation and six players scored tries—Blanchard Roberts, Percy, Bakalich, Butterfield and Maxwell—while Creedy landed five goals. A well-beaten home side scored through Jones,

Sullivan and Brown (tries), with two goals from Jones. The tour ended on this brief note of glory, but it had been a poor tour and receipts were £2500 down on the 1951 proceeds.

The Challenge Cup final at Wembley on Saturday, 28 April was a clash between St Helens and Halifax, watched by an 80 000 crowd. Mr R. Gelder was referee for the third year in succession and the teams were:

Halifax: Griffiths; Daniels, Lynch, Palmer, Freeman; Dean, Kielty; Wilkinson, Ackerley, Henderson, Fearnley, Pearce, Traill.

St Helens: Moses; Llewellyn, Greenall, Howard, Carlton; Finnan, Rhodes; Prescott, McIntyre, Silcock, Parsons, Robinson, Karalius.

Both these sides had suffered the disappointment of defeat in previous post-war finals, and the match was closely contested, with neither side able to get the other's measure. There were some interesting bursts in the first half, but no points were scored. The second half followed a similar pattern, and no score seemed likely until Carlton scored a brilliant and dramatic try for St Helens, receiving from Howard at half-way and sweeping past Griffiths and the limping Freeman for a try goaled by Rhodes. St Helens were now on top and Llewellyn and Prescott scored well-worked tries, Rhodes landing another goal. For Halifax, Griffiths kicked a goal as St Helens won their first Challenge Cup 13—2.

The inconsistency and bad luck which dogged Halifax in trophy finals harassed them again at Maine Road in the championship final against Hull. With only a minute to go they were leading 9—8, thanks to tries by Palmer, Daniels and Freeman against tries by Harris and Finn and a Hutton goal.

Then in the last minute Hull were awarded a penalty, wide out on the '25' line. It was a difficult, angled shot, but the Hull full-back, Collin Hutton, sent it straight through the posts and was promptly buried beneath his exultant team-mates. Seconds later the whistle sounded with Hull dramatic 10—9 winners.

The close season of 1956 passed quietly enough, and the 1956 Australian tourists did not arrive until October to play their shortened tour. Managers were Messrs. C. Connell and C.Fahy, with Ken Kearney, former Leeds hooker, as captain. Six players had made the 1952–3 tour—Churchill, Flannery, McGovern,

Holman, Bull and Kearney. The tourists were *Backs:* C. Churchill, G. Clifford, D. Flannery, D. Adams, D. McGovern, I. Moir, A. Watson, T. Payne, R. Poole, K. O'Brien, R. Banks, I. Johnston, K. Holman, C. Connell; *Forwards:* I. Doyle, T. Tyquin, N. Provan, K. O'Shea, B. Purcell, D. Furner, B. Davies, R. Bull, B. Orrock, W. Marsh, K. Kearney, E. Hammerton.

The Australians' schedule included only 19 games, including three Tests, compared with 27 on the two previous tours, and chances of a financial windfall were slight. Crowd interest in the Kangaroos began at a high level, but the tourists' form was scrappy and interest began to wane when victories at Liverpool, Hull, Barrow and Bradford were interspersed with defeats at Leeds, Whitehaven, Warrington and Oldham.

The first Test was played at Wigan on 17 November, and things were looking grim for the Australian party, whose receipts were £3000 down on 1952. Wet and drizzly conditions reduced the attendance at Central Park, and made the financial outlook worse.

The Aussies got off to a flying start when a quick passing movement sent Moir skidding over in the corner, but once Britain had recovered from this shock the home side took a grip on the game which never relaxed. Britain were beaten in the scrums, but elsewhere they were completely on top, and on the right wing barnstorming Billy Boston plundered the Kangeroos' defence at will. He scored two tries, and Davies, Sullivan and Grundy also touched down, Mortimer landing three goals. Poole got a try and Holman two goals for Australia, who were beaten 21—10.

The Aussies played two games before the second Test. In the first they beat Hunslet, in the second they took one of the most humiliating beatings handed out by a club side when St Helens pulverized them 44 points to 2.

It was not surprising after this that the Odsal Test on 1 December attracted only 23 000 spectators, but the spectators who did attend got a shock. Australia, who brought in Clifford, Flannery, McGovern, Furner and Doyle in a big reshuffle, gave Britain an unexpected run-around on a heavy, muddy ground in drizzly conditions. Britain, who had Turner (Oldham) replacing the injured Dawson, were level 7—7 at half-time, but in the second half the Australian pack went on the rampage and Britain's forwards crumpled surprisingly. Australia won 22—9 and squared the series with tries from Holman, Banks, Davies and Bull and five goals from Clifford. Stevenson scored a try and Mortimer kicked three goals for Britain.

After more in-and-out club form the Aussies squared up to Britain for the third and deciding Test at Wigan on 15 December. The public was still not convinced about the quality of the tourists' challenge, and the attendance was only 19 000. Their lack of interest was well justified by events, for Great Britain won without difficulty against a disappointing Australian team who were never in the hunt. Little, Turner, Gunney, Sullivan and Boston ran in the tries at regular intervals and Davies kicked two goals. The tour had been, to put it bluntly, a flop, and the Aussies left for France still needing £8000 to cover expenses. Receipts in Britain were down £7000 on 1952. With the World Cup due for Australia in 1957, the Kangaroos badly needed to rebuild their side.

The British party to defend the World Cup in Australia was announced on 1 April 1957. The side was much more experienced, on paper, than the 1953 side had been, and consisted of 18 players: G. Moses (St Helens), W. Boston, E. Ashton (Wigan), P. Jackson (Barrow), L. Jones, J. Stevenson (Leeds), R. Price (Warrington), M. Sullivan (Huddersfield), A. Prescott, T. McKinney, A. Rhodes (St Helens), T. Harris, J. Whiteley (Hull), S. Little, A. Davies, D. Turner (Oldham), G. Gunney (Hunslet), J. Grundy (Barrow). The tournament was due to begin on 15 June.

The 1957 cup final at Wembley on 11 May brought a clash between Barrow and Leeds, fine weather and a crowd approaching 80 000, which might have been higher had not both teams been beaten in the championship semi-finals the previous week, no doubt with their minds fixed on Wembley.

The Barrow team-choice for the final caused a stir when it was known that former Wigan front-row forward Frank Barton had been left out. Barton needed to play in this game to set up a new record of five Wembley appearances, and he was so upset by the decision to leave him out that he quit the game.

The teams were:

Barrow: Ball; Lewthwaite, Jackson, Rea, Castle; Horne, Harris; Woosey, Redhead, Parker, Grundy, Wilson, Healey.

Leeds: Quinn; Hodgkinson, McLellan, Jones, Broughton; Lendill, Stevenson; Hopper, Prior, Henderson, Robinson, Poole, H. Street.

Referee: Mr C. F. Appleton (Warrington).

The legendary 'Wembley nerves' played their part in preventing this match from being a great one, and tragic slips by Barrow gave Leeds victory. Leeds were the better side in a moderate first half and led at the interval by a Quinn try against a Horne goal. In the early stages of the second half Robinson scored a gift try for Leeds when Grundy, hearing a call 'Right, Jack!' slipped the ball to Robinson instead of to one of the Barrow players, and Robinson crashed over for a try. Jones made a try for Hodgkinson to put Leeds ahead 9—2, but then Jackson cut through for a try to Barrow, goaled by Horne, and with the score 9—7 Barrow got on top. Then came slip No 2. Rea, the Barrow centre, broke away in the last seconds of the game, but he could not see Castle on his left with the way clear, and his kick ahead was fielded as time ran out.

The Lance Todd Trophy for 1957 went to Jeff Stevenson, the elusive Leeds scrum-half.

The championship final at Odsal saw Oldham beat Hull in a heart-pounding finish. Oldham led deservedly 15—11 with minutes to go, tries by Etty, Ayres and Etty again and three goals by Ganley against a try by Turner and four goals from Hutton. Out of the blue, however, came an interception by Stan Cowan for a surprise try to Hull, and Hutton steadied himself for the conversion kick to repeat his sensational match-winning effort against Halifax. Fortunately for Oldham, his kick was just wide, and Oldham escaped on their merits.

The World Cup in June began with Britain beating France 23—5 at Sydney, while Australia beat New Zealand 25—5 at Brisbane. Two days later, on 17 June, Great Britain and Australia met for the match everyone regarded as the decider, and both sides were handicapped by injuries. Britain's position became worse when Davies was taken to hospital with a leg injury after 15 minutes, and Boston and Harris also received knocks which made them passengers. Britain's task was pretty hopeless, and in addition Australia played great rugby to sweep their way through to a resounding victory by 31 points to 6. Moir (2), McCaffery (2), Wells, Clay and O'Shea scored tries, and Carlson (4) and Davies goals. Britain's points came from three Jones goals.

The Australians now needed only to beat France, who had beaten New Zealand 14—10 at Brisbane, to make sure of the title, and they duly did so with another brilliant 26—9 win at Sydney to take the second World Cup tournament and wipe out memories of the 1956 tour. Meanwhile Britain went from bad to worse by losing 29—21 to New Zealand at Sydney three days later. Australia made it a clean sweep by beating the Rest 20—11 at Sydney, and with the tournament proving an immense financial success, the Kangaroos were back on top of the world.

On the way home from Australia, Britain and France played exhibition matches in the Rugby Union stronghold of South Africa, but the matches in Benoni and Durban were played in such a light-hearted manner that the South African crowds refused to take them seriously, and the propaganda scheme was not a great success. However, South Africa continued to arouse the interest of English clubs as a market for fine players, and soon Springbok internationals and club players were being signed up for League duty in Britain. A 'scoop' signing was made by St Helens, who signed up Tom Van Vollenhoven, Springbok Rugby Union star winger, in the teeth of vigorous opposition, and this spectacular signing set off a spate of activity in South Africa.

Wigan signed Fred Griffiths, full-back, and Tommy Gentles, scrum-half; Hunslet secured winger Ron Colin; Wakefield Trinity Jan Lotriet and Alan Skene, centres, and Ivor Dorrington, forward; St Helens, following up Vollenhoven, brought over Ted Brophy, forward, and Jan Prinsloo, winger; York signed winger Hugh Gillespie; Huddersfield winger Athol Brown; Leeds Wilf Rosenberg, winger, and the Deysel brothers, backs. This influx of Springboks undoubtedly proved a shot in the arm for Rugby League, for big crowds turned out to see the new overseas stars, Vollenhoven's spectacular right-wing runs proving a powerful magnet.

Season 1957–8 ended Jim Sullivan's record haul of 204 goals in a season when Bernard Ganley, the Oldham full-back, landed 219 goals in a season of wonderfully consistent kicking aided by some sparkling attacking football by Oldham. Oldham, who won the Lancashire Cup, were once again tumbled out of the Challenge Cup, a trophy which had eluded them since 1927, and which they had never won at Wembley. The 1958 finalists were Wigan and Workington Town, whose meeting at Wembley attracted an attendance of only 66 000, paying £31 030. This below-average gate was attributed to the fact that the whole of the game was televised.

Mr R. Gelder (Wakefield) was again chosen as referee, and the teams lined up as follows:

Wigan: Cunliffe; O'Grady, Ashton, Boston, Sullivan; Bolton, Thomas; Barton, Sayer, McTigue, Cherrington, Collier, Evans.

Workington Town: McAvoy; Southward, O'Neill, Leatherbarrow, Wookey; Archer, Roper; Herbert, Eden, Key, Edgar, Thompson, Eve.

The 1958 final provided an interesting contrast of styles. Wigan favoured speedy, open, attacking play, while Workington pinned their faith on a powerful, foraging pack to pave the way for the backs. Workington scored first when Edgar broke through to give Southward a try which the winger converted, but Wigan's great speed in attack was evident when Sullivan finished a movement with a try at the corner goaled by Cunliffe. Then Barton crashed over for Wigan and Cunliffe converted, but a goal by Southward made it 10—7 at half-time.

In the second half Town were weakened by injuries to Edgar and Archer, and McTigue finished another Wigan move with a good try. Another Southward goal made it 13—9, and then Workington made a last-ditch effort. A swift passing move gave Southward half a chance, and as he sped for the line he seemed certain to score until Charrington came across with a superb flying tackle to save the day for Wigan. The Lance Todd Trophy went to little Rees Thomas, the veteran Wigan scrum-half, for his continual prompting of the Wigan attack.

Town's ill-luck dogged them again in the championship final at Odsal on 17 May. Against the perennial Hull side they scored first through an identical Edgar-Southward try to that scored at Wembley, but then Cec Thompson, grafting Workington forward, was carried off with a leg injury, and Hull got on top of 12 men to score four tries through Cooper, J. Whiteley, Scott and Finn, and five goals from Bateson. After a season of splendid consistency unlucky Town were left with nothing to show but two sets of runners-up medals.

The 1958 annual meeting at Leeds brought an important development of the play-the-ball. To open up play and stop 'tuck-it-up-your-jersey' tactics, the acting half-back had to pass the ball or concede a scrum. Here was a further attempt to make playable one of the most criticized features of the game.

With the 1957–8 season over, thoughts turned with livelier interest than usual to the 1958 tour of Australia. The touring party had been announced, some controversy had been aroused by choice of officials and the World Cup fiasco of 1957 had to be avenged, if at all possible.

The managers were Messrs Bennett Manson (Swinton) and Tom Mitchell (Workington Town), with Jim Brough (Workington Town) establishing a precedent by travelling with the team as coach. Alan Prescott (St Helens) was appointed captain, and the party consisted of *Backs:* G. Moses, F. Carlton, A. Murphy and A. Terry (St Helens), E. Fraser, J. Challinor (Warrington), I. Southward, W. Wookey, H. Archer (Workington), M. Sullivan, E. Ashton, D. Bolton (Wigan), P. Jackson (Barrow), A. Davies, F. Pitchford (Oldham); *Forwards:* A. Prescott, V. Karalius (St Helens), B. McTigue (Wigan), B. Edgar (Workington), T. Harris, J. Whiteley (Hull), K. Jackson (Oldham), A. Ackerley (Halifax), R. Huddart (Whitehaven), M. Martyn (Leigh), D. Goodwin (Barrow). Four players chosen to go, J. Stevenson (Leeds), scrum-half, and forwards D. Turner, S. Little (Oldham), and J. Drake (Hull) were unable to travel, and Pitchford, Edgar, Goodwin and Terry took their places. Despite the withdrawals, it was a strong well-balanced party, charged with a big responsibility.

17

A Sensational Tour; the TV Years

THE tourists began well with a sequence of victories, but an unsatisfactory draw against Western Districts at Orange showed defensive weaknesses. A week before the first Test at Sydney the tourists beat New South Wales 19—10 in a rough, tough game in which three men were sent off, two Australians and Karalius, of England.

On the surface things looked reasonable, but behind the scenes disputes and discontent were weakening the spirit of the British party. When the officials had been announced there had been misgivings about sending a manager (Tom Mitchell) and coach (Jim Brough) from the same club, and the fact that these two did not see exactly eye to eye on relationships with the players rapidly became apparent. Jim Brough and Bennett Manson, the co-manager, came down hard on what were alleged to be serious breaches of discipline among the players, including alleged indulgence in too much Australian hospitality, which is always on a lavish scale.

Messrs Brough and Manson favoured greater discipline, and some of their 'curfew' measures did not go down too well with the players, who appear to have found a champion in Mr Mitchell.

When the first Test was played at Sydney on 14 June no compromise had been reached, and the split in the British camp was soon apparent on the field of play. Britain were never allowed to settle down, and mistakes, fumbling and hesitancy made matters worse. Full-back Fraser was not really fit to play, and had a poor game defensively. Australia were 17 points up in rapid time, and went on to win comfortably by 25 points to 8, with the typically large and enthusiastic Sydney Cricket Ground crowd roaring their heads off. From journalistic sources came allegations that the tourists had been 'kidded' and out-manoeuvred by Aussie tactics on and off the field, and referee Darcy Lawler was criticized for visiting the dressing-rooms of both teams and laying down the law before the game started.

After the first-Test disaster the British party left for Brisbane, where, behind closed doors, a top-secret meeting between players and management thrashed out current disagreements and disputes with no quarter asked or given. Coach Jim Brough gave the first-Test performance a thorough tongue-lashing, and business manager Bennett Manson pointed out that repetition of the form would kill any hope of financial reward from the tour.

The Queensland tour was a great success. All the 'country' matches were won, some by thumping margins. In one match Far North were trounced 78—8, and North Queensland also conceded more than 70 points, Eric Fraser landing 17 goals in this match. Then came a dramatic decision which played a vital part in the tour. Messrs Brough and Manson decided to take the players away from Brisbane to a special place of training—the 'millionaires' playground' at Surfers' Paradise beach, on the coast 50 miles from Brisbane.

A training schedule was applied and adhered to, excesses were avoided and team-spirit was improved beyond belief at Surfers' Paradise.

The Brisbane Exhibition Ground was too small for all who wanted to see the second Test. Gates were closed on 37 507 spectators, with many thousands still outside, and a sum of £13 101 was taken in receipts. The fans who got inside saw the most thrilling, heart-thumping, stirring game since the immortal 'Rorke's Drift' 1914 Test, a fantastic match in every respect.

Britain needed to win to save the Ashes and the tour, and after only four minutes they suffered a crippling blow when captain Alan Prescott fell awkwardly under an opponent and broke a bone in his forearm. Soon afterwards stand-off half David Bolton was bounced to earth by a fierce tackle and was taken to hospital with a fractured collar-bone. In addition, Fraser, Karalius and

Challinor all received hard knocks which reduced their effectiveness, yet Britain, with Karalius at half-back and Prescott tackling and passing with one arm, led 10—2 at the interval.

There was a dramatic scene in the English dressing-room at half-time. A doctor advised Prescott not to turn out in the second half. When the English skipper asked the British officials what chance the team would have without him, and heard the inevitable answer, he said: "I'll play on.' His decision saved the Tests for Britain.

In the second half the sight of the ginger-haired, red-faced forward from St Helens urging on his crippled team with one arm dangling helplessly inspired even partisan Aussies to cheer. Britain had a 10—2 lead with tries by Challinor and Sullivan and two goals from Fraser against a goal from Clifford, and, remarkably, within minutes of resuming, Southward scored a third try to make it 15—2 with Fraser's conversion. Australia hit back against this courageous 11½-man team, and forward Billy Marsh scored a try converted by Clifford. Staggeringly, Britain came back with another high-speed try by Southward, goaled by Fraser, and the score was 20—7. As excitement mounted, the Australians flogged home their attack against courageous tackling to score unconverted tries by Carlson and Dimond, but just as Britain seemed likely to crack, 19-year-old Alec Murphy, youngest player ever to tour Australia, corkscrewed his way through the Kangaroos defence for another great try converted by Fraser.

This try sealed the match, for although Holman got a late try converted by Clifford, Australia were beaten, and as the final whistle blew the crowd rose to the 'gallant cripples' who had squared the series against such overwhelming odds.

The victory had been won at great cost, for both Prescott and Bolton had to come home, and other stars were injured, but the victory put the Lions in tremendous heart for the third and deciding Test at Sydney Cricket Ground on 19 July. After the success of Surfers' Paradise the British party agreed to hold their training sessions at another resort, Cronulla, near Sydney, and again the tonic worked. For the third Test Phil Jackson replaced Bolton and Abe Terry took the place of Prescott, while a refereeing change brought in Mr Jack Casey, of Queensland, in place of Mr Darcy

Lawler, of New South Wales. This change did not go down too well in Mr Lawler's home state, and there were to be nasty repercussions. Before another huge crowd, 68 320, the third Test was played to decide the series, and produced almost as many sensations as the Brisbane battleground.

The first half of the game was closely contested, and when the teams went in at the interval Britain had a narrow lead at 14—12. Southward and Terry scored tries for Britain, with four goals from Fraser, while Provan and Holman scored for Australia, with three goals from Clifford.

The second half brought the sensations. Mr Casey got the bird from the partisan crowd when he gave Britain two penalties, and their temper did not improve when Murphy shot through for a try. By now Britain had the beating of Australia, and Sullivan scored a fourth try, goaled by Fraser. Then came the incident which caused the crowd to boil over. Australia were mounting a rally which might have swung the game, and Moir, the speedy winger, was badly obstructed by Southward as he kicked. However, Moir followed up, and almost got a touchdown for a try, bringing the ball back into play by touching it but failing to ground properly. Britain promptly seized possession and while the crowd howled for 'obstruction' Sullivan galloped almost the length of the field for a try. Pandemonium broke loose, and the spectators, howling with rage, let fly with everything they could lay their hands on. Bottles, oranges, orange peel, rolled-up newspapers, everything poured on to the pitch in a furious bombardment of Mr Casey. By a minor miracle, no one was hurt, and the British players helped to cool things down a little by clowning.

One Englishman picked up a bottle and pretended to drink from it, and another caused a laugh by catching an orange, peeling it and eating it. The crowd laughed in spite of themselves, and though Mr Casey continued to get the raspberry, the worst was over. Sullivan's try completely crushed the Aussies' spirits, and Davies, Whiteley and Sullivan added more tries, Fraser landing two goals. Hawick got a try for Australia goaled by Clifford, but the route was complete—a record 40 points to 17 win for Britain and the retention of the Ashes despite that disastrous first Test.

Unfortunately, the disputes and disharmonies of the tour were uppermost in the minds of League officials at home, who had been disturbed by reports from Australia of the earlier squabbles. The outcome was an inquiry held on Monday, 15 December 1958, under the chairmanship of Mr F. Ridgway (Oldham), chairman of the Council. The inquiry was held behind closed doors, and a full report of what was said inside has never emerged from official files. The result of the meeting was that Mr Manson was criticized for certain actions on tour, and Mr Mitchell for not revealing that he was unlikely to see eye to eye with the coach, Mr Jim Brough, at the time the appointments were announced. Mr Brough had a portion of his tour bonus impounded for his part in the creation of the discontent which had festered early in the tour. On the face of it, the decisions regarding Messrs Manson and Brough were a little harsh, and both men undoubtedly felt a sense of grievance.

The Council was occupied with another problem at this time—that of TV. Sport had entered the television era, and there had been criticism of the decision to allow live TV of matches during 1958–9. On one side were those who said that television ruined gates and took spectators from the terraces to fireside armchairs. Against these criticisms was the claim that national television of Rugby League was good publicity for the game.

The season brought several interesting moves in playing and coaching personnel. International forward Derek Turner moved from Oldham to Wakefield Trinity for £8000, while Oldham paid a world-record fee of £10 600 for Workington winger Ike Southward. St Helens coach Jim Sullivan joined Rochdale Hornets, while Alan Prescott took over at St Helens.

The 1959 Wembley final brought a match between the reigning holders Wigan and the reigning champions Hull. It was held on 9 May in perfect weather, and before a good crowd of 80 000. This was Hull's first appearance at Wembley and their first final since 1923.

Teams were:

Hull: Keegan; Cowan, Cooper, Saville, Watts; Matthews, Finn; Scott, Harris, J. Drake, Sykes, W. Drake, Whiteley.

Wigan: Griffiths; Boston, Ashton, Holden, Sullivan; Bolton, Thomas; Bretherton, Sayer, Barton, Cherrington, McTigue, Evans.

Referee: Mr C. Appleton (Warrington).

The Wigan machine began to function from the kick-off, but Hull seemed in the grip of the legendary 'Wembley nerves' and their play was nervy and shaky. Wigan, confident and snappy, with that we-have-been-here-before look, quickly took the lead with a fine Holden try and Griffiths goal, and Sullivan soon raced 60 yards to score after a dropped pass by Hull. From then on the result was never in doubt, and a superbly fit and confident Wigan swept to a 30—13 victory with further tries from Boston (2), Bolton and McTigue, and a total of six goals from Griffiths. For Hull, nothing went right, and their only try came near the end from scrum-half Finn, Keegan kicking five goals. The Lance Todd Trophy went to Brian McTigue, Wigan forward, for his ceaseless prompting and foraging.

The championship final at Odsal the following week brought a feast of good football. Contestants were St Helens and Hunslet, and in a wonderful display of open football by both sides 66 points were scored, a record aggregate for a championship final, with St Helens' 44 a record winning score and Hunslet's 22 a record for a beaten team. Hunslet swept to an early 12—4 lead, but the game was turned by a superb try by South African winger Tom Van Vollenhoven, who ran 75 yards and beat off five attempted tackles. From then on St Helens never looked back and Prinsloo, Vollenhoven (2), Smith, Murphy and Huddart touched down, Rhodes kicking 10 goals. For gallant Hunslet, who went down spiritedly, Gunney, Poole, Stockdill and Doyle scored tries and Langton four goals.

The visit of the Australian tourists in 1959 did not at first arouse much enthusiasm. Even in Australia the tourists were given little hope. They arrived on 7 September 1959, under managers Messrs Jack N. L. Argent and Ernest Keefer, and with former Test player Clive Churchill as coach. Captain was full-back Keith Barnes, a native of Port Talbot, and players were *Backs:* K. Barnes, D. Chapman, E. Lumsden, B. Carlson, D. Parish, K. Irvine, R. Gasnier, H. Wells, R. Boden, B. Clay, J. Riley, T. Brown, B. Muir, R. Bugden, P. Burke; *Forwards:* J. Raper, E. Rasmussen, R. Mossop, B. Hambly, J. Paterson, W. Wilson, G. Parcell, W. Delamere, D. Beattie, N. Kelly, I. Walsh.

This team of largely unknown quantities, with only Carlson, Wells and Mossop of seasoned experience, began well, with big and high-scoring wins over Leeds, Rochdale, Warrington and Salford, but then came heavy defeats against Lancashire and Yorkshire.

Despite these defeats, the young Aussies were looking good, with flying centre Reg Gasnier described as 'another Dave Brown'. Wins over Widnes and Oldham were followed by a magnificent morale-raising win of 15 points to 2 over champions St Helens, and this victory was just the tonic needed for the first Test, which was played at Swinton on Saturday, 17 October 1959.

The good form of the underrated Kangaroos proved no flash in the pan. Great Britain, who were expected to win easily, were in for a surprise. The Australians scored first when Gasnier took a high pass from Wells and romped past Fraser, and from then on Australia were on top. Their fine combination and speedy running threw the British team out of their stride, and when Wells went through for a second try there was no doubt about the result. Gasnier completed a hat-trick as Australia led 20—4, and it was only late in the game that Boston and Turner scored tries for Britain. Australia won 22—14, Barnes kicking five goals and Fraser four.

The series was now wide open, and as the tourists continued to play good football, beating France in a Test match and performing well against club sides, the English selectors had to think hard. There were several changes for the second Test at Headingley on 31 November. J. Whiteley (Hull), D. Vines (Wakefield T.) and D. Robinson (Leeds) came into the pack for Huddart, Martyn and Terry. J. Stevenson, the York scrum-half, got a surprise recall to Test football, and was chosen as captain, while N. Fox (Wakefield T.) and F. Dyson (Huddersfield) replaced Davies and the injured Fraser. Australia had Rasmussen in the second row, replacing the injured Beattie in a reshuffled pack, and Carlson returned for Riley.

This second Test was exciting and tense from first to last, with Britain constantly in trouble against the lively Aussies. Robinson plunged over to give Britain the lead, and another try by Fox against a goal by Barnes made it 6—2 for Britain at half-time. In the second half the Kangaroos showed their first-Test form, and two lovely swerving runs by Gasnier made openings for tries by Carlson. Carlson, who took over as kicker from the injured Barnes, hit a post with one easy conversion attempt, and this miss had vital consequences. With only minutes left to play, and Australia leading 10—6, Britain attacked desperately to save the Ashes. From a scrum near the tourists' line Stevenson got the ball and flipped a reverse pass to loose forward Whiteley. The powerful Hull man crashed over the line and Fox's simple goal gave Britain victory.

After this narrow, one-point and very streaky victory, Britain prepared for the third, deciding Test at Wigan. Britain had to make changes through injury, G. Round (Wakefield T.) replacing Dyson, and J. Wilkinson (Wakefield T.) taking over from the injured Karalius.

The match was a disappointment after the thrills of the first two Tests. The home team, coached by League secretary Bill Fallowfield, played a tactical game, holding the ball among the forwards and closing the game up so successfully that they gave the fast Australian backs no room in which to work. Referee Mr Eric Clay, who took over from Mr Gelder, gave Australian infringements short shrift, and Neil Fox banged over six match-winning goals for Britain. Early on, Fox was given the benefit of the doubt when he touched down a loose ball after an alleged knock-on, and another gift try near the end sealed Britain's 18—12 victory.

Australia fought back to 15—12 with two splendid tries by Raper and Carlson, plus three goals from Barnes, but when Raper dropped a pass on his own 25 Whiteley snapped it up and sent Southward (Oldham) over for a try.

At a meeting of the International Board during the tour arrangements were made for the 1960–1 World Cup in Britain, and it was agreed that no league matches should be played on World Cup dates. The Rugby League later made two important rulings. The tap penalty was abolished, as was the advantage rule at the scrum. It was hoped that the abolition of the tap penalty would prevent clubs holding the ball for long periods, while the end of the scrum advantage rule gave hopes of that as yet unattained goal—better scrummaging.

The closing days of the 1959–60 season saw Hull fight their way through to Wembley for the second successive year. Their opponents were Wakefield Trinity, and the game was given a tremendous boost by the news that Her Majesty the Queen and Prince Philip would attend the final, giving royal patronage for the first time since 1949.

The final was held on 14 May 1960, and the teams were:

Hull: Kershaw; Harrison, Cowan, Halafihi, Johnson; Broadhurst, Finn; Scott, Harris, Evans, Sutton, M. Smith, J. Whiteley.

Wakefield Trinity: Round; F. Smith, Skene, Fox, Etty; Rollin, Holliday; Wilkinson, Oakes, Vines, Firth, Chamberlain, Turner.

Referee: Mr Eric Clay (Rothwell).

Any luck Hull might have had in earlier rounds deserted them completely for the final. Injury after injury robbed them of half their first-choice side, and the Hull team contained several reserves and players called virtually out of retirement to play. Sam Evans and Tom Sutton in the pack were reaching the end of their careers, and Mike Smith and Jack Kershaw were young players pressed into service at the last minute.

Hull put up a great fight with depleted resources in the first half, but more injuries knocked the fight out of them in the second half, and Wakefield ran riot. At half-time it was 7—5 to Trinity, but head injuries to Harris and Whiteley and a chest injury to Cowan sapped Hull's strength as Trinity stormed in with incessant attacks.

Rollin, Fox (2), Skene (2), Holliday and Smith raced over for tries, some of them after movements covering half the length of the field, and Fox kicked seven goals. Wakefield's total of 38 points was a Wembley record, as was Fox's personal total of 20. A crumb of consolation for unhappy Hull was the award of the Lance Todd Trophy to their tireless and gallant hooker Tommy Harris, who had to leave the field near the end concussed and exhausted.

Trinity, triumphant at Wembley, sought the double at Odsal the following week. Their opponents were Wigan, and Wakefield made a great start with a try by F. Smith. Wigan then took control, however, and Wakefield's chances disappeared when Fox sustained a leg injury which crippled him. Wigan moved the ball with speed and power, and Boston (2), Ashton (2) and Sayer scored tries, Griffiths kicking six goals in a 27—3 win.

Events in the 1960 close season included an International Board meeting at which Britain asked for a contribution from France, Australia and New Zealand towards the cost of supporting the new developments in Italy. The other countries refused, and Britain, unable to pour money endlessly into Italy, had to cut down her support. Inevitably, progress in Italy slowed down, though Italian clubs continued to struggle to keep the game alive.

The big event of season 1960–1 was the third World Cup competition, with Australia defending her 1957 title. The Great Britain selectors chose the following panel: E. Fraser, J. Challinor R. Greenough (Warrington), E. Ashton, M. Sullivan, B. McTigue (Wigan), A. Davies (Oldham), A. Murphy, A. Rhodes, V. Karalius (St. Helens), F. Myler (Widnes), J. Wilkinson, D. Turner (Wakefield T.), T. Harris, J. Whiteley (Hull), J. Shaw (Halifax), B. Shaw (Hunslet). The two referees appointed for the tournament were Mr Eric Clay (Britain) and M. Edouard Martung (France).

It was announced before the series began that a sum of about £40 000 would be needed to cover costs and expenses, calling for an average attendance of 20 000 at each match. No league matches were to be played on World Cup dates, and despite the fact that key matches were being televised no difficulty was anticipated in raising the money.

In the first games on 24 September Great Britain beat New Zealand 23—8 at Odsal, and Australia narrowly beat France 13—12 in a thrilling match at Wigan. Results were going according to expectations, and Great Britain hammered France 33—7 at Swinton on 1 October, while Australia beat New Zealand 21—15 at Headingley. The way was paved for a Great Britain *v.* Australia decider at Odsal on 8 October.

At this stage attendances had failed to live up to expectations, and a lot depended on gates at the last three games, the matches on 8 October and the challenge match on Monday, 10 October. A sample of the below-average attendances was the 10 773 for Australia *v.* New Zealand, and once again television received its portion of blame for luring away spectators. In addition, the British spectator had shown once again that he was more interested in matches where he could show partisan feeling than in 'neutral' matches.

It needed a 50 000 attendance for Great Britain *v.* Australia at Odsal and 10 000 at Wigan for France *v.* New Zealand to give the tour finances a healthy surplus. Unfortunately, the weather played a scurvy trick on the Rugby League. Torrential rain poured down throughout 8 October, and while 33 000 braved the elements at Odsal, less than 3000 brave souls attended the Wigan game, fewer than normally attend many Wigan 'A' team games.

The Odsal game, which should have been a thrilling World Cup spectacle, became a brawl which is best forgotten.

Britain had the better of what might loosely be called the exchanges. They won by 10 points to 3, and won the World Cup for the second time in three attempts. Sullivan and Boston scored good tries, and Fraser added two goals against a Carlson try for Australia.

New Zealand beat France 9—0 at Wigan, and qualified for third place, France taking the wooden spoon.

On Monday, 10 October, there was another disappointment, for only 3908 turned up at Odsal to see the Northern Hemisphere *v.* Southern Hemisphere match which concluded the tournament. The match was a light-hearted romp which no one took very seriously, and Northern Hemisphere won by 33 points to 27.

There was no doubt the World Cup 1960 had not come up to expectations, although it was later revealed that television fees and programme proceeds, added to receipts, had enabled expenses to be covered, quelling earlier fears. With the next World Cup due to be played in New Zealand, the International Board faced some serious planning and thinking.

There could hardly have been a greater contrast than that between the spectator interest engendered by the World Cup and that created by the 1961 Challenge Cup final between St Helens and Wigan. This match between famous rivals, played at Wembley on 13 May, brought a capacity attendance of 95 000, the first since the immediate post-war years, and thousands more who sought tickets were unable to obtain them.

Saturday, 13 May, dawned with a cloudless sky and a promise of baking heat for the final. When the teams took the field the heat was so intense that spectators stood in shirt-sleeves, bathed in sweat, and it was so hot in London that the Piccadilly Underground line suffered delays due to buckled rails.

The teams were:

St Helens: Rhodes; Van Vollenhoven, Large, McGinn, Sullivan; Smith, Murphy; Terry, Dagnall, Watson, Vines, Huddart, Karalius.

Wigan: Griffiths; Boston, Ashton, Bootle, Carlton; Bolton, Entwistle; Barton, Sayer, McTigue, Collier, Lyon, Evans.

Referee: Mr T. W. Watkinson (Manchester).

In view of the intense heat, few expected the 26 players to stay the pace to the end, yet although the game did not produce the anticipated classic, there was plenty of excitement, a keen struggle and some fine football.

The game see-sawed dramatically until the last quarter, when St Helens got on top of a Wigan side who had shot their bolt in a fierce assault on the St Helens line early in the second half. At that stage the score was 5—4 for St Helens, a fine try by Murphy following a Huddart burst-through, and a Rhodes goal against two goals from Griffiths. In Wigan's tremendous assault on the St Helens line the turning point came when a penalty kick by Griffiths, which would have put Wigan ahead, hit the upright and bounced out again. From then on St Helens took a grip on the match, and the game was climaxed by a brilliant try. Large, the St Helens centre, burst through magnificently, interpassed with South African Van Vollenhoven, and finally gave a perfectly timed pass which sent the winger careering round to the posts for Rhodes to goal. This was the end for Wigan, for although Griffiths kicked another goal, they had no further steam left, and St Helens won the cup by 12 points to 6.

The championship final at Odsal the following week brought the first-ever championship title for Leeds, many times winners of the Challenge Cup. They easily beat Warrington by 25 points to 10 in a disappointingly one-sided game. Warrington, badly beaten for possession, never found their true form and were outpaced and outgunned by Leeds, for whom the mercurial Lewis Jones and forwards Fairbank and Goodwin were outstanding.

After a brief summer recess season 1961–2 opened, a season

destined to be one of the most exciting and eventful in Rugby League history. In July, at a momentous meeting of the Rugby League Council, it was agreed that two divisions would operate in the League in season 1962–3, with the League split in two on the basis of League positions at the end of 1961–2.

The excitements of 1961–2 continued with the visit of the New Zealand touring party, a young and enthusiastic side destined to give a salutary shock to British complacency. The Kiwis, with Mr C. H. Siddle as business manager and Mr W. 'Snow' Telford as team manager, were minus several famous names when they arrived in August, and a young and inexperienced party were not expected to set up much of a challenge to British supremacy.

The tourists had mixed fortunes in the games preceding the first Test. They lost the first game at Widnes, and had won roughly half their games before the first Test at Headingley.

The match was played on 30 September, and few members of the Headingley crowd gave the likeable young Kiwis much chance. Confident predictions of a big Great Britain win seemed well on the way to fruition when in the early minutes speedy football by the home team brought tries to Boston and Murphy and a goal to Rhodes. Then suddenly the Great Britain side seemed to lose their grip on the game. The keen, lively Kiwis began to throw the ball about with exhilarating abandon, taking chances galore, and suddenly the home bubble burst. After several chances had been missed by the over-eager Kiwis, Fagan kicked a goal, Edwards romped over for a try and Hadfield surprised the home defence with a quick dive over the line from a play-the-ball. Fagan landed four first-half goals in all, and at the interval New Zealand led 14—8. The fantastic turn-up continued in the second half, with the jubilant Kiwis finding everything going their way and the British team falling to pieces in both attack and defence. Although Boston got a crashing try for Britain, it was mostly one-way traffic towards the home line, and Reidy, M. Cooke and Hammond romped over for tries, Fagan completing a total of seven goals in a seemingly incredible 29—11 shock win. Equally as astounding as the result was the way in which the Headingley crowd cheered the 'underdogs', culminating in a fantastic ovation for the cock-a-hoop tourists at the end of the game.

Although the New Zealanders continued to have only mixed success in club games, they had boosted their Test reputation sky-high, and when the second Test took place at Odsal, on 21 October, changes had brought in Fraser (Warrington), Fox (Wakefield T.) and Sullivan (St Helens) for Rhodes (St Helens), Hallas (Leeds) and O'Grady (Warrington), and Whiteley (Hull) returned in a reshuffled pack. These changes proved master moves, as a more determined British side recovered from the shock of conceding five points in the early minutes to square the series 23—10. The Kiwis fought magnificently, and had Fagan been on kicking form they might have had the inspiration to make it a closer fight. But it was Britain's day, with half-backs Murphy and Bolton providing the speed in the backs, and Whiteley showing his generalship in the forwards. Sullivan scored two first-half tries, and Evans, Bolton and Ashton went over in the second half, with three goals from Fox. Roger Bailey got two tries for New Zealand and Fagan two goals.

Thus the third Test at Swinton on 4 November was vital, and in this deciding game Great Britain erased their first-Test failure with a brilliant display of football which overpowered the gallant but outplayed tourists.

New Zealand took the lead with two goals from Reg Cooke, but once Great Britain had taken a grip on the game there was no stopping the flow of brilliant attacking moves sparked by Murphy and Bolton at the scrum. Sullivan (2), Herbert, Murphy, Fraser, Ashton and Dagnall scored tries, and Fox kicked seven goals. For New Zealand, Edwards and Hadfield (2) scored tries and Cooke kicked five goals. It was a worthy end to a tour which had developed dramatically, and the tourists left for France with the best wishes of everyone in Britain, following their sporting and always enterprising displays. In France they won consolation for their series defeat in Britain by winning one and drawing two of the Tests against France.

In this continually eventful 1961–2 season developments came thick and fast. There was a setback in Italy when the Italian Government refused to recognize the infant Rugby League game there, but almost immediately this news was swallowed up by exciting reports from South Africa. In this stronghold of Rugby

Union, where opposition to Rugby League at times assumed fantastic proportions, a break-through at last seemed to have been made when two wealthy syndicates, backed by business men, announced their determination to launch Rugby League football in South Africa in 1962. Invitations were sent to star Springboks Tom Van Vollenhoven and Fred Griffiths in Britain, asking them to take a team of South African and British stars to the new republic in the summer of 1962 for exhibition games. Eventually Wakefield Trinity made a short tour, taking several 'guests'.

The trend towards Rugby League continued when it was announced in February 1962, that five Springbok Rugby Union stars had signed professional contracts with one of the two Rugby League organizations. They were Martin Pelser, Charlie Nimb, Hennie Van Zyl, Manetjie Gericke and Natie Rens.

Still the excitements and developments flowed. League secretary Mr Bill Fallowfield revealed that Rugby League gates were up by 25 per cent on the previous season, a sure sign of the increased competitiveness provided by the two-division plan.

The touring team to visit Australia and New Zealand in 1962 was chosen at Leeds in March, and there were the usual quota of surprises.

The choice of comparative 'unknowns', like Gary Cooper (Featherstone), Peter Small (Castleford) and Ken Noble (Huddersfield), caused controversy in areas where more popular suggestions had been overlooked. Manager was Mr S. Hadfield (Wakefield T.), assistant manager Mr A. Walker (Rochdale H.), and trainer-baggage man Collin Hutton (Hull K.R.).

The party consisted of: *Backs:* E. Fraser (Warrington), G. Round, N. Fox, H. Poynton (Wakefield T.), W. Boston, F. Carlton, E. Ashton (capt.), D. Bolton (Wigan), M. Sullivan, A. Murphy (St Helens), I. Southward (Workington T.), G. Cooper, D. Fox (Featherstone), P. Small (Castleford); *Forwards:* J. Wilkinson, D. Turner (Wakefield T.), B. McTigue, W. Sayer, R. Evans (Wigan), N. Herbert, B. Edgar (Workington T.), K. Noble (Huddersfield), J. Shaw (Halifax), R. Huddart (St Helens), J. Taylor (Hull K.R.), L. Gilfedder (Warrington).

The major trophies of 1961–2 produced some piquant situations. The Challenge Cup final became an all-Yorkshire battle between

Wakefield Trinity and Huddersfield after four Yorkshire teams, Hull K.R. and Featherstone Rovers being the others, had made the semi-finals. Then the same two clubs became championship finalists, Trinity again beating Featherstone and Huddersfield shocking Wigan at Central Park.

Interest lay in Wakefield's attempt to land the four cups—Yorkshire League, Yorkshire Cup, Challenge Cup and championship.

The Challenge Cup final at Wembley on 12 May 1962, attracted 85 000 spectators, and the teams were:

Huddersfield: Dyson; Breen, Booth, Haywood, Wicks; Deighton Smales; Slevin, Close, Noble, Clark, Bowman, Ramsden.

Wakefield Trinity: Round; Smith, Skene, Fox, Hirst; Poynton, Holliday; Wilkinson, Oakes, Firth, Williamson, Briggs, Turner.

Referee: Mr D. T. H. Davies (Manchester).

As a spectacle, the final was a disappointment. Tourist-studded Trinity were expected to make short work of a Huddersfield team lacking great names, but Huddersfield's teamwork tactics, dictated by shrewd Scots coach Dave Valentine, were to keep the ball tight and tackle like demons. They succeeded so well that Trinity were unable to move the ball freely, and the result was in doubt until well into the second half. Trinity won 12—6 after a hard struggle, and their matchwinner and Lance Todd Trophy winner was centre Neil Fox, with three beautiful drop goals and a try. Hirst got the other try after a 50-yard run, while Smales and Ramsden scored tries for a courageous and battling Huddersfield.

The following Saturday, at a rain-lashed Odsal Stadium, 37 000 spectators saw Wakefield's four-cup dream smashed by a ruthlessly determined Huddersfield, whose remarkable consistency was crowned by the championship title. Although a splendid Neil Fox try and goal gave Trinity a 5—2 lead, Huddersfield's almost fanatical tackling and harassing finally wore down Wakefield's resistance and completely disorganized the Trinity attack. Shortly before half-time Round was hustled off a pass by Ramsden, and Wicks scooped up the ball to score for Dyson to convert. In the second half Huddersfield camped out on the Wakefield '25', keeping the ball relentlessly tight and tackling like demons, and after a third Dyson goal Smales scooted over for a try that brought delirious Huddersfield fans swarming on to the pitch. Shock team Huddersfield took the last championship title before the return of two divisions by 14 points to 5, their seventh championship title in an illustrious club history stretching back to the golden era just before the First World War.

The 1962 tour brought its share of sensations and shocks. The preliminary games in Australia included a few flare-ups and dismissals, but the first Test at Sydney on 9 June brought no unpleasant scenes and Britain made a great start to the tour by winning easily 37—12, Sullivan (2), Ashton (2), Turner, Huddart and Boston getting tries and N. Fox kicking five goals.

Britain made sure of the Ashes by beating Australia 17—10 at Brisbane on 30 June. In another comfortable win, Britain's 'old guard', plus Gilfedder, replacing Turner, did the trick. The tourists, however, were denied the first-ever 'clean sweep' in Australia when in the third Test at Sydney on 14 July Turner and Sullivan were sent off and Britain were finally beaten 18—17, Irvine scoring a disputed try and kicking a touchline goal in the last minute.

An injury-hit touring side, minus injured captain Eric Ashton, who was flown home with a leg injury, went to New Zealand and were hammered 19—0 in the first Test at Auckland. In the second Test, at the same ground, a reshuffled and battered side, with Boston and Edgar playing though injured, were slammed 27—8, and the final humiliation was a record 46—13 beating by Auckland. It was a jaded party of 17 which went to South Africa for three exhibition games to end a tour of remarkably mixed fortunes.

18

Another Short-Lived Experiment

THE second attempt to float a two-divisions scheme with viable results began in 1962–3, though the start was delayed. Two new competitions were launched as pipe-openers to the season. They were named Eastern and Western Division Championships, with Yorkshire clubs playing in the former and Lancashire and Cumberland clubs competing in the latter.

There were no doubt excellent reasons for this, but the new divisional championships did not prove crowd-pullers as people awaited the return of two-division football. After a series of preliminary matches Widnes and Workington won through to the play-off of the Western Division Championship at Wigan, and Huddersfield met Hull K.R. at Headingley for the right to lord it over the eastern side of the Pennines.

The attendances at the play-offs were not encouraging. The gate at Headingley was less than 7000, and only a few hundreds more went to Wigan for the Western Final and midweek replay. Hull K.R. and Workington were the respective winners.

Perhaps one reason for the decision to delay the start of two divisions was the fact that the ambassadors from the Australasian tour were in South Africa playing light-hearted exhibition games, and were therefore unavailable for their clubs. Wakefield Trinity started their fixtures, against Batley, minus five Great Britain tourists.

However, once the divisional championships were out of the way, and the tourists back in England, the second experiment with two divisions began. It had been hoped, understandably, that competition in each division would be so needle-sharp and close that crowds would increase. In effect, after a few weeks of 'novelty' crowds, this only happened with clubs at the top of their respective tables. Good crowds were attracted to St Helens, Widnes, Leeds, Workington, Castleford and Warrington as these clubs made the early pace in the first division, but clubs who tumbled to the lower reaches of the division soon found crowds on the decline.

It was a similar story in division two. Hunslet, Keighley and Whitehaven did well as they set the pace, and Liverpool City had a short spell of success and clicking turnstiles. But second division failure ultimately proved punitive to club treasurers coffers.

These signs were ominous, for if the two-divisions experiment was to be successful, attendance figures had to increase with a degree of uniformity. The pattern of large crowds at the top games had been a feature of the previous one-division championship. A further complaint from the lesser second division clubs received renewed airing. Without visits from the attractive first division clubs, there were few 'special' gates. The signs and portents were not propitious.

There was optimism in another sphere, however. On the South African front it was stated that a Springbok touring team would make a short tour of Australia during the summer of 1963, and would be able to include players registered with English clubs.

Furthermore, an International Board meeting at Auckland declared that there were plans to invite South Africa to take part in a Rugby League World Cup tournament scheduled for 1965. Mr Fallowfield added the prophetic rider that this depended on the game being 'developed to a sufficiently high standard in South Africa'.

A less congenial atmosphere prevailed in another area of the international scene. Great Britain played France at Perpignan on 2 December, and this led to yet another outburst of criticism of French referees and their often blatant leaning towards Gallic sides. So low was the regard in which some French referees were held that one official, with an unfortunate legacy of an accident, was known as the 'one-armed bandit'.

There had been hopes that the Perpignan game would put an end to this unfortunate trend, since the appointed referee was

M. Edouard Martung, the Bordeaux inspector of police who had won high praise as a World Cup referee.

Sadly, and one must take into account inevitable British bias when assessing the reports, the pattern was painfully predictable. France were allowed every conceivable kind of mayhem, from scrum offences to stiff-arm tackles and blatant offside, while British errors, often non-apparent, were severely punished by M. Martung. France led 7—2 at half time through a try by Mantoulan and two goals from Benausse.

Poor Flanagan, the Great Britain hooker, had been flattened by an uppercut just before half-time. In these circumstances, he did well to be beaten by no more than 23—13 at the scrums. In the second half, tries from Bourreil and Carrere, both converted, put France ahead 17—2. In the last ten minutes M. Martung relaxed his vigil, and Great Britain, allowed to heel from four out of five scrums, scored tries through Ashton and Fox, with two Fox goals. In fact, with the last move of the game, Myler was crashed into touch at the corner flag.

A contentious defeat, later to be avenged in cruelly effective fashion by Great Britain.

The approach of Christmas, 1962, brought the wickedest weather conditions for many a long year. Snow, ice and fog enveloped the country, and grounds were frozen from Boxing Day onwards. The complete New Year's Day fixture list was abandoned, and this was the beginning of a long, cold, wearisome spell of non-playing lasting well into February.

So awful was the stagnation in fixtures, in all sports, that the League took the unusual steps of stating that home clubs in the Challenge Cup could switch to the grounds of visiting clubs if their own grounds were unfit.

The Management Committee also announced that in view of the wholesale cancellations, the season would be extended for league games until 31 May.

One club who beat the weather were Widnes, the well-named Chemics, who placed a chemical solution on their ground to enable matches to be played in the frostiest of conditions. The matches were, indeed, played, but there were some misgivings about the long-term effect of chemicals on the Naughton Park pitch.

At last, in late February, things got back to normal, though fixture lists were hastily revised to cope with League and Cup. On 3 April, at Wigan, Great Britain won revenge for their experiences at Perpignan. Without their own ground, their own crowd, and, let it be said, their own referee, France were humiliated and trounced to the tune of 42 points to 4. France went quietly, without a fight, and Great Britain could easily have doubled the score. Try scorers were Smales (2), Stopford (2). Bolton, Fox, Ashton and Boston, with nine goals from Fox.

With the fixture congestion resolved, and priority given to the Challenge Cup, the two semi-finals were played on 20 April 1963, and Wakefield Trinity reached Wembley for the third time in four seasons.

Trinity beat Warrington at Swinton and Wigan beat Hull K.R. at Headingley to reach the final, and Trinity's magnificent surge through the early 60s continued with this, their third opportunity to prove themselves the team of the decade and one of the great teams of all time.

The match brought yet another triumph to Ken Traill's team, although injuries again dogged their opponents. Wigan actually started favourites for the final, and for a spell during the first half their fine football matched that of Trinity to promise a well-matched and exciting final. But late in the first half David Bolton, the brilliant international out-half of Wigan, was concussed, and he had to leave the field. Although he came back in the second half, he was obviously affected by his injury, and this contributed to an incident of vital importance in the stages when Wigan were fighting to get back into the game. As Wigan broke on the right, the bemused Bolton turned a pass to that lively poacher Poynton instead of a colleague, and Poynton scooted away for a try. Trinity went ahead shortly before the interval, and when Pitchford scored a try for Wigan there was a brief suggestion that the Colliers might hit back. But the team shake-up caused by Bolton's injury had its effect, and Trinity romped away to win 25—10. Sampson, Coetzer (2), Poynton and Brooke got Wakefield's tries and Fox kicked five goals. Carlton scored Wigan's other try, and Ashton kicked two goals.

The teams were:

Wakefield Trinity: Round; Greenwood, Brooke, Fox, Coetzer; Poynton, Holliday; Wilkinson, Kosanovic, Sampson, Vines, Turner, Pearman.

Wigan: Bolton; Boston, Ashton, Davies, Carlton; McLeod, Pitchford; Barton, Sayer, McTigue, Collier, Lyon, Evans.

Referee: Mr D. T. H. Davies (Manchester).

On 19 May, Swinton, who had finished the season in breathtaking style, clinched the First Division championship at Widnes by beating their closest rivals. Swinton, playing superb football throughout, had won 17 consecutive games. Unfortunately, this crucial success had tragic accompaniment, for the club chairman, Mr W. C. 'Bill' Scholes, collapsed and died while watching the match.

Widnes finished runners-up. Relegated from Division One were Bramley and Oldham, while Hunslet and Keighley came up from Division Two. The first season of the experiment received a mixed verdict from administrators and public. While gates had certainly held up, and in some cases improved, among top teams in both divisions, gates elsewhere had declined, catastrophically in some Division Two centres. The worst situation seemed to be at Bradford, where Northern were in serious financial difficulties.

New Zealand toured Australia in 1963, but far more important in the long term, in view of the hoped-for expansion, was the promised tour of Australia by South Africa. The touring party included several players who had gained experience with English clubs, although one of them, Trinity's winger Gert Coetzer, dislocated his shoulder against Southern New South Wales. The tourists won this comparatively simple match by 41—2, but any feelings of euphoria the Springboks felt were quickly dissipated when Queensland beat them at Brisbane by 33 points to 16. Injuries dogged the tourists, and the two Test matches resulted in thorough hidings for the eventually demoralized pioneers. The scores were 34—6 at Brisbane and 54—21 at Sydney, a demonstration, if one was needed, that the infant South African Rugby League still had much to learn in the arts of survival.

Before the start of the 1963–4 season, the second term of the two-divisions experiment, there was a sudden surge of militancy from the players of several clubs, particularly the more successful first division outfits. St Helens, Wigan, Wakefield Trinity, Workington and Widnes players led the way in demanding improved terms. In fact, there was a note of industrial collective bargaining, disturbing in sport, about the way the players threatened to strike if improved terms were not offered. St Helens refused to play in a pre-season charity game, and the situation for a time looked rough, but eventually terms were negotiated between club committees and players which enabled a normal start to the season to be made. Widnes committeemen, a little ruefully perhaps, announced that the players' terms for the new season were the best in the history of the club.

Not all the militancy came from Division One, however. Whitehaven players also asked for more money, no doubt following the lead of neighbouring Workington, and their League game against Liverpool City was postponed.

The new season demonstrated the manner in which television was becoming a major influence within Rugby League. It was announced that the Challenge Cup semi-finals would be played on separate Saturdays during the 1963–4 season, in order that BBC and ITV could screen one semi-final each.

In September the Australian tourists arrived, and a major item of controversy referred, at least in part, to the emphasis placed by television companies on Rugby League. The first Test was scheduled by the Rugby League for Wembley, in midweek under floodlights, and although the major reason was stated to be propaganda value in the South of England, it was noticeable that the BBC would be screening highlights of the game.

This first Test took place on Wednesday, 16 October, and before the event gloomy predictions about the attendance came from Mr Len Went, the Wembley Press Officer, who reported that advance ticket sales were not promising. On the night the attendance was a mere 14 000, a figure hardly justifying the decision to take the game to Wembley.

The small attendance was not the only blow to the pride of the Northern Rugby League. The Great Britain side had suffered

Bobby Fulton, outstanding Australian player in the triumphant 1973 tour of Britain

Left: Cliff Watson, St Helens and Great Britain forward, charges into a ruck of Aussie defenders in a Test match at Headingley

Below left: Hull Kingston Rovers star half-back Roger Millward gets Great Britain's sole try in the Third Test of the 1973 tour

Below: Australian centre Starling crashes through a tackle by Hynes (Leeds) for one of Australia's five tries in the deciding Third Test of 1973

The Australian hooker helps himself to one of a nap hand of tries in the 1973 Third Test win.

New Zealand players perform their war dance before a Test match at Swinton in the last World Cup series

from the withdrawal of two key forwards, Huddart and Turner, and a vital injury during the game was to result in a staggering defeat for Great Britain, and a wonderful fillip for Australia.

The teams lined up as follows:

Great Britain: Gowers (Swinton); Burgess (Barrow), Ashton (Wigan), Fox (Wakefield Trinity), Field (Batley); Bolton (Wigan), Murphy (St Helens); Tembey (St Helens), Sayer (Wigan), Tyson (Hull K.R.), Measures (Widnes), Bowman (Huddersfield), Karalius (St Helens).

Australia: K. Thornett; Irvine, Langlands, Gasnier, Dimond; Harrison, Muir; Gallagher, Walsh, Kelly, R. Thornett, Hambly, Raper.

Referee: Mr D. T. H. Davies (Manchester).

There had been a heavy shower during the day, and the ball was slippery. Although this could be taken as a minor reason for Britain's bad handling, it could not entirely excuse a poor display by the home side. In addition, Great Britain lost the luckless David Bolton through injury, and Bowman went to centre with Ashton at stand-off half. Australia, revelling in both conditions and numerical superiority, swept to a 28—2 win with some fine, confident and speedy handling, inflicting on Great Britain a record home defeat, and threatening to become the first all-Australian side to win a Test series in Britain. The try scorers were Gasnier, with a typical hat-trick, Langlands, Irvine and Ken Thornett, with five goals from Langlands. Fox landed a lonely penalty goal for Great Britain.

Australia's cards were on the table. They were going for the first-ever Ashes victory of an all-Australian touring side, and the second Test at Swinton was vital. As a contrast to the Wembley attendance, over 30 000 attended the game. The Australian side included skipper and hooker Ian Walsh as the result of a remarkable example of disciplinary tit-for-tat. Walsh had been sent off at Wakefield, but had been adjudged 'sending off sufficient' by the disciplinary committee, whose chairman stated that this was a reciprocal gesture in view of the fact that on the last Great Britain tour of Australasia the first five tourists to appear before an Australian committee had received similar leniency.

After the Wembley defeat, Great Britain had made many changes. The teams were:

Great Britain: Gowers (Swinton); Sullivan (York), Ashton (Wigan), Fox (Wakefield T.), Stopford (Swinton); Myler (Widnes), Murphy (St Helens); W. Robinson (Leigh), McIntyre (Oldham), Watson (St Helens), Morgan (Swinton), Measures, Karalius (Widnes).

Australia: K. Thornett; Irvine, Langlands, Gasnier, Dimond; Harrison, Muir; Quinn, Walsh, Kelly, R. Thornett, Hambly, Raper.

Referee: Mr D. T. H. Davies (Manchester).

No one could have conceived or anticipated the shattering result of this game, not even the Australian party in their wildest daydreams.

The game started promisingly for Great Britain with a try to Stopford in the first ten minutes, an early score that momentarily aroused hopes of the home comeback. Then came the first of two crippling and vital blows. Centre Ashton was heavily tackled, and was led from the field with severely bruised ribs and concussion. Once again the rhythm of the Great Britain side was disturbed, and worse was to come later in the half when Myler was similarly crash tackled, and suffered an almost identical fate. In the second half the demoralized home side was reduced to 11 men, and the Australians gleefully made most of their good fortune to run up the almost incredible Test match total of 50 points.

It was total humiliation for Great Britain as their tired and outnumbered players were outflanked and overwhelmed, and yet another record score was piled on the overworked scoreboard. In fairness to Australia, the pace and skill of their running and handling indicated that the result would still have produced a first-ever Ashes win in England, but the size of the score was ludicrous, and perhaps this game was a watershed in the later call, a successful one, for substitutes in Rugby League.

Langlands scored two tries and seven goals for Australia, and further tries were added by Irvine (3), Gasnier (2), Dimond (2), Kelly, R. Thornett and Harrison. Great Britain's token reply came from tries by Stopford and Measures, with three goals from Fox.

With their historic Ashes win safely under their belts, the Aussies could afford to take things a little more easily, and, not surprisingly, the third Test was something of an anti-climax, bringing some restoration of pride to British Rugby League.

This was badly needed, for after the Swinton debacle, Mr Bill Fallowfield, who had acted as team manager for the Great Britain side, offered to resign after criticism of his handling of the team. The selection committee gave him a vote of confidence, and in the third Test at Headingley bruised egos were restored.

Great Britain could afford to make more sweeping changes, and try out new faces. Into the side came backs Geoff Smith (York), Keith Holden (Warrington), and Alan Buckley (Swinton), while the pack included Frank Collier (Wigan), John Ward (Castleford). Ken Roberts (Halifax) and Don Fox (Featherstone Rovers). The new captain was Huddersfield half-back Tommy Smales.

The match was played on 30 November, and Great Britain won by 16 points to 8. It was not a satisfactory win, however, since three men were dismissed, two Australians and one Briton, and referee Eric Clay constantly had to break up feuds and fights. The Kangaroos dismissed were Hambly, who went early, and Muir, while Watson was sent off in the incident involving Muir.

Nevertheless, a win was welcome for Great Britain, and satisfaction could be gained by the debutants. Smith, Don Fox and John Ward scored tries, Stopford getting the fourth, and Don Fox emulated brother Neil by kicking two goals. The attendance was 20 000.

Following the third Test a meeting of the International Board considered Australian proposals to amend the much-abused play-the-ball rule. It was proposed that the ball should be released in the tackle, and then played by either hand or foot of either side, but like so many other propositions centred around this aspect of the game, it was of short duration, and ultimately died quietly. Scrummaging and the interchange of players between Australia and Britain were again raised, again somewhat inconclusively.

The successful Australians went to France, and a stormy beginning to the tour saw a free fight develop in the match against Basque-Bearnais. In the first Test at Bordeaux, more rough exchanges ended in the dismissal of France's Georges Fages, but France won 8—5. Later the tour cooled down, and it all ended satisfactorily for the Kangaroos, who won the second and third Tests at Toulouse and Paris.

Back in Britain, distress signals were flying above Odsal, the famous home of Bradford Northern. Once-great Northern were losing vast sums of money, with gates down under the 1000 mark, and talk of dissolution led to a special management committee meeting.

This was held after Bradford Northern had made it known that the fixture with Oldham on Saturday, 14 December, would not be fulfilled. The management committee called for public meetings to be held in Bradford to measure the support for the retention of the club, and to discover whether new directors would come forward to take the reins.

The matter went a step further on 10 January when Northern officially gave up membership of the Rugby League, and Mr Fallowfield, in an official statement, expressed regret, with an optimistic rider. He said: 'Possibilities of forming a new club are being investigated'.

January brought a further sad demise. Harry Sunderland, the peppery, lovable Queensland Aussie, pioneer of the game in France, and former Australian touring team manager, latterly a journalist and broadcaster, died at the age of 74. His memory was to be commemorated in a Rugby League Writers Association award to the best and fairest player in the championship final each season, an award to be known as the Harry Sunderland trophy.

The third sad event came in February. It was the death of the two-divisions scheme which had been launched with such optimism in 1962. The failure of Bradford Northern had, perhaps, underlined the parlous financial state of many clubs, particularly those existing on tiny gates in the lower reaches of the divisions. At a vital meeting on 12 February in Leeds, clubs voted by the huge margin of 23 votes to 4 to abandon the two-division experiment and return to one division for 1964–5. The unloved and disregarded Eastern and Western Division Championships would also disappear. The second two-division experiment of the century had lasted no longer than the first.

With the decision to end two divisions, all interest disappeared in promotion and relegation issues, and the championships of the two divisions remained the only League honours worth the seeking. The brilliantly attractive Swinton side deservedly retained their First Division title, and Oldham galloped away with Division Two, in which Bradford Northern's results were expunged.

The Challenge Cup, however, retained its perennial crowd-pulling appeal, and there were some thrillingly close matches as Hull Kingston Rovers and Widnes fought their way through to the Wembley Final.

Widnes had to fight their way through cliff hanging replays with Swinton in the third round and Castleford in the semi-final. Hull K.R. figured in a dramatic and controversial semi-final with Oldham.

After a 5—5 draw at Headingley the teams replayed at Swinton. With the scores tied 14—14 after 80 minutes, Oldham went ahead with a try in the opening half of extra time, but by then the light had become so bad that the referee, Mr D. T. H. Davies, abandoned the match.

The following Monday, at Fartown, Huddersfield, the result was clear cut, Rovers winning by 12 points to 2.

A crowd of 84 000 saw the Wembley Final in May.

The teams were:

Hull K.R.: Kellett; Paul, Major, Elliott, Blackmore, Burwell, Bunting; Tyson, Flanagan, Mennell, Palmer, Clark, Poole.

Widnes: Randall; Chisnall, Briers, Myler, Thompson; Lowe, Smith; Hurstfield, Kemel, Collier, Karalius, Measures.

Referee: Mr R. L. Thomas (Oldham).

Hull K.R., having shown freer scoring propensities in the earlier rounds, were favourites to win the Cup, but the Yorkshire side was shaken both by the keen tackling of the Lancastrians, and by some brilliant and unexpected second half football by the Chemics. At half time it was 2—0 to Widnes, Randall having landed a goal, and neither side had really opened up, with the speedy Rovers wingers, Paul and Blackmore, well watched.

Then, in the second half, Widnes, inspired by skipper Vince Karalius and the forward signing from Wigan, Frank Collier, turned on some splendid combined handling and running. Briers, Collier and Myler scored tries, and Randall kicked another goal. Widnes won 13—5, Burwell scoring a brilliant individual try and Kellett a goal for Hull K.R.

International football at the close of the 1963–4 season brought home and away games between Great Britain and France. The first match was at Perpignan, on Sunday, 8 March, and Great Britain, given a much better deal from the French referee than had been customary, won by 11 points to 5, their first win in France since 1960. Shelton (2) and Buckley scored tries and Gowers kicked a goal. For France, Verge scored a disputed try, and Villeneuve kicked a goal.

The return match was at Leigh on 18 March, and this was a procession. Away from their own pastures, the French again put up merely token opposition, and were soundly trounched by 39 points to nil. Dixon, Hardisty (2), Smith, Parker, Fox and Jordan got the tries, and Neil Fox kicked nine goals.

19

World Cup Shock: Enter Substitutes

DURING the summer of 1964 France toured Australia and New Zealand with dismally unsuccessful results, and this precipitated another of those crushing decisions that Rugby League legislators were anxious to do without.

After Australia had whipped France with ease in all three Tests, and thereby won a series against France in Australia for the first time in four tours, the Australian Board of Control stated through their president Bill Buckley that in view of the poor form shown by France on the Australasian tour, the proposed 1965 World Cup in Australia and New Zealand should be postponed to give France time to rebuild.

This was a crushing blow to French pride, and Great Britain reacted strongly to the prospect of the postponement, since the World Cup was a great boost to players' performances in the domestic game, and an added interest at the season's end. The British Rugby League Council proposed several solutions, including one that suggested a separation of the tourney into Northern and Southern Hemispheres, but failed to sway Australia. The World Cup was shelved, and would not reappear until 1968.

Echoes of another Test series were heard in Britain, and an important change in the laws resulted. Britain's 11-man humiliation at the hands of Australia at Swinton had caused hard thinking about substitutes, and these were introduced in the 1964–5 season, two substitutes being allowed before and during the half-time interval. Eventually substitution was to be allowed at any stage of the game.

A splendid piece of news with which to start the season came from the city of Bradford, where the great Northern side resumed fixtures under new management. Public meetings had elicited tremendous support, and former Northern players of immense popularity, Joe Phillips and Trevor Foster, led a virile new team of directors. It was a Cinderella-like revival, for crowds of 10 000 and above flocked to Northern's matches and, indeed, the winter of 1965 was to bring a true fairy-tale climax to the revival. The Rugby League Management Committee helped out by voting a purchase of £500 worth of shares.

The return to one-division football brought innovations in a top-16 championship to replace the old top four, and, later, a bottom-14 championship which was short-lived, hardly surprising in view of the fact that it was an obvious sop to the lower clubs. In addition, the bottom-14 matches were to be used for play-the-ball experiments.

Swinton installed floodlights of such high quality, certainly of better standard than the pioneer Bradford Northern and Leigh lights, that Oldham must have wished devoutly that they had been available at the time of the previous season's abandoned semi-final. St Helens followed with good quality lights, and another major development was increasing its momentum.

International competition in 1964–5 consisted of home and away games between Great Britain and France, and the first-ever Under-24 international between these countries. In the first full international at Perpignan, France, no doubt smarting under Australia's implied snub, beat Britain 18—8, the only outstanding feature of Britain's play being a brilliant long-distance try scored by Berwyn Jones, Olympic sprinter who had joined Wakefield Trinity and who had quickly won recognition. In the return match, Great Britain won 17—7 at Swinton, but the result was lost in a ferocious controversy which almost caused the abandonment of the match.

The game was frequently stopped by referee Mr Davies for infringements, and eventually he lost patience with French forward Bescos and sent him off. Bescos refused to go and stood arguing. Eventually he was persuaded by his countryman and touch judge, M. Jameau, to go to the touchline, but immediately changed his mind and rushed angrily back. So Mr Davies left the field and walked to the dressing room, to be followed by the gesticulating and arguing French team.

Mr Arthur Walker, chairman of the Rugby League, went down to the dressing rooms and succeeded in getting everyone back on the field 'for the sake of international Rugby League'. It had been a nasty scene, and did little to make the game's image attractive. Eight minutes were lost, and much goodwill.

Rather more encouraging, in terms of spectator appeal, was a second round Challenge Cup tie at Central Park between Wigan and St Helens. Wigan won 7—2 before a magnificent 40 000 crowd. Wigan went on to reach the Cup final, not an unusual event for this everlastingly consistent side, by beating Swinton 25—10 in the semi-final at St Helens. The other semi-final brought a surprise, Hunslet's tigerish pack taming Wakefield Trinity in an 8—0 win.

A fine crowd of 92 000 saw the Wembley final in excellent weather on Saturday, 8 May, and the game proved as exciting and memorable as the Warrington *v.* Huddersfield final of revered memory.

The teams were:

Wigan: Ashby; Boston, Ashton, Holden, Lake; Hill, Parr; Gardiner, Clarke, McTigue, Stephens, Evans, Gilfedder.

Hunslet: Langton, Griffiths, Shelton, Preece, Lee; Gabbitas, Marchant; Hartley, Prior, Eyre, Gunney, Ramsey, F. Ward.

Referee: Mr J. Manley (Warrington).

Gilfedder promptly put Wigan ahead with a prodigious penalty from half way, but Langton quickly equalized. A Holden try for Wigan was followed by another Langton penalty.

Then Wigan shot into a big lead, with Gilfedder kicking a goal and converting a sinuous run and try from Lake. At 12—4 Hunslet were rocking, but they came back brilliant with a superb sidestep and try at the post by Shelton which Langton converted.

In the second half Wigan again piled up the points. A 45-yard try by Gilfedder, converted by Ashton as Gilfedder took deep breaths, and a try by Lake made it 20—9, but in a breathtaking finish Griffiths weaved his way round to the Wigan posts and Langton kicked two goals. A wonderful match, and two men, one from each side, shared the Lance Todd trophy, Ashby of Wigan and Gabbitas of Hunslet.

The season ended on a note of disappointment for St Helens, who had been the outstanding League side. Although they won the secondary honour of heading the League, having at one stage gone 17 League matches without defeat, they were beaten in the Swinton top-16 play-off by Halifax. For Halifax, pulling off one of those frequent play-off surprises, Burnett (2) and Jackson scored tries and James three goals in a 15—7 win. Killeen got a try and two goals for St Helens, who took a little consolation from the fact that earlier in the season they had won the Lancashire Cup for the fifth successive season.

The continually maligned play-the-ball rule figured largely at the annual meeting of the League at Leeds in June, and no fewer than four attempts to change the rule were made, all without securing the necessary majority vote.

Among the four amendments was a proposal that the Rugby Union rule should be adopted, and a further proposal that the bottom-14 experiment of the past season should be made law. In the end, the meeting agreed that the Wigan *v.* Hunslet cup final at Wembley had produced such brilliant rugby that, perhaps, there was no need to change the rules.

The Australians toured New Zealand in the summer of 1965, and after Australia had won the first, the Kiwis squared the series in enthusiastic style by winning at Auckland. This 7—5 win was a notable fillip.

The New Zealanders arrived for their tour of Britain with a lively young side, and high ambitions, but these were to be crushed by the experiences of a poor tour, both financially and in the playing sense. The New Zealanders were beaten in nearly half their games, including two of the three Tests, and did not prove a major spectator attraction. In the first Test at Swinton on 25 September a rather uninspiring game ended with victory for Great Britain by 7 points to 2. Although the home side were rarely in difficulties, tries were hard to create on both sides. Smales got the only one three minutes from half time, and Holliday kicked two goals. Tait kicked a goal for New Zealand.

In the second Test at Odsal on 23 October, Great Britain had a similarly comfortable victory, but again without producing exhilarating rugby. The score was 15—9, Burgess, Shelton, and Stopford getting tries with three goals from Holliday, while New Zealand's points came from a try by W. T. Schultz and Fagan's three goals.

The third Test at Wigan salvaged a little pride for New Zealand. They were the brisker side in a 9—9 draw, and with steadier finishing might have won the match against a Great Britain side once again in disjointed and lethargic mood.

Burgess scored a try for Great Britain, Gowers kicking three goals, while the replies came from a Tait try and three goals from Fagan.

The attendances for the Tests were derisory, being respectively 8497, 15 849 and 7919, and much of the blame was placed on live television.

This latter medium had introduced a new competition to Rugby League. With more and more clubs installing floodlights, BBC2 enterprisingly introduced the Floodlit Trophy to be played on midweek evenings and televised.

October 1965, brought the climax of the Bradford Northern revival. In the Yorkshire cup final at Headingley amid, as they say, scenes of wild rejoicing, the reconstituted side beat Hunslet by 17 points to 8 in a most exciting and fluctuating game in which Hunslet missed sufficient chances to have robbed the match of its fairy-tale result. Brooke scored a brilliant 80-yard try for Northern and Australian winger Lionel Williamson scored two more tries, with Clawson adding four goals. Lee and Thompson scored tries for Hunslet, and Langton kicked a goal. It was a weekend of celebrations in Bradford, and proud days for Joe Phillips, Trevor Foster and company.

In the search for major honours, 1965–6 was undoubtedly the year of St Helens, who once again set a blistering pace in the League and brought the season to a wonderful climax by winning all four major trophies.

The Saints won the Lancashire League, the League Leaders Trophy, the Challenge Cup and Championship in irresistible style, yet several arguments and debates clouded their great achievement.

These were centred on the Challenge Cup, in which St Helens reached, and won, the Wembley final via a third round game which ended in furious argument, and a semi-final in which ugly personal rivalries exploded on the field of play. Then, in the final, the St Helens tactics were widely criticized.

The third round game between St Helens and Hull K.R. produced a finish which had home supporters whooping with incredulous delight, and Hull Kingston Rovers' players and directors virtually in tears.

With 80 minutes gone, Hull K.R. led 10—7 and seemed certain to win. Referee Eric Clay, however, allowed up to five minutes of injury time, and in that time Murphy took an up-and-under free kick for St Helens, followed up, and disappeared under a mass of bodies behind the Rovers' posts. Mr Clay awarded a try as the mêlée broke up, and the try was goaled to give St Helens a totally unexpected, and bitterly disputed, win. So angry were Hull K.R. officials that after the game they stated that Mr Clay would never again be accepted as referee for a Rovers' game. An inquiry was called for at Council level, but, sadly for Rovers, the only outcome was an implied censure on their own officials for publicly abusing the referee. St Helens marched on to Wembley, but not without incurring the ire of Dewsbury in the semi-final after a bruising match in which Mick Sullivan, Dewsbury coach and skipper, was carried off the field.

The Wembley final on 21 May brought a record attendance of 100 000 to Wembley and record receipts. This was in anticipation of a magnificent open game between two great and prestigious sides, but it did not materialize.

The teams were:

St Helens: Barrow, Van Vollenhoven, Murphy, Benyon, Killeen; Harvey, Bishop; Halsall, Sayer, Watson, Warlow, French, Mantle.

Wigan: Ashby; Boston, D. Stephens, Ashton, Lake; Hill, Parr; Gardiner, Woosey, McTigue, A. Stephens, Gilfedder, Major.

Referee: Mr H. Hunt (Culcheth).

Wigan were handicapped from the start by the fact that Clarke, their hooker, was unable to play, and Woosey, a prop forward, was pressed into service. In addition, one or two members of the Wigan side were not 100 per cent fit through nagging injuries.

To add to Wigan's woes, St Helens played a tactical game which involved a great deal of calculated offside play. It all added up to a one-sided game, and a decisive and crushing 21—2 win for the Saints. Killeen scored a try and kicked five goals for St Helens, Mantle and Bishop added tries, and Murphy dropped a goal. Wigan's solitary reply was a penalty by Gilfedder.

St Helens' tactics brought considerable Press and private calumny, and their persistent offside running at play-the-balls precipitated a rule change where a scrum was replaced by a kick to touch, and a tap penalty from the point where the ball was kicked into touch.

St Helens completed their quartet of triumphs, richly deserved despite the controversies, by gaining revenge over Halifax in the Championship final at Swinton. The score was 35—12.

It was a good year for French Rugby League. After completing the New Zealanders' gloom by winning all three Tests in France, the team despised as 'not yet up to standard' by Australia's World Cup planners completed a double over Great Britain. The score at Perpignan on 16 January was 18—13, and in the return at Wigan in March, France won 8—4 in yet another dull international, one which did little good for Britain's Australian tour prospects. A desirable and necessary innovation in these internationals saw an English official, Mr Clay, take charge of the game in France, and a Frenchman, M. Martung, officiated in England.

The influence of television brought a minor revolution when Wigan refused to allow a game to be televised, describing TV as a 'creeping paralysis which in time will destroy Rugby League'. The reference was to live TV, and although other clubs supported Wigan's stand, television continued unabated, the official view being that the Wigan case was not proved, and that other social factors affected attendances.

In Australia, the Board of Control made another attempt to open out play from the play-the-ball, suggesting to the other international bodies that the acting half-back should stand five yards back from the heel, instead of three.

Australia was to be the scene of the summer's major tour, with

Great Britain arriving to try to regain the Ashes and wipe out the humiliations of 1963. One absentee from the British party was to be Alex Murphy, who cried off for 'business reasons' after being overlooked as captain.

The skipper was Harry Poole, of Leeds, and the party was: Gowers (Swinton), Keegan (Hull), Burgess (Barrow), B. Jones (Wakefield T.), Shelton (Hunslet), Myler (Widnes), Brooke (Bradford N.), Buckley (Swinton), Wrigglesworth (Leeds), Hardisty (Castleford), Aspinall (Warrington), Dooler (Featherstone), Bishop (St Helens), Roberts (Halifax), Edgar (Workington T.), Flanagan (Hull K.R.), Clarke (Wigan), Watson (St Helens), Crewdson (Keighley), Ramsey (Hunslet), Mantle (St Helens), Bryant (Castleford), Fogarty (Halifax), Robinson (Swinton), Poole (Leeds). Managers were Messrs Wilf Spaven (Hull K.R.) and J. Errock (Oldham).

It had been quite a year for controversies of one kind and another, and the Australasian tour brought more. Some of the personal battles of 1963 spilled over into this series, and the Test series brought further refereeing disputes, with the British team feeling thoroughly aggrieved about their treatment at the hands of the appointed official in the vital second and third Tests.

The Australian referees' interpretation of the rules were frequently bones of contention in the early part of the tour, with British skipper Harry Poole occasionally involved verbally. The tourists suffered several defeats in the early stages, and it was a surprise when, in the first Test at Sydney on 25 June, Great Britain emerged victors by 17 points to 13.

Poole was unable to play because of tonsillitis, Robinson taking his place. It was not an inspiring or particularly exciting match, with Australia playing a robust forward game entirely lacking in the speedy attacking play that had characterized the 1963 Ashes tour of Britain.

Barnes kept Australia in the game with a series of penalties, but Britain scored tries through Watson, Hardisty and Burgess, with goals from Keegan (3) and Bishop. Banks got a late up-an-under try for Australia, and Barnes kicked five goals.

The referee for this game was Mr J. Bradley. For the second Test at Brisbane the Australian Board made a change, Mr C.

Pearce taking over. The change was greeted cynically by the British party, who felt that Mr Pearce's appointment presaged a strict Australian interpretation of the rules for the second Test.

In the event, Australia won 6—4 in a bruising, brawling, match and Ramsey, the British second row forward, was sent off after four minutes of the second half. At one stage Britain led 4—2, two goals against one, but two easy penalties, awarded near the posts, enabled Barnes to kick the Kangaroos to victory.

It was a third Test decider at Sydney, with Mr Pearce again nominated as referee. Before a 65 000 crowd Australia produced a better, more attacking performance to retain the Ashes by a score of 19 points to 14, but again defeat left a nasty taste in British mouths. Again Britain finished a man short, Watson being sent off after kicking at Dimond, and again controversy surrounded Australian scores, particularly a try by winger Irvine, which appeared to come after a knock-on. Irvine got a hat-trick of tries, and Lynch and King also crossed for Australia, with two goals from Johns. Britain kept in touch for most of the game despite Watson's dismissal, but fell away at the end. Hardisty scored two tries for Britain, Gowers landing four goals. The Kangaroos had retained the Ashes.

The tourists, licking their wounds, went to New Zealand, where they won both Tests comfortably. Again, however, there were refereeing difficulties. In the second Test at Auckland, referee John Percival penalized Britain 24 times to New Zealand's 8, and Harry Poole was again moved to dissent.

The 1966–7 season began without the returning tourists. It also began with a notable achievement by Bradford Northern, and a new ruling in force. Northern, due to the re-seeding of Odsal, played their first six matches away from home, and won them all.

The new ruling, surely associated with St Helens's tactics in the cup final, introduced the rule whereby a penalty kick could be taken into touch, with a play-the-ball to the non-offending side at the point of entry.

The play-the-ball rule was under continual fire, and at a management committee meeting Mr W. Fallowfield presented statistics regarding the number of play-the-balls in an average game, and 'serious concern' was expressed at the way sides kept possession. An experimental rule was introduced into the floodlit tournament, with a scrum after every three play-the-balls, the 'fourth-tackle rule'. The first result was an increase in scrums, hardly a desirable product.

Rugby League played its part in precipitating a social revolution in December 1966, when at a special general meeting of club representatives approval was given for Sunday football. Clubs voted for the right to stage League matches on Sundays despite the misgivings of a small minority of clubs who harboured religious and social objections to the move. The decision brought nearer the Friday night, Saturday and Sunday era of fixtures, with the threat of fixture congestion and confusion.

In addition, the experimental play-the-ball rule which had applied in floodlit competition was ratified for all competitions This called for a scrum after four consecutive tackles by defenders, unless the attacking side had kicked or otherwise given away possession. The search for fluidity of movement and the opening-up of play continued.

The internationals between Great Britain and France took Britain to Carcassonne on 22 January, and brought France's first defeat since January 1965. Great Britain, despite playing under the recently discontinued play-the-ball rule, won by 16 points to 13. The highlight was a brilliant try by Hull winger Clive Sullivan, who ran half the length of the field, beating four men by speed and swerve. Sullivan scored two tries, Hardisty two more, and Fox kicked two goals. France's points came from a try by Ferren, and five goals from Lacaze.

In the return at Wigan on 4 March, France won ample revenge, the score being 23 points to 13. With the scores at 13—13 Castleford forward Bill Bryant broke a leg, and with Hardisty also injured, Great Britain fell away. Keegan, Hardisty and Robinson scored tries, with two goals from Fox, while Clar, Marracq and Lecompte, with seven goals from Lacaze, were France's scorers.

In the Challenge Cup semi-finals Barrow beat the gallant Dewsbury side 14—9 at Swinton and Featherstone Rovers pulled off a major shock by beating the favourites Leeds at Huddersfield.

It was very much South Yorkshire's year in the battle for major honours in 1967. Wakefield Trinity took the championship, but only after two battles with St Helens. The first game at Headingley was drawn 7—7, but in the replay at Swinton in midweek, Trinity returned to their best form to win 21—9. Brooke (2), Owen, Poynton, and Hirst scored tries, and Fox kicked three goals. Vollenhoven scored a try for St Helens, with two goals from Killeen and a dropped goal from Bishop.

The Challenge Cup final brought a first-ever win for Featherstone with a surprisingly easy victory over a disappointing Barrow.

The teams were:

Featherstone Rovers: Wrigglesworth; Thomas, Cotton, Jordan, Greatorex; M. Smith, Dooler; Tonks, Harris, Dixon, Morgan, Thompson, Smales.

Barrow: Tees; Burgess, Challinor, Hughes, Murray; Brophy, G. Smith; Hopwood, Redhead, Kelland, Sanderson, Delooze, Watson.

Referee: Mr Eric Clay (Ossett).

Barrow started promisingly enough. After Smales had kicked a goal for Rovers, Delooze equalized with a similar effort, then a brilliant handling movement was superbly finished off under the posts by Brophy, and Delooze converted. However, Barrow faded, and a powerful, surging run by Morgan brought a try converted by Smales. Then Dooler dropped a smart goal, and gave Rovers a lead they never lost. Thomas and Smales added further tries, with a goal from Smales, and the Barrow scoreline was no more than improved by a last minute try by Watson, converted by Tees. It was 17—12 to Featherstone, and triumph for this splendid nursery of Rugby League players among the pithead winding engines.

Several amendments to the laws were made at the annual meeting at Leeds. The two really notable ones stated that after an unsuccessful drop goal attempt, the defending side could re-start with a play-the-ball on the '25', and that when a penalty try was awarded, the kick at goal would be from under the posts.

When the Australian tourists arrived in Britain in September 1967, they were seeking to become the first-ever Australian side to win three successive Tests series against Great Britain. They were managed by Messrs Jack Drewes and Harry Schmidt, and made an unpromising start to the tour with unimpressive displays against club sides.

The first Test was held at Headingley on 21 October, and this was hardly a propitious sign for the Kangaroos, since they had never won in eight Tests at the Leeds ground.

The teams were:

Great Britain: Keegan (Hull); Young (Hull K.R.), Price (Rochdale Hornets), Brooke (Wakefield Trinity), Burgess (Barrow); Millward (Hull K.R.), Bishop (St Helens); Holliday (Hull K.R.), Flanagan (Hull K.R.), Watson (St Helens), Mantle (St Helens), Irving (Oldham), Robinson (Swinton).

Australia: Johns; McDonald, Gasnier, Langlands, King; Gleeson, Smith; Gallagher, Kelly, Manteit, Lynch, Rasmussen, Raper.

Referee: Mr F. G. Lindop (Wakefield).

The Headingley hoodoo dogged the tourists once again, for injuries robbed them for the best part of the game of their two star men, Gasnier and Raper, and Great Britain made a healthy start to the series by winning 16—11. Indeed, Australia started with a try from King, but an apparently sound effort was disallowed by Mr Lindop for a forward pass. Britain then went into a 7—0 lead with a try from Young, converted by Millward, and a drop goal from Bishop. Australia hit back with a try and two goals from Langlands, but a brilliant, curving run by Millward brought him a try, which he converted. Millward added a penalty, as did Holliday, and Langlands provided two late penalties for Australia. To add to Australia's woes, Manteit was sent off.

The Rugby League made another propaganda gesture for the second Test. This was played at London's White City, on Friday, 3 November, under floodlights, avoiding clashes with soccer and international Rugby Union fixtures.

Australia had McDonald at centre for the injured Gasnier, Greaves on the wing, and Coote and Noel Gallagher in the pack for Manteit and Raper. On the British side Neil Fox returned at centre for Price, and Foster, of Hull Kingston Rovers, replaced Robinson. There was an alarm for Britain before the game, for Burgess cried off at the last minute with a leg injury. The reserve, Jordan (Featherstone) could not be contacted, and Wigan's Bill

Francis, answering an urgent telephone call, had to drive 200 miles to play on Britain's wing, hardly the best preparation for an international game.

A crowd approaching 20 000 saw Australia square the series with a score of 17 points to 11. Nevertheless, the Kangaroos only got in front and on top seventeen minutes from the end after Britain had twice led at 7—2 and 9—7. Bishop scored a try and Fox four goals for Great Britain, while Langlands, King and Coote scored tries for Australia, with Langlands kicking four goals.

Australia's search for a hat-trick of winning series came to fruition at Swinton on 9 December. Price, Jordan and Millward came into the British back division, with Valentine of Huddersfield getting a cap in the pack. Johnny Raper returned to give experience and guile to the Australian pack. It was not an outstanding game, and the only real satisfaction was obtained by the tourists, who won 11—3 and achieved their ambition. Coote, substitute Branson, and King scored tries for Australia, with a goal from Langlands. Millward made a fine try for Price for Great Britain, breaking from his own '25', but that was a rare flash of home brilliance to warm a crowd of 12 515.

After their success in Britain, Australia went off to France to figure in a great anti-climax.

After the first Test had been drawn at 7—7, France won the two remaining Tests by 10—3 and 16—13, and this took a great deal of the warmth out of the home reception for the tourists. Worse was to come, for after serious allegations of rowdyism and orgies of destruction by the tourists at the Ilkley Moor Hotel in Yorkshire, the Australian players were reprimanded, and their bonuses were reduced.

20

Sunday Football: Wales Revived

In mid-December came the major change in spectator habits that had been foreshadowed when Sunday football was sanctioned. The first senior games were held on Sunday, 16 December. They were Bradford Northern *v.* York, Featherstone *v.* Salford and Leigh *v.* Dewsbury, and with good attendances recorded, including over 10 000 at Bradford, the way was clear for regular Rugby League fixtures on the sabbath. The development produced a curio, for Bradford Northern and Doncaster later played two games each within 24 hours, a cup fixture on a Saturday in January, followed by a Sunday League game. Lucrative for the players, but exhausting.

The internationals between Great Britain and France turned form upside down. France, having thoroughly whacked the Aussies, were expected to beat Great Britain, but in Paris on 11 February the visitors won by 22 points to 13 in a fine, exciting game for which both teams had special training as they looked ahead to the 1968 World Cup. Millward, Risman (2) and Burwell got the British tries, and Risman five goals. Sabatie and Pellerin (2) scored tries for France, with two goals from Mantoulan.

Great Britain achieved the double at Bradford on 2 March in a less exciting game. Millward, Young, Burwell (2) and Morgan scored tries for Britain, and Risman two goals in a 19—8 win Mazard and Pellerin were try-scorers for France, Capdouze landing a goal.

The domestic season in Britain ended with the cup final at Wembley, and it produced the most dramatic and bizarre cup final ever, and certainly the most breath-catching finale. Leeds and Wakefield Trinity were the finalists, Leeds having beaten Wigan in the semi-final and Trinity beating Huddersfield.

People will talk about the 1968 cup final as long as Rugby League is talked about. A remarkable match of incident ranging from the farcical to the tragi-comic and back to the bizarre. An attendance of 90 000 saw the West Riding Derby at Wembley. Mr J. P. Hebblethwaite was the referee, and the teams were:

Leeds: Risman; Smith, Hynes, Watson, Atkinson; Shoebottom, Seabourne; Clark, Crosby, K. Eyre, Ramsey, A. Eyre, Batten.

Wakefield Trinity: Cooper; Hirst, Coetzer, Brooke, Batty; Poynton, Owen; Jeanes, Shepherd, D. Fox, Haigh, McLeod, Hawley.

Although the sun was shining in typical cup final fashion at the start of the game, there had been a prodigious thunderstorm shortly before three o'clock and both ground and spectators were soaked. The ground was consequently slick and skiddy, and players found it hard to keep their feet. Indeed, Trinity went ahead when Atkinson, moving across to tackle Hirst, slipped and the winger scored. Little sustained constructive football was possible, and the remaining scores of the first half were two goals from Don Fox for Wakefield and two from Risman for Leeds.

During half-time there was yet another monstrous deluge of rain, and the pitch became so waterlogged that many on the Wembley terraces were convinced that Mr Hebblethwaite would abandon the match. The official, obviously reluctant to make history in an unpopular and unsatisfactory manner, decided to play on, and the game was decided by the resultant aquatic farce. Leeds went into an 11—7 lead when Atkinson kicked ahead, and as everyone slithered about, appeared to be obstructed. Mr Hebblethwaite awarded a try, Risman converted it and Risman then added a penalty.

Then came the dramatic finish which is recorded for ever in television archives and in the memory of everyone who saw the game in the flesh or on TV. Straight from the kick-off from Risman's penalty, Hirst gathered and kicked ahead. Again defenders floundered and splashed as Hirst got his toe to the ball, sent it over the line, and made a spray-covered dive to touch down. It was 11—10 and the result depended on Don Fox's conversion.

It was so easy, alongside the posts, a formality. Fox placed the ball in the wet, stepped back, moved forward, slipped and sliced the ball wide. He buried his head in his hands, and Leeds defenders danced the Highland fling.

Consolation for the near-inconsolable Fox was the Lance Todd trophy.

The championship final had been held at Headingley on 4 May, Trinity receiving pre-consolation for cup defeat by beating Hull K.R. 17—10.

Attention now switched to Australia and New Zealand, where the first World Cup for eight years was to take place. The British party, captained by Bev Risman, was: D. Edwards (Castleford), C. Young (Hull K.R.), I. Brooke (Wakefield Trinity), A. Burwell (Hull K.R.), C. Sullivan (Hull), J. Atkinson (Leeds), R. Millward (Hull K.R.), T. Bishop (St Helens), M. Shoebottom (Leeds), M. Clark (Leeds), P. Flanagan (Hull K.R.), K. Ashcroft (Leigh), C. Watson (St Helens), R. French (Widnes), A. Morgan (Featherstone R.), J. Warlow (St Helens), R. Haigh (Wakefield Trinity), C. Renilson (Halifax). Managers were Messrs W. Fallowfield and C. Hutton (Hull K.R.).

It was reasonably predicted that Australia and Great Britain would once again work their respective ways through to the play-off, but this did not happen. The Great Britain side reacted bitterly to the handling of their first game, against Australia at Sydney. New Zealand referee John Percival applied the rules mercilessly against Britain, to the extent of awarding frequent 'double penalties', alleging that the Lions were slow to get back 10 yards after a penalty award. Simms, the Australian full-back, had a field day, kicking eight goals in Australia's 25—10 win. Smith, Raper and Coote scored tries for Australia, while Brooke and Sullivan touched down for Britain and Risman kicked two goals.

Worse was to come for Britain, for in their game against France at Auckland torrential rain reduced the pitch to a swamp, and France won 7—2, Ledru scoring a try, and Garrigues and Capdouze goals, against a Risman goal. Australia won all their games against Britain, France and New Zealand, scoring more than 30 points in each of their games against the latter two countries.

In the final at Sydney, France, who had also beaten New Zealand, met Australia and a crowd of 54 290 saw the expected easy win for the home country by 20 points to 2. Britain ended with a hollow consolation win, 38—14 against New Zealand at Sydney. Australia had retained the Ashes and won the World Cup.

Since good crowds had watched the series, particularly in Australia, the International Board countries considered a quick follow-up with a World Cup in Britain in 1969, but with France vacillating, and Australia slow to straighten the financial accounts for 1968, the suggestion petered out, and 1970 was agreed.

The constant search for a new and acceptable fixture formula brought a management committee proposal in October 1968, to split up the League into top-15 and bottom-15. There was yet again insufficient support, for this and for other formulae, at a special meeting of club representatives in November.

The revival of the Welsh international side came at Salford on Thursday, 7 November. For the first time since 1953 a side bearing the name of Wales appeared in an international fixture. The selectors had more than forty Rugby League-playing Welshmen to choose from, and they did their job well, since Wales beat England 24—17. England were 10 points down in eleven minutes and never got on terms. Dixon (Salford), Rees (St Helens), Watkins (Salford) and Sullivan (Hull) scored the Welsh tries, with six goals from Price (Bradford Northern). For England Atkinson, Taylor, Smith (2) and Watson scored tries, one goal coming from Jefferson.

A Great Britain side, with the Welshmen playing alongside the Englishmen, comfortably accounted for France at St Helens on 30 November. The score was 34 points to 10, Burgess getting a hat-trick of tries and Gemmell two.

The return game took place at Toulouse early in 1969, and France turned the tables in a 13 points to nine win.

The 1969 Challenge Cup final produced finalists who were making their first appearance at Wembley since the 30s. Castleford beat Wakefield Trinity 16—10 at Headingley and Salford's revival took them to the final when they beat Warrington 15—8 at Wigan in the other semi-final. In the Salford side was their latest big-fee signing from Rugby Union, England forward Mike Coulman, who joined Salford at a time when Wigan joined the big-name hunt by signing Welsh international winger Keri Jones.

A capacity crowd of 100 000 saw the final on 17 May. Unfortunately the spectacle was not commensurate with the size of the attendance, for neither Castleford nor Salford produced the scintillating attacking form that had been their trademark on the way to the final.

The teams were:

Castleford: Edwards; Briggs, Howe, Thomas, Lowndes; Hardisty, Hepworth; Hartley, Dickinson, Ward, Redfearn, Lockwood, Reilly.

Salford: Gwilliam; Burgess, Whitehead, Hesketh, Jackson; Watkins, Brennan; Ogden, Dickens, Bott, Coulman, Dixon, Hill.

Referee: Mr D. S. Brown (Preston).

Salford's hopes of outspeeding Castleford on the flanks suffered an early blow when Test winger Burgess was flattened by a heavy tackle and was reduced in effectiveness. Castleford's close marking similarly stifled all Salford's danger men, and with 'Cas' content to wait for the chances, the expected classic did not materialize. Hill gave Salford an early lead with a penalty goal, but a Hardisty pass sent Howe through two tackles for a Castleford try. Hill landed another penalty for Salford, but Castleford got a grip on the game when powerful loose forward Reilly, who later went to Australia for a considerable signing-on fee, blasted an opening for the fast supporting Hardisty. Redfearn converted, and although Hill kicked a third goal for Salford, Castleford got the clinching try through Hepworth after superb ball handling by Ward.

Castleford had won their way through to the championship final at Odsal, but their hopes of a double were dashed with four minutes to go. They were leading Yorkshire rivals Leeds 14—11, and seemed certain to secure the double, when Shoebottom broke through for Leeds, Risman gathered a loose ball and kicked ahead, and the ball bounced like a dog sitting up to beg for Atkinson. The Leeds winger went round near the posts and

Risman converted. Before that Dickinson and Hardisty had scored tries for Castleford, with three goals from Redfearn and a drop goal from Hardisty. Cowan scored a first half try for Leeds, with two goals from Risman, who added a third just after the interval to make the score 11—9 to Castleford. Ramsey's late drop goal for Leeds, making the score 14—11, proved vital in that last-gasp finish.

The substitute rule was taken a stage further in July. It was decided that a substitute could be allowed at any stage in the game, not merely after half time.

The three-cornered tournament between England, France and the revived Wales team, was October's replacement for the proposed World Cup tournament. It was not over-successful. Attendances were small, with TV again taking much of the blame, and the matches alternated between high-scoring exhibitions and low-scoring yawns.

Faced with alarming reports from some clubs of staggering declines in attendance, an extraordinary general meeting of clubs in November considered several proposals for re-structuring fixtures. The management committee suggested three divisions; Castleford two divisions, and Widnes three regional leagues. The Castleford proposal got most support, putting the age-old two-division controversy back on the agenda.

As an antidote to the gloom about attendances, secretary Mr W. Fallowfield, said that attendances in the first three months of the 1969–70 season were, in overall terms, higher than the corresponding period of 1968.

Star names were regarded as useful crowd-pullers and there were more big money forays into Wales. Barrow paid £14 000 to Keith Jarrett, the big international centre from Newport, and Leigh paid £6000 to secure Swansea and Welsh trialist full back Stuart Ferguson.

In December, 1969 the French Rugby League suggested that there should be a European championship play-off between the top four clubs in England and France. This was rejected by the English League on the grounds that there was a 'considerable difference in playing standards' between the two Leagues.

Whatever the difference in playing standards at League level, international matches between the countries could still provide upsets, vagaries and surprises.

The triangular tournament between England, France and Wales was held between January and March, 1970. The first game brought a major surprise, with Wales going to Perpignan on Sunday, 25 January and beating France 15—11, Sullivan (2) and Price getting tries, and Price three goals. However, this success had to take second place in the headlines behind the sensations as the match finished. Referee Mr Dickie Thomas, of Oldham, was attacked by spectators as he left the ground, knocked unconscious, and detained overnight in hospital. Later Mr Thomas declined to take action against the offenders, offering a stiff, and rather swollen, upper lip.

Topsy-turvey form continued, with England beating Wales 26—7 at Headingley on 24 February, and then losing to France 14—9 at Toulouse on 15 March. England won the tournament with the superior points average.

The 1970 cup final brought together Castleford, making their second successive appearance, and the ever-consistent Wigan, with St Helens and Hull K.R. the beaten semi-finalists. Once again the match was to prove a big disappointment, with an early incident clouding the whole game and aftermath.

Mr F. G. Lindop (Wakefield) was the referee, and the teams were:

Castleford: Edwards, Briggs, Thomas, Stanton, Lowndes; Hardisty, Hepworth; Hartley, Dickinson, Redfearn, Kirkbride, Lockwood, Reilly. sub. Hargrave.

Wigan: Tyrer; Jones, Francis, Rowe, O'Loughlin; D. Hill, Parr; Ashcroft, Burdell, Hogan, Ashurst, Robinson, Laughton. sub. C. Hill.

The unpleasant, and vital, incident occurred in the eighteenth minute when Tyrer, the Wigan full-back regarded as a key figure, was flattened by a late, high tackle from Hepworth and carried off the field with jaw injuries. He was replaced by Cliff Hill, but Wigan had lost their goal-kicker and surprise attacker, and it cost them dearly. Francis took over as goal-kicker, but missed a couple of simple kicks at vital stages. Castleford got the only try of a poor game when Reilly, Kirkbride, and Hepworth sent over

Lowndes while Redfearn kicked two penalty goals. Tyrer had kicked an early penalty for Wigan. Castleford had won the cup for the second successive year, but in controversial manner.

The Yorkshire side was involved in a further controversy, this time in more favourable light, during the championship semi-final with St Helens. After the teams had drawn at Castleford, the replay was fixed for Monday, five days before Wembley. Not surprisingly Castleford fielded a reserve team at St Helens, and almost pulled off the shock of the century. With seven minutes left, Castleford 'reserves' led 12—10 and only two desperate late tries by St Helens made sense of the game. St Helens went on to make no mistake in the championship final, playing superbly, with Myler the star, in beating Leeds 24—12 at Odsal.

This year of 1970 was a hectic one. Further meetings regarding fixture formulae were held, and a special general meeting turned aside the top-15/bottom-15 structure in favour of a more orthodox 16/14 structure. It was still uncertain when precisely the new formula would begin to operate.

The summer brought another Australasian tour, with Great Britain travelling out very much the underdogs under manager Jack Harding (Leigh) and his assistant John Whiteley (Hull).

The touring party was D. Edwards (Castleford), T. Price (Bradford Northern), R. Dutton (Widnes), J. Atkinson, A. Smith, S. Haynes, M. Shoebottom, B. Seabourne (Leeds), R. Millward (Hull K.R.), F. Myler, captain, (St Helens), C. Sullivan (Hull), K. Hepworth, A. Hardisty (Castleford); C. Watson (St Helens), J. Ward (Salford), D. Chisnall (Leigh), P. Flanagan, P. Lowe (Hull K.R.), A. Fisher (Bradford Northern), D. Hartley, M. Reilly (Castleford), D. Robinson, D. Laughton (Wigan), J. Thompson (Featherstone R.), R. Irving (Oldham).

The tourists swept through their opening matches, but were rudely shattered in the first Test at Brisbane on 6 June, which went very much according to plan for the Kangaroos. Australia thrashed Britain 37—15, walking through some pretty feeble tackling. Langlands kicked three penalties to set Australia going, and he eventually completed nine goals, with two drop goals from Hawthorne. The Australian tries came from Morgan (2), King (2) and McDonald. Britain's token efforts consisted of tries from Watson, Flanagan, and Laughton, with three goals from Price.

If there was trouble on the field, there was trouble off it, too, with Castleford's Malcolm Reilly involved in two incidents. In each case the big forward was said to have assaulted another man, once in a social club, and Mr Harding, the tour manager, fined him £75 after ruffled Australian feelings had been soothed with difficulty.

Things brightened for the British party in the second Test at Sydney on 20 June. Playing with great spirit and determination, Great Britain found the Australians in slipshod mood, and squared the series at 28—7 before a crowd of 60 692. Australia missed the injured Langlands, and could only manage a try by King, and goals by McDonald and Hawthorne. For Britain the star was Millward who scored two tries, kicked six goals from six attempts and dropped a goal for a record-equalling tally of 20 points. Atkinson and Fisher also got tries and Hynes a drop goal. One blemish to the display was that Hynes was sent off.

The build-up for the deciding Third Test at Sydney on 4 July was not too pleasant for Great Britain. Just before the Test a game was played at Wagga Wagga against Riverina, and such was the mayhem and skullduggery that tour manager Jack Harding was moved to say that Riverina had deliberately set out to maim members of the British Test side. 'We will never play here again,' he added.

However, things worked out well for the tourists with a third Test win that was much more convincing than a four-point margin, 21—17, would indicate. Britain, in fact, scored five tries to one and only a series of penalty goals from McKean, who landed seven goals from nine attempts, kept Australia in the match. McKean's kicking gave Australia an early lead, but once Hartley had charged down a kick and scored, Great Britain's fast, flowing attacking play produced the tries. Australia could only match this style with tough forward play, and Hepworth, Myler, Hynes and company easily outpaced these sort of tactics, with Millward again a particular thorn in Kangaroo flesh. Atkinson (2), Hynes and Millward scored further tries and Millward two goals. McCarthy got a late disputed try for Australia to make the score

18—17, a travesty of a scoreline, but Britain's fifth try made the score a genuine reflection of a one-sided Test.

The tour continued on a high note in New Zealand, all three Tests, at Auckland twice and Christchurch, being won by big margins, with the tourists twice coming from a nine points deficit to win handsomely.

Such splendid form boomeranged when it was learned in England that several members of the Test side had been given big financial inducements to join Australian clubs. The Rugby League expressed its displeasure, but the wedge had been driven firmly home.

There was only a brief respite from Test football, for the postponed World Cup tournament was held in Britain from 22 October to 7 November 1970.

The Australian party was without the injured Langlands, and after Britain's Ashes victory the home side began the series at short odds. The organizers were anxious to attract good crowds, both to justify the tournament and cover costs, although television was again present and the fees were expected to bridge any gap that might occur at the turnstiles.

Whether the television fees made up for the possibility of TV stay-aways, a continuous sore point among Rugby League clubs, remained arguable throughout the tourney. Specimen attendances of 3900 at Hull for France *v.* New Zealand and 6215 at Bradford for Australia *v.* France could hardly be termed successful. Even the Great Britain *v.* Australia play-off brought no more than 18 776 to Headingley, a good attendance by some Test standards but well below capacity.

This play-off came in unfortunate circumstances for Great Britain, who won all their three games, yet by the rules of the competition, had to play off against Australia. Australia's only win in the preliminaries was 47—11 against New Zealand before a crowd of 9586 at Wigan, but the Kangaroos won through on points average when France and New Zealand won one game each.

The final was doubly unfortunate for the home team. Not merely did they lose, they did so in a brawling, punching, fighting match that was no credit to the code.

Players fought out personal rivalries, echoes perhaps of the tour, and there were many ugly mêlées. It was 1960 at Odsal all over again. In the fracas, Australia, the better side on a not very auspicious day, won the game and the cup. Cootes and Williamson got tries, with three goals from Simms. Atkinson got a late try for Great Britain, Dutton kicking a penalty and Hynes dropping a goal.

The attendances at the matches may well have been one of the reasons for a December outburst by a Hull K.R. director Mr Ron Chester, who declared that television presented the game as 'comic relief', and that the game was being adapted to the requirements of television.

21

Sponsorship, Two Divisions, Six Tackles

WHEN France beat Great Britain 16—8 at Toulouse in February 1971, a French referee officiated. Britain had decided to revert to the principle of a home referee on the grounds that French referees' control of games in England had not always been of the desired quality.

The 1971 Challenge Cup brought a major surprise through the appearance in the final of Leigh for the first time in fifty years. They beat Huddersfield 10—4 in a drab semi-final at Wigan, while the star-studded Leeds outfit beat Castleford's attempt at three in a row by winning 19—8 at Odsal.

Leigh's inspiration was the brilliant, aggressive, cunning and vastly experienced Alex Murphy, the former St Helens and Great Britain half-back who was coaching and leading the Lancashire side. Before the Wembley game he oozed confidence, a confidence assisted by the fact that Leeds were without the injured Shoebottom, Smith and Batten.

Mr W. H. Thompson (Huddersfield) was referee, and the teams were:

Leeds: Holmes; Langley, Hynes, Cowan, Atkinson; Wainwright, Seabourne; Burke, Fisher, Barnard, Hick, Haigh, Ramsey. Subs.: Dyl, Cookson.

Leigh: Eckersley; Ferguson, Dorrington, Collins, Walsh; Barrow, Murphy; Watts, Ashcroft, Fiddler, Grimes, Clarkson, Smethurst. Subs.: L. Chisnall, Lester.

Murphy's optimism was totally and crushingly justified as injury-hit Leeds failed to find any sort of cohesion, and Leigh enjoyed themselves in a 24—7 victory. Although Leigh scored only two tries, with five goals and four drop goals, they were always comfortably in front, and Murphy out-generalled his opposite numbers. In fact, Hynes became so exasperated by Murphy's tactics that he was involved in an incident with the Leigh coach, and when Murphy fell to the ground as if poleaxed, was ordered off the field. Dorrington and Eckersley, by a brilliant late run, scored the Leigh tries, with five goals from Ferguson, and drop goals from Murphy (2) Fiddler and Eckersley.

Ferguson became the third British player to score in every game of a season.

For Leeds, Wainwright scored a try and Holmes kicked two goals. The great and much-celebrated Leigh victory had a somewhat deflating aftermath, for Murphy signed as player-coach for Warrington almost immediately.

The championship final brought a piece of desperately bad luck for Wigan. In the final at Swinton they led St Helens 12—11 in the last seconds of the game, and deservedly so. Walsh, the St Helens centre, tried a drop goal attempt which swerved yards wide, only to bounce on the Wigan line and plop into the waiting arms of fellow centre Benyon, who scored for Coslett to convert. It was a cruel blow for Wigan, who claimed that Benyon was yards offside in accepting the lucky chance.

The movement towards a further two-divisions scheme was becoming a hardy monthly, and the annual meeting discussed it in June. Bradford proposed the latest scheme, but the move was defeated. However, the two-division momentum was gathering pace, and the management committee sent out circulars testing club reaction in late 1971. Replies were 'encouraging.'

Sponsorship in Rugby League arrived as a major force in 1971–2. There had been some sponsorship of smaller competitions, but a total of £11 000 was pumped into the game as prize money by the John Player organization. Another knockout competition, to be played in the early part of the season, was the result, with a first prize of £3000. The money and the incentive were welcome, but the county cups had to be brought forward to accommodate the John Player Trophy, and Leeds promptly opted out of the Yorkshire Cup on the grounds that it was too early. Leeds were censured for their action.

Two events shook the world of Rugby League in 1971. One

was the Caine Report, the other the unexpected Test series success of New Zealand.

The Caine Report, named after the Manchester public relations company, John Caine Associates, was a commissioned series of recommendations and observations, made at the behest of the Rugby League.

The report was presented to the full Council in two stages, a preliminary survey followed by a document titled *The Future.* The first report cited the problems of lack of good communications, and poor public relations, and also criticized the presentation of the game on television. *The Future* went into detail with recommendations including a change to Sunday Rugby League; the formation of two or more divisions; the introduction of a six-tackle rule, and the publication of a regular magazine. It also went further in its criticism of TV presentation. Ironically, although the Caine Report was not exactly received with acclamation in some official quarters, all main recommendations were ultimately accepted in whole or part.

The telephone and newspaper wires hummed for some considerable time after the publication of the report, with more than a degree of acrimony. Mr Eddie Waring gave a spirited defence of his commentary technique, stating that he had received no complaints from official Rugby League sources in nearly twenty years of commentating, and had helped introduce Rugby League to an audience well beyond the North of England.

The Test series brought the first-ever win by a full Kiwi team in England. The 1907–8 tourists had won a series, but this party had included several Australians.

In the first Test at Salford on 25 September, New Zealand won 18—13, a victory all the more surprising in that several club matches had been lost before the Test. Britain were foiled by fierce, keen tackling and lively handling, as well as their own disjointed form.

Williams, Whitaker, P. Orchard and R. Orchard scored the tourists' tries, Tatana landing three goals. Great Britain scored tries through Benyon, Ashurst and Hesketh with two goals from Whitehead.

The second Test at Castleford on 16 October confirmed the

evidence of the first, but the Kiwis' series-winning victory aroused enormous controversy. Great Britain players' claimed that they were unlucky to get the rough edge of referee Deryk Brown's most difficult decisions. Britain led 11—0 at one stage, but New Zealand fought back to 11—10. Then the controversial judgments began. Walsh and Benyon, of Great Britain, had touchdowns disallowed for 'failing to ground properly' and P. Orchard was given a try for New Zealand when the British players were convinced he had stepped into touch. To make matters worse for the home side, Haigh broke an arm. New Zealand won 17—14, P. Orchard (2) and Tatana getting tries, and Tatana four goals. Coulman, Walsh, Millward and Sullivan got Britain's tries, with but one goal from Watkins.

The third Test at Headingley on 6 November brought minor consolation for Britain in a 12—3 win, but it was not a sparkling game. Atkinson scored two tries and Holmes three goals for Britain, Greengrass a try for New Zealand.

If the results were bad for Britain the attendances were equally staggering. They totalled 3764 at Salford, 4108 at Castleford and 5479 at Headingley.

The New Zealanders completed a triumphant tour by winning two and drawing one of their games in France.

In the Challenge Cup, Leeds reached the final for the second successive year, and faced St Helens in an attractive inter-county battle. Leeds had beaten Halifax in the semi-final, while St Helens beat Warrington after a replay.

The game was played at Wembley on Saturday, 13 May, with Mr E. Lawrinson (Warrington) as referee.
The teams were:

Leeds: Holmes; Smith, Hynes, Dyl, Atkinson; Hardisty, Hepworth; Clawson, Fisher, Ramsey, Cookson, Haigh, Batten. Subs.: Langley, Eccles.

St Helens: Pimblett; Jones, Benyon, Walsh, Wilson; Kelly, Heaton; Rees, Greenall, Stephens, Mantle, Chisnall, Coslett.

For the second successive year Leeds frustrated and disappointed their followers. It was another below-average display, and a particularly bad afternoon for goal-kicking forward Terry

Clawson, who had a most unhappy time, missing several easy kicks, including one from in front of the posts.

St Helens, skilful and composed as ever, ran in tries through Rees and Jones, and Coslett kicked three goals, while Clawson managed three goals from a seeming multitude of chances. It was 12—6 at half-time, then Cookson scored a try under the posts, and Clawson missed the most crucial and easy kick of all. Leeds' chance had gone, and although Coslett and Clawson each landed two more goals, St Helens won 16—13. However, Clawson's pride was repaired, along with that of the whole Leeds side, when in the championship final at Swinton Leeds beat St Helens 9—5, Clawson landing three fine goals, including a touchline conversion of a try by Atkinson.

The Great Britain *v.* France Test matches, regarded as trial horses for the proposed 1972 World Cup in France, resulted in a fine double for Britain, 10—9 at Toulouse and a sweeping 45—10 at Bradford.

The two-divisions serial story went one stage further with a meeting of clubs in March at which St Helens and Wigan sponsored the move. Surprisingly, the vote was 18—11 against, but the fight for two divisions continued with vigour.

The summer of 1972 brought further depressing news from Hunslet, the club whose directors, faced with mounting losses and gates of under 1000, were contemplating selling the Parkside ground and moving to Leeds Greyhound Stadium. Hunslet reported debts of £16 500 and borrowed £10 000 from the Rugby League.

Season 1972–3 began with the introduction of the six-tackle rule in place of the existing four-tackle rule. This meant that a scrum or change of possession had to take place after the sixth successive tackle by one side, and was designed to give sides more time to develop attacks.

Another major development was the introduction of the Australia-style system of having timekeepers at matches with a hooter to signal the end of the game. This system took a great deal of responsibility from referees, and avoided arguments, often fierce, about time allowed for stoppages.

The 1972 World Cup was played in France in October and

November. After their defeat at the hands of New Zealand, and failure at the last fence in 1970, the Great Britain side stood well behind Australia in the ante-post betting. But, as in 1954 when a young, scratch side triumphed, Great Britain upset the odds. In their first game Britain beat Australia at Perpignan by 27—21 in a magnificently thrilling game. The Aussies, who had been given special training for the World Cup, were leading 21—17 in a pulsating match when Nicholls put in a superb kick which enabled his Widnes team-mate O'Neill to gather and score. Then hooker Mick Stephenson scored near the posts, and with both goals kicked Britain had won. In this game the French referee M. Teissere had pundits reaching for their rule books. After Atkinson had gone round near the posts for a try, converted by Clawson, he awarded Britain a penalty at the half-way line because Elford had lunged dangerously at Atkinson over the line. Clawson kicked the goal for the first seven-point try.

France beat New Zealand 20—9 in their opening game, and then Britain beat France at Grenoble by 13 points to 4. True to form, Australia beat New Zealand 9—5 in Paris, though not convincingly, and it must have been a tremendous psychological boost for Britain when New Zealand were put to the sword by the Lions to the tune of 53—19 at Pau, with Holmes (Leeds) setting up a world individual record of 26 points, two tries and ten goals.

Australia qualified to meet Britain in the final by beating France comfortably at Toulouse, although there was an amazing incident involving the English referee, Mr Mick Naughton of Widnes, and a French touch judge. Australia scored what appeared a perfectly good try by Branighan. The French touch judge put up his flag for some offence, foot in touch the likely one. There was a five-minute argument in midfield between Mr Naughton and French officials, the touch judge threatened to leave the field, and the Aussie skipper, Graeme Langlands was consulted before the try was disallowed. Justice triumphed when Australia later ran away with the game 31—9.

The final at Lyons gave Australia the opportunity for revenge. It proved a bruising, bitter battle, as many of these games had done in the past, and when the game was drawn 10—10 after extra time, Britain won back the trophy on a superior points average. Clawson kicked a penalty for Britain, then O'Neill, a powerful forward, raced 25 yards to score, with Branighan converting. Australia hammered at the British line, but lost possession, and British winger Sullivan gathered the ball to race 80 yards, pursued by half-a-dozen Kangaroos, to touch down. Beetson restored the Australian lead with a try, converted by Branighan, but a great fight back by Britain saw hooker Stephenson back up brilliantly to take a pass from Lockwood and score, Clawson converting to equalize. There were no further scores in extra time, but it was a tense twenty minutes.

The British win was a great fillip for the game in England, while defeat for Australia, who had trained so hard and so confidently, was a bitter pill.

Perhaps a crumb of consolation could be obtained 'down under' from the brilliant performances of a pioneer team of touring Australian schoolboys, who came to Britain in December. The High Schools' tour romped through a twelve match itinerary, including three Tests at Wigan, Wakefield and in pioneer land at Hayes, Middlesex, and won all twelve with a points aggregate of 402 against 17. The Australian boys were, on average, bigger and slightly older than the English boys because of a difference in schools' leaving ages, but even allowing for this, they played superb rugby, and deserved both bigger gates and a greater share of publicity.

On 16 February 1973, yet another special general meeting was called to decide on a two-divisions scheme or alternative structure. The meeting was held at Salford, whose chairman, Mr Brian Snape, had actually put forward an earlier scheme for three divisions. This time the vote was in favour, and it was agreed that a two-division scheme, top-16 and bottom-14, would operate in season 1973–4, with a four up and four down system. This latter decision proved controversial, for clubs foresaw an undignified scramble for survival in the bottom half of the first division.

The 1973 Challenge Cup final was very much a Yorkshire affair, with four Yorkshire clubs fighting out the semi-finals. Bradford Northern beat Dewsbury and Featherstone Rovers beat Castleford in the semi-finals. Although the Wembley attendance in May was 74 000, some 25 000 below capacity, receipts were a world record for a Rugby League game at £125 000.

Mr Mick Naughton (Widnes), who had made a big name in the World Cup, was referee, and the teams were:

Bradford Northern: Tees; Lamb, Stockwell, Watson, Redfearn Blacker, Seabourne; Hogan, Dunn, Earl, Joyce, Pattinson, Fearnley. Subs.: Long, Treasure.

Featherstone Rovers: C. Kellett; Covenby, M. Smith, Newlove, K. Kellett; Mason, Nash; Tonks, Bridges, Farrar, Thompson, Rhodes, Stone. Subs.: Hartley, Hollis.

This was a final for records. It produced the highest-ever points tally in a Challenge Cup final, and a record-breaking goalkicking performance from the veteran Cyril Kellett, of Featherstone.

As a contest the match was finished within twenty minutes. In that time a rousingly confident Featherstone side ran up 17 points against a nervous, hesitant, fumbling Northern. Brilliant backing-up by centre Newlove brought him two tries, and a powerful charge from forward Farrar, a real pocket battleship of a man, brought the third, with four goals from Kellett.

Northern substituted Long for Earl, and attempted to get to grips with a game which had already run away from them. However, they could manage only three penalty goals from Tees before half-time.

The second half was much more of a contest, with both sides throwing the ball about freely. Points flowed to each side in turn, though it was always obvious that Rovers had something in reserve if required. Mick Smith scored a superb individual try for Featherstone, beating half the Bradford team, and Hartley, a substitute, also got on the scoring sheet. Kellett completed eight goals in eight shots, a record, and Nash dropped a goal. Redfearn and Fearnley scored tries for fighting Bradford, and Tees kicked another goal.

The championship final brought one of those major surprises that are the life blood of any sport. The unfancied Dewsbury side fought through to the final to face Leeds. After being slaughtered earlier in the season by Leeds in the Yorkshire Cup, Dewsbury played an inspired game, led by hooker and inspiration Mick Stephenson, and won 22—13, with Stephenson scoring a brilliant individual try, and the other Stephenson, Nigel, getting a try and five goals. It was unfortunate for Leeds that Alan Hardisty was sent off for the first time in a distinguished and non-controversial career, but Dewsbury were better on the day.

It was quite a season for records. David Watkins, Salford and former Wales Rugby Union skipper, set up a new world season goal-kicking record by landing 221 and beating Bernard Ganley's haul of 219.

The new season of 1973–4 held promise of a new two-divisions scheme, the second in just over a decade, and the visit of the Australian touring team thirsting for revenge for World Cup defeat.

The arrival of two divisions created an attendance pattern similar to that of 1962. Top First Division games drew crowds, while bottom Second Division games had wretched attendances. These latter figures cast serious doubts on the ability of some small clubs to survive.

One club which survived most bravely was Hunslet. The Parkside ground had been sold by the previous directors, yet a nucleus of players led by long-serving player Geoff Gunney, backed by some keen, generous and optimistic Leeds businessmen, opened up as New Hunslet at Leeds Greyhound Stadium, with limited success but happily unlimited enthusiasm and ambition.

The arrival of the Australian party caused some consternation at League headquarters. Anxious to have the tour over and finished by Christmas, the Kangaroo party had left their precise time of arrival in England in some doubt right up to the last minute. They arrived, in fact, on Monday, 24 September, and took up residence in a Huddersfield hotel.

There were more controversies to come. Australian manager Mr Charlie Gibson complained that the fixtures had been badly arranged, with games often conflicting with attractive nearby League fixtures. In addition, the tourists created a stir by insisting that the first Test should be at Wembley Stadium rather than at Wigan. Mr Gibson felt, and declared, that there were sufficient Australians in London to justify the propaganda, and anticipated a crowd of 30 000. The Australians were anxious to play a game at the showplace of the Commonwealth.

The plan, and high hopes, misfired. Whether it was lack of adequate publicity, or the fact that television covered the game, or merely southern apathy, only 10 000 turned up, and Mr Gibson's gravest criticism afterwards was directed against TV.

The match was played on 3 November, and Great Britain upset the odds by beating the Australians, who had successfully marched through their club games, by 21—12. Lowe, the big Hull K.R. forward, was outstanding in a magnificent British pack performance, and scored two tries. Hooker Clarke also went over, and Lockwood, in the second row, made it a happy afternoon for the Lions' pack with the fourth try. Clawson kicked four goals, and Nash got a drop goal, worth one point.

For a staggered Australia, Branighan and Fulton scored tries and Langlands three goals. Australia at one stage fought back to 14—12, but a tremendous try by Lowe finished them.

The Kangaroos, however, had learned their lessons well. They made six changes for the second Test at Headingley, including an enforced one, Eadie for the injured Langlands at full back. On a wild, windy and gale-ridden day, Australia squared the series at 14—6, Lockwood, the British second row forward, getting marching orders. McCarthy scored a try for Australia, with five goals from Eadie and a one-point drop goal from Fulton. The attendance was 16 000.

The third Test was played at Warrington, and brought further argument and controversy. The ground was frozen solid, and there were many who felt the game should not be played on such a hard surface. However, the Australians had their tight itinerary, and were anxious to play, and after much discussion, the decision to go ahead with the game came about twenty-five minutes before the kick-off. On the rocklike surface, before a crowd of 10 000, Great Britain where never able to get to grips, and an early interception try by Fulton set the pattern.

The man who sent out the stray pass, Terry Clawson, had left his goal-kicking boots behind, quite literally, and had to play in a borrowed pair.

With Fulton the fearless inspiration, Australia won with ease.

In fact, they scored five tries to Britain's one, and only the fact that no goals were kicked by Australia kept down the score to 15—5. Millward got Britain's consolation try, and Clawson kicked a goal.

In a tour of continuing controversy, Australia had won back the Ashes, and had gained revenge for World Cup defeat.

Also, Australia seemed to be slowly winning off-the-field battles. Big financial inducements to British players had long been in the pipeline, and among star names who accepted appetizing bait to join Australian clubs were Mick Stephenson (Dewsbury), Doug Laughton (Widnes), Bill Ashurst (Wigan), Phil Lowe (Hull K.R.), and Alan Hardisty (Leeds), with more threatened as Australia skimmed the cream off British Rugby League.

However, the League soldiered on, with a new sponsored competition, the Captain Morgan Trophy, which congested fixtures still more, but whipped up undoubted interest.

The televised floodlit trophy brought a welcome new winner. Bramley, the small Yorkshire club in the shadow of Leeds for ninety-four years, emerged from those shadows to beat Widnes at Naughton Park and win their first-every trophy. Except in Widnes, the victory was widely celebrated.

Big-money signings from Rugby Union helped stimulate interest, too, with Keith Fielding, England winger, joining Salford, and British Lions' star winger, the welsh John Bevan, joining the equally enterprising Warrington. Fielding went to the top of the try-scoring table, and Bevan scored four tries in a match as they justified their fees.

In fact, Salford and Warrington could quite reasonably claim that their considerable outlay on signing-on fees was amply recouped in the first season. Fielding's 49 tries helped Salford win the First Division Championship and John Bevan's 22 tries helped Warrington towards a mammoth haul of four major trophies in a season.

In January, 1974, Jim Challinor was appointed coach to the Great Britain side to tour Australasia, and Reg Parker, former Barrow forward and Blackpool Borough director, was appointed team manager.

Because of the Australasian tour, the Test matches against

France assumed the mantle of Test trials. In the first game at Grenoble on Sunday, January 20th, Great Britain won by 24 points to 5, with the highly successful Rugby Union convert Fielding getting a hat-trick of tries. In the return game at Wigan in February, Great Britain won easily by 29 points to nil. Charlton (2), Redfearn (2), Laughton, Willicombe and Gray scored tries, with two goals from Clawson, and one each from Gray and Watkins.

The search for the ideal scoring formula, a quest over half a century old, continued at an international committee meeting in January, whose recommendations were later endorsed at Council level. It was recommended that a try should be worth four points instead of three, and that the value of a drop goal should be reduced to one point, as it had been in the Great Britain v. Australia Tests. The number of tackles before a scrum or change of possession also came under discussion. A reduction from six to four was first to be mooted, and at a later date a proposal to introduce a three-tackle rule was given strong support.

A further proposal of mildly revolutionary import was that the scrum formation should rule out the "detached" loose forward. The back row of the scrum was to consist of three men behind the front row, with the scrum half leaning one hand against the back row before the emergence of the ball.

In the major competitions of 1973–74, Warrington swept the board under the highly controversial leadership of Alex Murphy, whose own printed boast that he was "the finest player of the last 10 years" was amply justified, though not always attractively.

The remarkable career of the volatile Murphy had taken him to Australasia as a precocious 17-year-old Test player, to League and Cup successes with St. Helens, and to Challenge Cup success with Leigh. Brought by wealthy industrialist Mr. Ossie Davies to Wilderspool Stadium, he dragged Warrington upwards from a mediocre outfit with a great tradition, and led them to victory in the John Player, Captain Morgan, Challenge Cup and Club Championship finals.

Yet, such is the nature and personality of Murphy, undoubtedly one of the greatest and most charismatic players ever to play

Rugby League, that considerable controversy and ill-feeling was aroused by Warrington's success.

Murphy, an experienced tactician, created a ruthlessly functional side consisting of a fierce, marauding, spoiling pack, behind which Murphy's tactical manoeuvres created drop goals and sudden, unexpected try-scoring bursts of open football. Unfortunately for Warrington's popularity, the emphasis on bruising forward play, and preference for tactics rather than spectacular back play, irritated both opponents and spectators.

This was amply demonstrated in the Wembley Cup Final, watched by 8 oooo people who paid record receipts of £131 000. The referee was Mr. Sam Shepherd, of Oldham, and the teams were:—

Featherstone Rovers:—Box; Dyas, Smith, Hartley, Bray; Newlove, Nash; Tonks, Bridges, Harris, Thompson, Rhodes, Bell.

Warrington:—Whitehead; M. Philbin, Noonan, Whittle, Bevan; Murphy, Gordon, Brady, Ashcroft, Chisnall, Wright, Nicholas, B. Philbin.

Featherstone were seeking their second consecutive trophy, and at half-time they led 9–8, scoring the only try of the first half when Murphy was off the field injured. Whitehead had landed four goals for Warrington, one from half way, and Box two for Featherstone. Murphy came back for the injured Gordon after the interval, and immediately took the game by the scruff of the neck, making a try for Ashcroft within three minutes. Featherstone never got back into the game, and with Whitehead kicking three goals, Murphy typically dropping two, and Nicholas storming over for a try, Warrington won 24–9. However, it was not an attractive performance by Warrington, and ill-feeling reached such a pitch that in one second half brawl, a dozen players punched and wrestled, Tonks and Bridges left the field injured, the latter unconscious, and Nicholas and Thompson were also hurt.

Several days after the game letters were sent by the Rugby League to both clubs deploring unsavoury incidents, and David Watkins, Salford skipper, attacked Murphy for his concentration on victory at the expense of open football.

Needless to say, this elicited a tart reply from Murphy, who said that Rugby League was not a game for girls, and that he would only use "fancy" players like Salford's Watkins if the game was "tig-and-pass".

A week after Wembley, in a game which produced many more thrills and much more open football, Warrington made it four major trophies by beating St. Helens 13–12 in the championship final, the climax of a rather weird "merit competition". The fixtures had been arranged according to a points system awarded for successes in previous competitions of the season.

The match was played at Central Park, Wigan, before 18 000 spectators. Warrington led 13–7 with 20 minutes to go, having scored tries from Mike Philbin, Brady and Noonan, plus two goals from Whitehead, against a try from Wilson and two goals from Coslett. Then Wilson got a second try for St. Helens, goaled brilliantly by Coslett to make the score 13–12, and there was a cliff-hanging 20 minutes before the whistle finally blew and Murphy was again hoisted shoulder high by Warrington supporters. The amazing Alex had threatened to retire from playing, but not everyone took the threat seriously. Indeed, such a player and personality, however controversial, would be hard to replace.

The final act of the 1973–74 season was the departure of the tourists. Missing were Laughton, who had joined the emigration exodus to Australian teams, Fielding, who dropped out for business reasons, and the unfortunate Nicholas, injured in the cup final.

The party which flew out to attempt to regain the Ashes was: Backs: K. Willicombe (Wigan), C. Hesketh, capt., P. Charlton, D. Watkins, K. Gill (Salford), F. Eckersley (St. Helens), J. Butler (Rochdale Hornets), D. Redfearn (Bradford N.), J. Bevan (Warrington), J. Atkinson, L. Dyl (Leeds), R. Millward (Hull K.R.), A. Bates (Dewsbury), S. Nash (Featherstone Rovers). Forwards: T. Clawson (Oldham), J. Gray (Wigan), J. Mills (Widnes), G. Nicholls, E. Chisnall (St. Helens), J. Bridges, J. Bates, J. Thompson (Featherstone Rovers), K. Ashcroft (Warrington), C. Dixon (Salford), P. Rose (Hull K.R.), S. Norton (Castleford).

The party included brothers John and Alan Bates of Dewsbury, and two of the three outstanding signings from Rugby Union, Fielding, Bevan and Gray.

The end of the season brought to an end a great career in Rugby League administration. Mr. William (Bill) Fallowfield retired after 28 years as secretary, maintaining the remarkable longevity of the office. He was replaced by Mr. David Oxley, like Mr. Fallowfield an M.A., from the Duke of York Military School in Dover.

The effort to introduce a four-point try failed at the League's annual meeting in June, but the value of a dropped goal was reduced to one point. An attempt by Halifax to revert to one division was defeated.

In the Australian Tests, an injury-strewn Britain lost the first at Brisbane 12—6, but fought back magnificently, with the injured Gray the hero, to square the series by a score of 14—11 at Sydney.

However, in the closely fought Sydney decider on July 20, Australia won the series, beating Great Britain by 22 points to 18. Australian referee Keith Page gave Australia a second half spate of penalties in vital positions, and Australia took the ascendancy while Britain crumbled. Langlands crowned a great career by completing over 100 points in tests against Britain, but British tour manager Reg Parker gave a telling and justifiable postscript: 'After this we will have neutral referees in World Championships.'

Appendix

Chairmen of the Rugby League Council

1895–7: H. H. Waller, Brighouse Rangers
1897–8: J. E. Warren, Warrington
1898–1900: J. H. Smith, Widnes
1900–1: H. Hutchinson, Leeds
1901–2: J. H. Houghton, St Helens
1902–3: J. Clifford, Huddersfield
1903–4: R. Collinge, Rochdale Hornets
1904–5: F. Lister, Bradford
1905–6: J. H. Smith, Widnes
1906–7: J. B. Cooke, Wakefield Trinity
1907–8: H. Ashton, Warrington
1908–9: J. Nicholl, Halifax
1909–10: J. H. Houghton, St Helens
1910–11: J. Wood, Leeds
1911–12: G. Taylor, Wigan
1912–13: W. D. Lyon, Hull
1913–20: J. H. Smith, Widnes
1920–2: W. Fillan, Huddersfield
1922–3: J. Counsell, Wigan
1923–4: J. H. Dannatt, Hull
1924–5: R. Gale, Leigh
1925–6: J. F. Whitaker, Batley
1926–7: E. Osborne, Warrington
1927–8: C. Preston, Dewsbury
1928–9: F. Kennedy, Broughton Rangers
1929–30: W. J. Lingard, Halifax
1930–1: F. Mattinson, Salford
1931–2: E. Brown, Millom (Cumberland)
1932–3: W. Popplewell, Bramley
1933–4: W. M. Gabbatt, Barrow
1934–5: J. Lewthwaite, Hunslet

1935–6: T. Ashcroft, St Helens Recs.
1936–8: A. A. Bonner, Wakefield Trinity
1938–40: G. F. Hutchins, Oldham
1940–2: A. Townsend, Leeds
1942–5: R. F. Anderton, Warrington
1945–6: R. Lockwood, Huddersfield
1946–7: W. H. Hughes, Salford
1947–8: W. A. Crockford, Hull Kingston Rovers
1948–9: T. Brown, Liverpool Stanley
1949–50: H. Hornby, Bradford Northern
1950–1: A. Widdeson, E. Lancs. Amateur Representative
1951–2: Sir Edwin Airey, Leeds
1952–3: B. Manson, Swinton
1953–4: C. W. Robinson, York
1954–5: J. Hilton, Leigh
1955–6: G. Oldroyd, Dewsbury
1956–7: H. E. Rawson, Hunslet
1957–8: C. E. Horsfall, Halifax
1958–9: F. Ridgway, Oldham
1959–60: W. Cunningham, Huddersfield
1960–1: J. S. Barritt, Bradford Northern
1961–2: T. Mitchell, Workington
1962–3: W. Spaven, Hull Kingston Rovers
1963–4: Dr H. Roebuck, Liverpool City
1964–5: A. Walker, Rochdale Hornets
1965–6: A. B. Sharman, Leeds
1966–7: J. B. Harding, Leigh
1967–8: J. N. Smallwood, Keighley
1968–9: J. Jepson, Featherstone Rovers
1969–70: J. J. Davies, Widnes
1970–1–2: H. Lockwood, Huddersfield
1972–3: R. Simpson, Castleford
1973–4: G. B. Snape (Salford)

Challenge Cup Finals (1897–1974)

YEAR	WINNERS	RUNNERS-UP	VENUE
1897	Batley	St Helens	Leeds
1898	Batley	Bradford	Leeds
1899	Oldham	Hunslet	Fallowfield
1900	Swinton	Salford	Fallowfield

YEAR	WINNERS	RUNNERS-UP	VENUE
1901	Batley	Warrington	Leeds
1902	Broughton R.	Salford	Rochdale
1903	Halifax	Salford	Leeds
1904	Halifax	Warrington	Salford
1905	Warrington	Hull K.R.	Leeds
1906	Bradford	Salford	Leeds
1907	Warrington	Oldham	Broughton
1908	Hunslet	Hull	Huddersfield
1909	Wakefield T.	Hull	Leeds
1910	Leeds	Hull	Huddersfield
Replay:	Leeds	Hull	Huddersfield
1911	Broughton R.	Wigan	Salford
1912	Dewsbury	Oldham	Leeds
1913	Huddersfield	Warrington	Leeds
1914	Hull	Wakefield T.	Halifax
1915	Huddersfield	St Helens	Oldham
1916–19	No competition		
1920	Huddersfield	Wigan	Leeds
1921	Leigh	Halifax	Broughton
1922	Rochdale H.	Hull	Leeds
1923	Leeds	Hull	Wakefield
1924	Wigan	Oldham	Rochdale
1925	Oldham	Hull K.R.	Leeds
1926	Swinton	Oldham	Rochdale
1927	Oldham	Swinton	Wigan
1928	Swinton	Warrington	Wigan
1929	Wigan	Dewsbury	Wembley
1930	Widnes	St Helens	Wembley
1931	Halifax	York	Wembley
1932	Leeds	Swinton	Wigan
1933	Huddersfield	Warrington	Wembley
1934	Hunslet	Widnes	Wembley
1935	Castleford	Huddersfield	Wembley
1936	Leeds	Warrington	Wembley
1937	Widnes	Keighley	Wembley
1938	Salford	Barrow	Wembley
1939	Halifax	Salford	Wembley
1940	No competition		
1941	Leeds	Halifax	Odsal
1942	Leeds	Halifax	Odsal

YEAR	WINNERS	RUNNERS-UP	VENUE
1943	Dewsbury	Leeds	Dewsbury and Leeds (two-leg)
1944	Bradford N.	Wigan	Bradford and Wigan (two-leg)
1945	Huddersfield	Bradford N.	Huddersfield and Odsal (two-leg)
1946	Wakefield T.	Wigan	Wembley
1947	Bradford N.	Leeds	Wembley
1948	Wigan	Bradford N.	Wembley
1949	Bradford N.	Halifax	Wembley
1950	Warrington	Widnes	Wembley
1951	Wigan	Barrow	Wembley
1952	Workington T.	Featherstone R.	Wembley
1953	Huddersfield	St Helens	Wembley
1954	Warrington	Halifax	Wembley
Replay:	Warrington	Halifax	Odsal
1955	Barrow	Workington T.	Wembley
1956	St Helens	Halifax	Wembley
1957	Leeds	Barrow	Wembley
1958	Wigan	Workington T.	Wembley
1959	Wigan	Hull	Wembley
1960	Wakefield T.	Hull	Wembley
1961	St Helens	Wigan	Wembley
1962	Wakefield T.	Huddersfield	Wembley
1963	Wakefield T.	Wigan	Wembley
1964	Widnes	Hull K.R.	Wembley
1965	Wigan	Hunslet	Wembley
1966	St Helens	Wigan	Wembley
1967	Featherstone R.	Barrow	Wembley
1968	Leeds	Wakefield T.	Wembley
1969	Castleford	Salford	Wembley
1970	Castleford	Wigan	Wembley
1971	Leigh	Leeds	Wembley
1972	St Helens	Leeds	Wembley
1973	Featherstone R.	Bradford N.	Wembley
1974	Warrington	Featherstone R.	Wembley

Rugby League Champions (1902–1974)

YEAR	WINNERS	RUNNERS-UP
1901–02	Broughton R.	Salford
1902–03	Halifax	Salford

YEAR	WINNERS	RUNNERS-UP
1903–04	Bradford	Salford
1904–05	Oldham	Bradford
1905–06	Leigh	Hunslet
1906–07	Halifax	Oldham
1907–08	Hunslet	Oldham
1908–09	Wigan	Oldham
1909–10	Oldham	Wigan
1910–11	Oldham	Wigan
1911–12	Huddersfield	Wigan
1912–13	Huddersfield	Wigan
1913–14	Salford	Huddersfield
1914–15	Huddersfield	Leeds
1919–20	Hull	Huddersfield
1920–21	Hull	Hull K.R.
1921–22	Wigan	Oldham
1922–23	Hull K.R.	Huddersfield
1923–24	Batley	Wigan
1924–25	Hull K.R.	Swinton
1925–26	Wigan	Warrington
1926–27	Swinton	St Helens Recs.
1927–28	Swinton	Featherstone R.
1928–29	Huddersfield	Leeds
1929–30	Huddersfield	Leeds
1930–31	Swinton	Leeds
1931–32	St Helens	Huddersfield
1932–33	Salford	Swinton
1933–34	Wigan	Salford
1934–35	Swinton	Warrington
1935–36	Hull	Widnes
1936–37	Salford	Warrington
1937–38	Hunslet	Leeds
1938–39	Salford	Castleford
1945–46	Wigan	Huddersfield
1946–47	Wigan	Dewsbury
1947–48	Warrington	Bradford N.
1948–49	Huddersfield	Warrington
1949–50	Wigan	Huddersfield
1950–51	Workington T.	Warrington
1951–52	Wigan	Bradford N.
1952–53	St Helens	Halifax

YEAR	WINNERS	RUNNERS-UP
1953–54	Warrington	Halifax
1954–55	Warrington	Oldham
1955–56	Hull	Halifax
1956–57	Oldham	Hull
1957–58	Hull	Workington T.
1958–59	St Helens	Hunslet
1959–60	Wigan	Wakefield T.
1960–61	Leeds	Warrington
1961–62	Huddersfield	Wakefield T.
*1962–63	Swinton	St Helens
*1963–64	Swinton	Wigan
1964–65	Halifax	St Helens
1965–66	St Helens	Halifax
1966–67	Wakefield T.	Hull K.R.
1968–69	Leeds	Castleford
1969–70	St Helens	Leeds
1970–71	St Helens	Wigan
1971–72	Leeds	St Helens
1972–73	Dewsbury	Leeds
1973–74	Warrington	St Helens

**Division One.*